Chicago, Illinois
Sights Discovery, A Travel Guide

Author
Lucas Ball

Publisher:
SONIT
2162 Davenport House, 261 Bolton Road. Bury. Lancashire. BL8 2NZ. United Kingdom.

Table of Content

Summary

On the surface, travel is about seeing new places and (if you're heading abroad to volunteer) giving a bit back at the same time. But underneath it is so much more, opening your horizons to experience completely different cultures, cuisines and landscapes. While photos are proof that you went and saw, it's the transformation that takes place within that is often the strongest evidence of why travel is important.

Some argue that it's an indulgent expense, spending money to travel that could be spent saving for a home loan or "building for the future", but travel addicts would debate a strong case against this. It's not about ticking off the "bucket list" and being able to recount all the countries you've visited, but the way travel impacts you as a person, your interactions with others and your humanity towards the rest of the world.

So if you need a little help convincing yourself or others why traveling is a worthy pursuit, here are ten reasons why it's importan

Introduction

Chicago, city, seat of Cook county, northeastern Illinois, U.S. With a population hovering near three million, Chicago is the state's largest and the country's third most populous city. In addition, the greater Chicagoland area which encompasses northeastern Illinois and extends into southeastern Wisconsin and northwestern Indiana is the country's third largest metropolitan area and the dominant metropolis of the Midwest.

The original site for Chicago was unremarkable: a small settlement at the mouth of the Chicago River near the southern tip of Lake Michigan. Indeed, a common notion for the origin of the city's name is an Algonquian word for a wild leek (or onion) plant that grew locally. However, Chicago's location at the southwestern end of the vast Great Lakes system could not have been more ideal as the country expanded westward in the 19th century, and perhaps this is reflected in another interpretation of the Native American term as meaning "strong" or "great." Regardless of which derivation is correct, it was soon recognized that the Chicago River formed a critical link in the great waterway that arose mid-century between the Atlantic Ocean and the Mississippi River. With the rise of railways soon thereafter, the young city became the country's railway hub, which helped diversify the city's rapidly growing industrial base. Chicago continued as America's crossroads with the explosive growth of air travel after World War II, which eased the city's transition into a postindustrial economy.

Chicago sprawls along the lakeshore and extends inland to meet its suburbs in a ragged line. At its greatest extent, the city is some 25 miles (40 km) from north to south and 15 miles (25 km) from east to west. Area 228 square miles (591 square km). Pop. (2000) 2,896,016; Chicago-Joliet-Naperville Metro Division, 7,628,412; Chicago-Joliet-Naperville Metro Area, 9,098,316; (2010) 2,695,598; Chicago-Joliet-Naperville Metro Division, 7,883,147; Chicago-Joliet-Naperville Metro Area, 9,461,105.

Character of The City

A drive across Chicago's lively immigrant neighbourhoods is a trip around the world: the cultures of virtually every country can be found in food stores, restaurants, clothing shops, music and video dealers, places of worship, and street-corner conversations. Chicago's dizzying growth in the 19th century led to a reputation not only for disorder and political corruption but also for creativity in the arts, architecture, and business. The resulting economic opportunities also contributed to the diversity of the city's population.

Chicago never fulfilled its dream of becoming the largest American city, but between 1890 and 1982 it was second only to New York City. That fact has contributed much to the city's reputed personality. In the 19th century it had the image of being aggressive and self-promoting, stealing population and businesses from the East. Chicago's "Windy City" nickname, in fact, came not from lake breezes but from its braggadocio exhibited most dramatically in the 1890s, when it pushed aside New York and St. Louis, Mo., in the competition to become the site of the World's Columbian Exposition of 1893. Poet Carl Sandburg hailed it as the "city of the big shoulders," cunning and cruel, yet creative and strangely attractive. It was the "toddlin' town" of the 1920s tune, and Frank Sinatra famously proclaimed it "my kind of town." New York writer A.J. Liebling belittled its provinciality in a stinging series of magazine articles, collected in the 1952 book Chicago: The Second City. Chicagoans eventually forgot the book, but the adopted epithet stuck. Under the regime of the late mayor Richard J. Daley, efficient municipal services made it the "city that works."

Chicagoans still like to refer to it as the "city of neighbourhoods," even though that description can carry connotations of segregation by race, ethnicity, and social class.

Few cities evoke as many contrasting pairs of images as Chicago. During the 19th century it was regarded as exceptional for the speed of its growth and the diversity of its population, yet its interior location supposedly made it a much more "typically American" city than New York. One-third of Chicago lay in ashes in the wake of the Great Fire of 1871, but it was rebuilt in record speed during the onset of an economic depression. It was the city of the humble immigrant and the new millionaire, the home of brazen criminals such as Al Capone and of great humanitarians such as settlement-house pioneer Jane Addams and child-welfare crusader Lucy Flower. There were raucous saloons under the watchful eye of temperance leader Frances Willard. Fetid wooden slums and horrific public housing high-rises have coexisted cheek by jowl with a uniquely innovative architectural tradition and the beautiful Gold Coast lakefront neighbourhood just north of the river. Chicago traditionally has been a shot-and-a-beer town whose best-known culinary inventions include a deep-dish pizza and a hot dog elaborately overloaded with garnishes. At the same time, it has long enjoyed a reputation for cutting-edge innovation in the arts, and the Chicago Symphony Orchestra has maintained a high level of international renown.

Chicago has been a stranger's town throughout its history. Its position as a hub for rail and air travel has always meant that at any one time a large portion of the people in the city are out-of-towners. Over the years its location has fostered a lively convention trade a fact that has led hundreds of organizations and corporations to call it home. As the metropolis of the country's midsection, from the southern Great Plains to Canada and as far west as the Rocky Mountains, Chicago ranks among the country's top tourist destinations. On any given day, the parking lots of its museums are filled with cars from dozens of surrounding states, while its varied retailers and wholesalers have long been an interstate and international magnet for shoppers.

Landscape

City site

Chicago lies mainly on a relatively flat glacial plain on what was once the bottom of Lake Chicago (the precursor of Lake Michigan) averaging between 579 and 600 feet (176 and 183 metres) above sea level. Much of the site remained swampy, only a few feet above the lake level, before the central part of the city was filled in during the 19th century. Chicago is divided roughly into thirds by the North and South branches of the Chicago River, which join together about 1 mile (1.6 km) west of the lake. The original meandering river mouth was straightened soon after the town's founding, while a mile-long bend on the South Branch was eliminated to accommodate maritime traffic. A second important body of water, Lake Calumet, is located in the industrial southeastern part of the city; it is connected to the Chicago Sanitary and Ship Canal by the Calumet Sag (Cal-Sag) Channel and to Lake Michigan by the Calumet River.

Downtown Chicago occupies the area between the lakeshore and the northern end of the South Branch and extends south from the river for a mile or so. Within this is the Loop, named in the 1880s for the square of blocks originally enclosed by streetcar tracks and now generally defined by the elevated tracks of the rapid-transit system. The Loop and the adjacent North Michigan Avenue corridor stretching north along the lakefront form the commercial and financial heart of the city.

Climate

Chicagoans have a pair of old adages about the local climate. The first "If you don't like the weather, wait an hour and it will change" may have something to do with the fact that temperature and precipitation, borne by prairie winds from Iowa or Minnesota, routinely collide with conditions generated by Lake Michigan to produce abrupt weather alterations. The second "There are two seasons in Chicago: Christmas and the Fourth of July" refers to the sometimes stark extremes in the weather. About 50 °F (28 °C) separate the January average of 28 °F (−2 °C) and the July average of 75 °F (24 °C). The average annual precipitation is 35 inches (900 mm). Chicagoans can enjoy lying on the beach in summer and skating in the parks in winter.

The expansive Chicago region, however, is large enough to see simultaneous double-digit differences in temperature. Although city pavements are known to absorb and radiate enough heat to affect local meteorological patterns, the lake often provides a moderating influence, slightly warming the areas near it in winter, cooling them in summer, and generating occasional lake-effect showers and snowfalls.

City layout

Chicago presents a different face in each direction. One of the city's most attractive features is its miles of well-used parks and other public facilities along the lakeshore. Other parts of the city can be dismal. Sporadic industrial buildings, many of them abandoned, line the railroad routes and river branches that radiate out from the centre. The industrial landscape of the southeast portion of the city dominates the vista from the east. The western and northern approaches to Chicago present a vast expanse of tree-lined residential neighbourhoods, leading to a dramatic skyline of towering office, hotel, and apartment buildings that are concentrated downtown and along the lake.

Thousands of tourists come each year just to view the architecture. The reconstruction of the city after the Great Fire of 1871 initiated a pattern of building innovation that expanded in the late 1880s with a wave of new office structures that were dubbed skyscrapers, a term reputedly coined in Chicago but which New York also claims. The steel frames of skyscrapers removed height limitations previously imposed by solid load-bearing masonry walls and allowed the use of large expanses of glass, terra-cotta facing, and other types of curtain walls.

A generation of 1920s-era Art Deco office towers may be found principally in the LaSalle Street financial district, while the influence of Ludwig Mies van der Rohe, the German-born Chicago architect of great worldwide influence, can be seen in the 1950s–80s generation of International-style buildings. Scores of major structures have been constructed since the early 1970s. The 110-story, 1,450-foot (442-metre) Willis (formerly Sears) Tower (1974) remains one of the tallest in the world. Also ranking among the country's tallest buildings are the 100-story John Hancock Center (1969), the 98-story Trump International Hotel and Tower (2009), the 83-story Aon Center (originally Amoco Building; 1974), the 61-story AT&T Corporate Center (1989), and the 65-story 311 South Wacker Building (1990). Dozens of newer postmodern designs continue to remake the skyline.

As Chicago grew rapidly in the 1880s, places that were once rural quickly became part of the city. In 1869, public health advocates, who called for Chicago to purify its air with a "green crown" of trees, joined with real estate interests to badger the state government into creating a ring of major parks linked together by broad boulevards. Growth led to a patchwork of neighbourhood green spaces. In 1934 the city consolidated 22 smaller park administrations to create the Chicago Park District, which operates more than 500 parks covering some 7,000 acres (2,800 hectares). Beyond the city, county forest preserve districts and the federal government have set aside thousands of acres of natural woodlands and have re-created prairies.

A major outdoor gallery for the people, the city's parks and public plazas feature dozens of monuments and sculptures. Nineteenth-century works in bronze honour such figures as Presidents Abraham Lincoln and Ulysses S. Grant; immigrants have commemorated heroes and cultural figures including Johann Wolfgang von Goethe and Hans Christian Andersen. The philanthropist Kate Sturges Buckingham donated one of the world's largest fountains Clarence Buckingham Memorial Fountain (dedicated 1927), which graces Grant Park just east of downtown. Beginning in the 1960s, Chicago acquired contemporary sculptures by Alexander Calder, Claes Oldenburg, Henry

Moore, Marc Chagall, Richard Hunt, and others. The most famous is the Pablo Picasso sculpture in Daley Center Plaza, fabricated of steel designed to weather and once described by an unappreciative alderman as "six stories of rusting boiler-plate."

Like all cities, Chicago is still deeply affected by the physical artifacts of its history. The street pattern is basically an extension of the first city plan of 1830. It is a grid layout, eight blocks to a mile, with major commercial streets around the perimeters of each square mile (2.5 square km). Not all streets conform, some having evolved from meandering Native American trails radiating outward from the river mouth and others having paths determined by the presence of the river and the lake.

Chicago can perhaps be thought of as a fragmented city, with the river branches, major streets, railroad embankments, and (more recently) expressways dividing it into a diversity of neighbourhoods and housing types. There are lakefront high-rises, including Lake Point Tower once among the tallest apartment buildings in the country and now only one of many such structures in its increasingly fashionable district east of Michigan Avenue in sharp contrast to thousands of smaller stone-front or brick flats farther inland. Constantly improving public transportation and seemingly unlimited supplies of affordable land have long made single-family housing in the city relatively attainable for many. Outlying neighbourhoods still consist of tens of thousands of bungalows, built narrow and deep to fit city lots. Many of these homes were built in massive subdivisions where developers replicated the same basic house dozens of times.

Chicago sprawls in all directions from the curving lakefront. The vast public-transportation and expressway networks have allowed the metropolitan area, popularly called Chicagoland, to stretch from Kenosha, Wis., around the south end of the lake through northwestern Indiana to the Michigan state line. Early suburban development gave the appearance of a wagon wheel. On the outer rim is a broad arc of older industrial cities Waukegan, Elgin, St. Charles, Geneva, Aurora, Joliet, and Chicago Heights that were once independent of Chicago; these cities formed part of a ring that informally defined the outer boundary of the metropolitan area until the latter part of the 20th century. Immediately surrounding the city are such communities as Evanston, Oak Park, Cicero, and Blue Island, all of which resisted annexation by their larger neighbour. Connecting the hub and rim are a number of other older residential suburbs that developed as part of spokelike strings of towns extending outward from the city along several commuter rail lines.

The wheel pattern gradually broke down after World War II, when automobile commuting on a growing network of expressways allowed new subdivisions to displace the farms that lay between the spokes of the older rail-commuting suburbs. After 1960 the presence of O'Hare International Airport spurred businesses and light industry to concentrate in the northwest suburbs. New high-technology research facilities and offices developed after 1970 along the "Silicon Prairie" corridor stretching west of the city. As a result, the formerly quiet village of Naperville has been transformed into a sprawling "technoburb" with one of the largest populations in the state. Conversely, some of the older suburbs have replicated the inner-city pattern of aging structures, obsolete industrial buildings, and social problems, while the outward shift of jobs has accelerated the dispersal of residential development far beyond the ring of old industrial towns.

People

The most important fact about Chicago's population is its historic and rich diversity. Early Chicago was inhabited by the Sauk (or Sac), Fox, and Potawatomi peoples, and the first permanent nonnative resident, Jean-Baptist-Point Du Sable (or DuSable), was of French-African heritage by way of the West Indies. French Canadian traders mixed with settlers from New England and the Middle Atlantic states. Irish, German, and Scandinavian immigrants began to pour in during the 1840s. In 1850 more than half of the population was foreign-born. During the latter half of the 19th century, arrivals from Italy, Poland, Russia, Ukraine, Greece, Lithuania, Bohemia, China, and smaller countries entered the city through diverse portal neighbourhoods that were located just northwest and southwest of downtown. As they moved outward, they created communities that were virtually self-contained enclaves of commercial, social, and cultural activity. Elaborate churches and synagogues, many of which still survive, were often the centre of their lives.

Race became a divisive issue after the turn of the 20th century. Job opportunities during World War I and restrictions on foreign immigration after 1924 lured tens of thousands of African Americans from the South. These new arrivals poured into a community on the city's South Side that had existed since the mid-19th century. Soon dubbed Bronzeville, it became a centre of vibrant African American culture, amusement, and entrepreneurship. Mounting racial tensions, exacerbated by overcrowded and segregated housing on the South Side and the return of former soldiers, exploded in July 1919 into one of the country's worst race riots, which claimed 38 lives. Meanwhile, Mexican Americans, who had responded to the same wartime opportunities and who were exempt from the 1924 legislation, came by the thousands, attracted by jobs in railroading, steel, and meatpacking.

The Great Depression of the 1930s effectively halted the city's growth, but World War II again attracted thousands of African Americans to work in defense plants and initiated a new wave of migration that grew rapidly during the 1950s. Refugees from Lithuania, Poland, and other eastern European countries also arrived after the war, as did newcomers from the U.S. territory of Puerto Rico. At the same time, a thriving Japanese American community sprang from the relocation of workers from wartime internment camps to Chicago.

Since the latter part of the 20th century, the city's population growth has been fueled by migrants from both around the country and around the world. By the early 21st century, African Americans made up roughly one-third of the population, and whites constituted some two-fifths. Mexican Americans, whose numbers have mushroomed faster than those of any other group, have settled in a corridor extending southwestward from the Pilsen and Little Village neighbourhoods near downtown to suburban Cicero. They have been joined by others from every country in Central and South America.

African immigrants have come from all regions of that continent. Hispanics now make up a growing one-fourth of the city's population. The relaxation of immigration restrictions in the mid-1960s brought a substantial wave into the South Asian community, making Devon Avenue on the far North Side its arrival portal and main shopping street. There sari stores coexist with Jewish delis, Russian bookstores, and Palestinian markets. Meanwhile, Korean Americans also have prospered in small businesses scattered across the city. In 1975, arrivals following the Vietnam War created an instant neighbourhood centred near the lake on Argyle Street, where Cambodians, Thai, Hmong, and other Southeast Asians leaving their homelands have found opportunity.

Change has been a constant factor in the ethnic and neighbourhood makeup of the city, forcing many groups to struggle to maintain their communities. Urban renewal for expressways and public housing was the major destabilizing factor during the 1950s and '60s, notably for African Americans and Puerto Ricans. The loss of industrial jobs also devastated neighbourhoods, while chain stores drew money out of local circulation. Federal home loans which restricted where and how funds could be spent along with increased capacity on commuter rail lines and new expressway construction encouraged the post-World War II generations to build new homes in the suburbs, leaving behind aging parents in declining city neighbourhoods.

In many areas the thousands of bungalows that had been built in a relatively short period of time all started to deteriorate. Without new housing stock to replace decaying structures, the downward cycle toward abandonment began in many areas of the South and West sides. The departing families were replaced by newly arrived minorities, whose poverty and race were disadvantages in an increasingly segregated city.

The destruction of the old housing stock produced a loss of population, which led to the closing of such community anchors as churches, schools, and hospitals. Politicians and planners tried to contain the African American communities by constructing expressways around those areas and concentrating the residents of minority neighbourhoods in rows of monolithic public-housing high-rise apartment buildings. The Robert Taylor Homes near the lakefront on the South Side was the largest such project ever built in the country.

The most recent destabilizing factor in some areas of the city has been gentrification. Conveniently located old houses and apartment buildings have lured enough financing to transform once-abandoned districts into communities of upscale housing units. Since the last decades of the 20th century, thousands of new residents have moved into the light-manufacturing belt surrounding the Loop. Where immigrant workers once carried their lunch pails to work in factories, these young urban professionals clutch briefcases and talk on their cell phones as they walk to work in downtown office towers.

Similar developments are transforming the housing and manufacturing districts along several rapid-transit (popularly, "L," for "elevated") lines and in parts of the traditionally African American communities along the south shore of the lake. Boutiques and coffeehouses have displaced small grocers and other marginal merchants. While the process has saved neighbourhoods in one sense and brought back large numbers of affluent residents to the city, it has also tended to increase property values and tax assessments to the point where longtime residents of more-modest means are displaced. Indeed, many of the 1960s-era public-housing projects (including Robert Taylor) have now been razed, although some provisions have been made for housing the former tenants.

Economy

Besides church steeples and skyscrapers, smokestacks have long dominated the Chicago horizon. The city's position as a rail hub and a port aided its use of the Midwest's raw materials to produce a wide range of goods: light manufactures such as food, food products, candy, pharmaceuticals, and soap; communication equipment, scientific instruments, and automobiles; and refined petroleum, petroleum products, and steel. The city also became a major printing and publishing centre. This diversity originally grew out of Chicago's role as a transshipment point for eastbound grain and lumber as well as meat, which was smoked or packed in salt. The city assumed a new role as manufacturer of military supplies during the American Civil War, adding leather goods, steel rail, and food processing. Although railroading, steel, and meatpacking continued to be the largest employers, by the late 19th century manufacturing was branching into chemicals, furniture, paint, metalworking, machine tools, railroad equipment, bicycles, printing, mail-order sales, and other fields that were considered the cutting edge in their day. The production of most of the country's telephone equipment made Chicago the Silicon Valley of an earlier era. Industrial diversification also depended on a skilled workforce, whose numbers were enhanced through a tradition of innovative vocational training.

Manufacturing

Although Chicago failed to attract the automobile-manufacturing dominance it sought, its other industries thrived through much of the 20th century. It became a major radio and electronics centre during the 1920s. Like all manufacturing cities, Chicago was devastated by the Great Depression. The World War II boom involved more than 1,400 companies producing a wide range of military goods. Diversification, however, also made Chicago's job market vulnerable to changes in almost any industry. In addition, the city's abundant multistory factory buildings, which were often located in congested districts, could not compete with newer suburban industrial parks that had their sprawling single-story plants and access to expressways. Many companies sought new (and cheaper) labour markets south and west in the Sun Belt or overseas while keeping their headquarters in Chicago. Estimates of industrial jobs lost during the first four postwar decades run as high as one million, but manufacturing has remained a significant if diminished component of the regional economy.

Finance and other services

The drop in manufacturing's preeminence has been mirrored by a dramatic rise in the service sector, which now employs some one-third of the city's workforce. Notably, Chicago has fallen back on its original preindustrial role as a trading centre. The city's rapid early growth and its location as the rail hub amid the country's farm belt made it the logical site for commodities trading. In 1848, traders created the Chicago Board of Trade to rationalize the process of purchasing and forwarding grain to Eastern markets. Over the years the scope of its trading expanded to include a number of commodities, and in 1973 it spun off an independent Chicago Board Options Exchange to regularize trading of corporate stock options. Meanwhile, in 1874 the new Chicago Produce Exchange began providing trading services for butter, eggs, poultry, and other farm product markets; in 1919 it changed its name to the Chicago Mercantile Exchange. The fourth trading institution, the Chicago Stock Exchange, was organized in 1882 to handle corporate securities; mergers with exchanges in other cities led to it being renamed the Midwest Stock Exchange in 1949, but the original name was restored in 1993. All four of these institutions along with trading, banking, and other financial functions have made the downtown LaSalle Street district synonymous with Chicago's regional dominance, though the long-standing tradition of face-to-face trading that built them has experienced increased competition from electronic trading.

Chicago, with dozens of major banks, remains second only to New York City as a national financial hub. However, local wholesaling and retailing have fallen increasingly under the control of out-of-town interests, which have either bought out or squeezed out department stores and retailers in several product lines.

Chicago's position as a national transportation hub has long guaranteed the city a steady stream of conventions and trade shows. It has hosted numerous national political conventions since the one in 1860 that nominated Abraham Lincoln for the presidency. Older venues such as the Coliseum, the International Amphitheater, and the Chicago Stadium have given way to the United Center and the UIC Pavilion in the city and the Allstate Arena in suburban Rosemont, near O'Hare. McCormick Place, the lakefront convention complex just south of downtown, has been expanded several times to remain among the largest trade-show facilities in the country. Each year, McCormick Place alone hosts dozens of conventions and trade shows that draw many hundreds of thousands of people and pump considerable revenue into the local economy. Millions more businesspeople, tourists, and other short-term visitors come to the city annually to shop, dine, visit museums, and take in sporting and musical events, many of them staying in the region's tens of thousands of hotel rooms.

Transportation

Chicago continues to be the country's rail transportation hub. Each day thousands of Amtrak passengers arrive or change trains at Union Station, much as railway travelers did 150 years ago. The shift of freight carriers to containers has meant that rail yards and tracks are more likely to be filled with tractor trailers and stacks of giant boxes than boxcars and gondolas. Belt railways that circle the region still provide interchange between lines, but, as rail lines have consolidated, the corporate headquarters for much of the rail industry have left the city. Despite the preeminence of the railroads in handling freight, maritime industries survived and expanded to remain competitive in high bulk–low value hauling.

From the early days of commercial aviation, Chicago's city government has recognized and capitalized on the advantageous flexibility of air routes over more-or-less permanent railroad tracks. During the 1920s the city established Municipal Airport on the Southwest Side, which quickly developed into one of the country's busiest air hubs. However, by the end of the 1950s, the advent of jet airliners and their requirement of longer runways threatened to make landlocked Municipal obsolete. After long debate, the city chose to build a new facility by utilizing the old Orchard Field (hence the official acronym "ORD" used on luggage tags) in northwest suburban Park Ridge. In 1949 the new airport was named in honour of Lieutenant Commander Edward ("Butch") O'Hare, a wartime naval air hero, while Municipal was renamed Midway for the critical 1942 Allied battle victory in the Pacific. Long the undisputed busiest airport in the country, O'Hare more recently has competed with other large facilities across the country for the distinction, while a rejuvenated Midway became a regional hub. For decades the city has debated the issue of constructing a third major airport.

The move toward publicly operated mass transit grew out of adversity, as the Great Depression forced a collection of private streetcar and elevated-rail companies into bankruptcy. Public funding allowed the construction of a long-delayed subway system. Work began in 1938 on a north-south line under State Street that was completed in 1943, and a second, parallel route under Dearborn Street opened in 1950. These lines and the Loop elevated ("L") structure completed in 1897 and still the essential downtown link in the system constitute the core of a network of rapid-transit rail lines that came to include service to O'Hare and Midway. Meanwhile, in 1945 the Illinois state legislature, the General Assembly, created the Chicago Transit Authority (CTA) to take over operation of the "L" carriers; independent bus companies were absorbed in 1952.

Although Chicago grew most rapidly while it rode "L" trains and streetcars, it also fell in love with the automobile. Chicago's expressway system dates to the 1920s, when Lake Shore Drive was rebuilt as a divided highway. (Some claim it to be one of the country's oldest expressways.) But the postwar rush to suburbia, automobile commuting, and the 1956 Interstate Highway Act brought about the construction of the modern network. The Congress Street (later Eisenhower) Expressway to the west, completed in 1956, was the region's first interstate highway. During the following decade, a spiderweb of Loop-directed expressways and encircling bypass routes was superimposed on the region, which roughly followed the outlines of the original wagon-wheel pattern of settlement.

The move to the automobile left public transit in crisis. In 1973 the Illinois General Assembly created the Regional Transportation Authority (RTA) and gave it the power to levy a sales tax to support the CTA as well as a failing commuter rail system (which was unified and named Metra). Privately owned and municipal bus routes in the suburbs were similarly united under the name of Pace (1983). The RTA has revitalized the system and even expanded it, notably into areas northwest and southwest of the city not previously served. In addition, there is one independent commuter rail line, the heavily subsidized South Shore Line to South Bend, Ind., the country's sole surviving electric interurban line.

Occasionally, Chicagoans run the risk of being "bridged" shut out of the Loop because bridges in the central area must be raised to allow passage of river traffic. There are several dozen movable bridges over waterways within the city. Two of the most noteworthy are the large double-deck Michigan Avenue and Outer Drive (or Link) bridges, the latter connecting the northern and southern parts of Lake Shore Drive.

Although bridge raisings are now rare confined largely to specified times to allow the passage of tall-masted sailboats the river bustles in warmer weather with pleasure craft, sightseeing boats, and the occasional barge.

An aging remnant of Chicago's infrastructure came to light dramatically in April 1992, when an under-river tunnel was punctured, leading to massive flooding in downtown basements. A system of freight tunnels had been constructed below Loop streets at the beginning of the 20th century to haul cargo, coal, and ashes to and from downtown buildings. Eventually abandoned after having served its original purpose, the system found new life carrying communications wiring and fell into obscurity until the flood. There are also unused remains of three vehicular tunnels downtown that were built under the river before 1900 because the river's heavy shipping traffic so disrupted the use of the bridges.

Administration and Society

Government

Chicago's government is as complex as its people, with layers of shared responsibility created by its history. The city itself is divided into 50 wards and is led by a mayor who is elected to a four-year term. However, many powers belong to the aldermen, one elected from each ward, who sit on the city council and must approve most mayoral actions. This arrangement has meant that historically the city has been governed either by forming loose coalitions and making deals or especially during the heyday of the Democratic Party's political "machine" (1931–78) by controlling who got elected alderman. Mayoral control reached its zenith during the era of Richard J. Daley. The cry of one supporter that "Chicago ain't ready for reform" began Daley's 21-year reign, which ended with his death in December 1976.

After him followed a series of short mayoralties, including those of Michael Bilandic (1976–79) and Chicago's first female mayor, Jane Byrne (1979–83), both of whom faced unprecedented fiscal problems. During the first term of Harold Washington (1983–87), the city's first African American mayor, conflict with a coalition of white aldermen, known locally as "Council Wars," brought city business almost to a halt. Another African American, Eugene Sawyer, served briefly as mayor after Washington's sudden death, but he was defeated in 1989 by Richard M. Daley, son of the former mayor. The second Daley also was able to govern with little opposition, in large part because he, like his father, developed considerable influence over the city council.

Meanwhile, a series of semi-independent departments and agencies oversee such governmental responsibilities as parks, public transit, education, community colleges, water reclamation, and mosquito abatement.

Cook county, organized in 1831, reaches out well beyond the city limits, especially in the northwest. Its board is responsible for the operation of the county's health system and extensive forest preserve district, and the county sheriff's department patrols primarily unincorporated areas and aids in the operation of a large court system. The suburban "collar counties" of Lake, McHenry, Kane, DuPage, Will, and Kendall were once entirely rural with low population densities, but the massive influx of residents and businesses has forced them to expand services. Over time, the city and these counties together developed an identity that is distinct from "downstate," the remainder of Illinois.

The government of the state of Illinois has a presence in Chicago not only in the form of the architecturally distinctive James R. Thompson Center downtown but also in such responsibilities as welfare, employment, and state police patrols of expressways. The overwhelmingly Democratic city and the heavily Republican downstate and suburban constituencies have long been at odds. The population parity among the three that prevailed during the mid-20th century has given way to a surging suburban presence in the legislature and a subsequent decline in power statewide by Chicago and downstate interests.

Municipal services

Gas, electric, and cable-television utilities are operated by franchised private corporations, but the water system is city-owned. Chicago not only supplies its own drinking water (drawn from inlets in the lake far from shore) but also provides it to dozens of suburbs through an extensive pipeline network. The city is also responsible for collecting trash and maintaining Chicago's vast network of streets and alleys and its sewer system. However, wastewater treatment is the responsibility of a separate regional water-reclamation district. With well over 10,000 sworn officers on the streets, the Chicago Police Department is the biggest in the Midwest and one of the largest nationally. That status is shared by the city's fire department, which has nearly 100 engine companies.

Drainage has been a chronic problem in Chicago. An approach taken in the late 19th century was to raise the street level several feet in the central area (many of these older structures with a below-grade first floor can still be found). The major engineering marvel of the turn of the 20th century was reversing the flow of the Chicago River so that the sewage and runoff water dumped into it no longer ran into the lake except after heavy storms, when the locks had to be opened. The problem of untreated storm water flowing into the lake was addressed by an ambitious project popularly called Deep Tunnel. It consists primarily of a vast system of large tunnels bored in the bedrock deep beneath the region that collects and stores storm water until it can be processed at treatment facilities.

Health

During the city's early decades, its citizens suffered through periodic epidemic scourges that killed thousands, but by the turn of the 20th century these outbreaks were largely under control, thanks mainly to improved sanitation, water filtration, and the reversed flow of the river away from the lake. Chicagoans also may feel secure in the quality of medical care available. The first line of defense is the city health department, which annually administers hundreds of thousands of immunizations at its primary care clinics and conducts tens of thousands of inspections of the city's food establishments. The county operates an extensive system of public health-care facilities, which provide much of the treatment for the poor. The system is anchored by John H. Stroger, Jr. Hospital of Cook County (formerly Cook County Hospital), one of the largest such public institutions in the country with one of the busiest emergency rooms; it also operates a branch at Provident Hospital, a historic African American institution. Stroger Hospital is part of the massive Illinois Medical District on the Near West Side, a concentration of hospitals, medical schools, and other facilities. Medical schools affiliated with the University of Illinois at Chicago, Northwestern University, Loyola University, Rush University, and the University of Chicago are national leaders in several fields. In addition, dozens of hospitals are scattered throughout the metropolitan region, although hospital closings and cutbacks in federal spending have left some areas underserved.

Education

Chicago's enormous school system has laboured to overcome long-term problems with its quality while attempting to serve diverse ethnic and social class groups. About 500 elementary and 90 secondary schools serve more than 400,000 students, many of them from impoverished families. Another 200 parochial and private schools serve some 70,000 more students.

Higher education has always lured the young to Chicago. Private church-related institutions emerged in the region during the mid-19th century, including Northwestern University, founded by Methodists in 1851, in Evanston; Lake Forest College (Presbyterian; 1857), farther up the North Shore in Lake Forest; and Wheaton College (Wesleyan Methodist; 1860), in west-suburban Wheaton. Two institutions destined to become world-renowned were founded on the city's South Side in 1890: the University of Chicago (the second school of that name; the first, founded by Baptists in 1857, closed in 1886) and the Armour Institute of Technology (which merged with another institution in 1940 to form the Illinois Institute of Technology). Roosevelt University (1945), which occupies the historic Auditorium Building, and Columbia College (1890) are located downtown, as are branch campuses of Northwestern and of the two principal Roman Catholic institutions, DePaul (1898) and Loyola (1870) universities. Public higher education in the city took longer to emerge. The University of Illinois at Chicago (1867), which started as a two-year branch campus for World War II veterans, is the flagship among the public institutions, which include Northeastern Illinois University (1961), Chicago State University (1867), and the seven City Colleges of Chicago.

Cultural Life

The cultural life of any major city involves two sharply different activities. The first is the creative act of composing, writing, or producing an artistic work. The second consists of collecting, displaying, and performing the various artistic creations. Chicago has long been a leader in both categories.

The arts

From the 1890s through the 1920s, Chicago was a magnet for artistically ambitious and talented but often little-known writers, many of whom had fled the Midwest's dusty country towns. Theodore Dreiser, Sherwood Anderson, George Ade, and Opie Read produced a gritty form of urban literature rooted in the everyday lives of ordinary people, as did Chicago-born Henry Blake Fuller, Finley Peter Dunne, and I.K. Friedman. Their works, which often debuted in newspapers, expressed a sense of awe at the skyscrapers, factories, varied people, and hectic pace of urban life. Novelist Hamlin Garland, meanwhile, emphasized negative aspects of farm and small-town life in his works. Most of the first generation of writers had left by 1910, but the city attracted iconoclastic poets. Carl Sandburg, Vachel Lindsay, and Edgar Lee Masters helped Harriet Monroe launch the influential Poetry magazine.

The Great Depression of the 1930s reoriented another generation of writers away from awestruck downtown views. Such literary giants as James T. Farrell, Saul Bellow, and Nelson Algren set their stories of life's struggles in their own ethnic working-class neighbourhoods. The emergence of Richard Wright heralded the arrival of African Americans to the literary scene, which included young postwar talents such as novelist Willard Motley, poet Gwendolyn Brooks, and playwright Lorraine Hansberry. These same ethnic, racial, and social class themes continued to dominate 20th-century Chicago literature in the works of Harry Mark Petrakis, Stuart Dybek, Cyrus Coulter, William Brashler, Leon Forrest, Sandra Cisneros, and Ana Castillo. Meanwhile, other Chicago writers have drawn upon the gritty personality of the Windy City as a backdrop. Sara Paretsky and Scott Turow helped to create a new Chicago mystery genre. Studs Terkel elevated the oral history of ordinary people to an art form, much as Mike Royko, who revived the newspaper column as urban literature, used common sense to deflate pompous politicians.

Theatre in Chicago is also balanced between the lavish downtown venues and a tradition of low-budget experimentation among outlying groups that number more than 200. In the early 1970s, several small acting companies created storefront theatres in the Lincoln Park neighbourhood on the North Side. These include the Steppenwolf and Body Politic theatres, as well as the Organic Theatre, which was one of the first to showcase the plays of David Mamet. These off-Loop (often non-Equity) groups gained national acclaim for their productions and performers (many of whom later became famous in film and on television). Soon, actors who came out of the Chicago theatre scene carried a certain cachet. The famed Second City, which for decades has been performing improvisational comedy in the Old Town neighbourhood, spawned spin-off groups and inspired similar companies elsewhere. Meanwhile, dance has become increasingly important in Chicago, with the Hubbard Street Dance Company offering contemporary performances, the River North Chicago Dance Company producing hip-hop, house, and jazz dancing, Chicago Moving Company with modern dance, and the Muntu Dance Theater showcasing traditional and contemporary African American forms.

On any given day virtually all genres of music are performed somewhere in Chicago. There are specialized classical ensembles such as the Newberry Consort for Renaissance music, Music of the Baroque, and the Chicago Opera Theatre, which performs 20th-century and Baroque operas. The Old Town School of Folk Music (1957), on the far North Side, is the world's largest permanent centre for the study of both traditional and contemporary folk music. The many African Americans who moved to Chicago in the 20th century have had a dynamic impact on music. As the home of Muddy Waters, Howlin' Wolf, Buddy Guy, and other greats, the city has long been internationally known as a centre for the blues, which can be heard in clubs throughout the city. Chicago has also played a critical role in the development of American jazz, through the work of such pioneers as Louis Armstrong, Benny Goodman, and Jelly Roll Morton and, later, such innovative groups as the Jazz Ensemble of Chicago. Gospel music traces its roots to the city in the late 1920s, when Thomas Andrew Dorsey, the musician son of a Baptist preacher, combined blues with church music. During the summer Chicagoans can hear music at two long-established outdoor music venues. Ravinia Festival (1903), in north suburban Highland Park, is the summer home of the Chicago Symphony Orchestra; it also features performances of popular music. The lakefront Grant Park area east of downtown has been the home of free classical concerts since 1935. It is also the site of a lively series of city-sponsored festivals of blues, jazz, gospel, Latin American, and other specialized music as well as the Taste of Chicago, one of the largest outdoor food festivals in the country.

Art and Artistic History

Early in the twentieth century, Chicago artists and civic leaders believed that the city's accumulating wealth and their own ambitions soon would make it, in novelist Theodore Dreiser's words, "first in art achievement." Chicago did win renown for its art collections and schools for educating artists. This renown seldom extended to Chicago's art makers, yet by the beginning of the twenty-first century this increasingly diverse group of artists had created a substantial legacy. The city's limitations, as much as its strengths, shaped this legacy. New York always far surpassed Chicago in the number and overall importance of its patrons, galleries, critics, and art publications, as well as artists. Chicago's outside-the-spotlight position could be an asset for artists who wished to develop gradually maturing personal styles, be playfully irreverent toward prevailing practices in the arts, or expand the definition of art. Yet Chicago artists also connected with kindred spirits in their city and with national and international art worlds, participating in ongoing debates such as the persistent one between defenders and critics of tradition.

These connections developed slowly. The external world felt Chicago's influence in politics and industry decades before the city became a presence in the arts, initially as a market for works produced elsewhere. Although by the mid-1850s Chicago had attracted well-known portrait painter G. P. A. Healy and sculptor Leonard W. Volk, well-to-do citizens who sought art usually looked to Europe or the East Coast. This remained true at the time of the 1893 World's Columbian Exposition, described by sculptor Augustus Saint-Gaudens as "the greatest meeting of artists since the fifteenth century." Most were only visitors and less then 10 percent of the artworks on display were by Chicago artists, trained mainly in Paris, Munich, Düsseldorf, and Rome. Yet works at the exposition by painters and sculptors such as Alice D. Kellogg and John Donoghue gave promise of things to come.

Although Paris-trained, Donoghue and Kellogg initially had studied at the Chicago Academy of Design. Artists formed the academy in 1866 (incorporated in 1869) to offer art classes and exhibitions. Business leaders supplanted this financially troubled organization by incorporating in 1879 a new Chicago Academy of Fine Arts, renamed the Art Institute of Chicago in 1882. It included a museum and a school. Subsequently the School of the Art Institute became one of the most influential in the country, as did the museum, for which patrons such as Martin Ryerson and Bertha Honoré Palmer acquired works by Degas, Manet, and many others.

The Art Institute seldom acquired works by Chicago artists, who received some support from a variety of other institutions such as the Newberry Library, which first purchased and exhibited local work in the 1880s. The following decade a range of creative activities received nourishment at the 57th Street artists' colony, which later attracted writers Floyd Dell and Henry Miller. Also important were the low-rent studios erected in 1894 by Judge Lambert Tree and the Fine Arts Building, designed to bring together artists, musicians, writers, and craftspeople. Jane Addams added the Butler Art Gallery (1891) two years after opening Hull House. There in 1897 artists and supporters created the Chicago Society of Arts and Crafts, which championed decorative arts and a nonhierarchical definition of art, as Addams did by encouraging immigrant crafts. At the Little Room, artists such as painter Ralph Clarkson mingled with Addams and writers Henry Blake Fuller, Hamlin Garland (who credited impressionist painters with teaching him to see anew), and poet Harriet Monroe.

The number of artists available to participate in such interchanges grew. Between 1865 and 1900 the number of Chicagoans listed as "artists" in city directories increased from dozens to several hundred. Many, whose professional and social lives were likely to be quite different from the artists who met in the Little Room, were engaged in such specific commercial tasks as hand painting factory-produced ceramic pieces. Women did this hand painting; men usually received commissions for portraits, designed stained glass, and taught advanced students. The burgeoning publishing industry also mostly employed men, although women served as book illustrators. By the 1890s fields such as advertising, crystal cutting, furniture and leather product design, and metalwork, along with the emerging institutional support, made the artist's life more viable in Chicago than in St. Louis or Cincinnati, and comparable to that in Philadelphia or Boston. Chicago augmented New York's preeminence by launching the careers of many fine and commercial artists who then moved there.

Perhaps the most prominent Chicago artist at this time was Lorado Taft, who in addition to making monumental sculptures and teaching at the School of the Art Institute published in 1903 his influential The History of American Sculpture. The first work completed with support from the Ferguson Fund, created in 1905 to finance public monuments and sculptures in the city, was his Fountain of the Great Lakes, dedicated in 1913. Taft's vision of an uplifting high culture grounded in classical principles of artistic order and harmony received a challenge in that year from the Armory Show. The show featured works that made unconventional use of color and form and refused to idealize the human form. European artists created most of the controversial works, although one of the few nonrepresentational paintings in the exhibition was by Chicago resident Manierre Dawson. Earlier, the W. Scott Thurber Gallery (designed by Frank Lloyd Wright) and one or two others had exhibited works by local modernists such as Jerome Blum, and a few collectors, notably Arthur Jerome Eddy, purchased modernist work. Most of Chicago's 10 or so commercial galleries, and dozens of art-related associations such as the Friday Club, favored traditional styles.

However, the Armory Show encouraged dissident artists such as Stanislaus Szukalski, who arrived from Poland in 1913. Because the Art Institute's Annual Exhibition of Artists of Chicago and Vicinity slighted modernist work, abstract artist Rudolph Weisenborn and others created a Salon des Refusés and the Chicago No-Jury Society of Artists. They exhibited works in the 1920s at sites such as Marshall Field's. The more traditional Palette and Chisel Club, founded in 1895 by artists who wanted to share the cost of models, offered another venue. The Renaissance Society, traditionalist when founded at the University of Chicago in 1915, began in the late 1920s to challenge prevailing conceptions of art, leading to such exhibitions as American Primitives (1931). The Arts Club, promodernist from its founding in 1916, brought Fernand Léger to Chicago in 1930 to show his film Le Ballet Mécanique.

As encoded in its name, during its brief existence Neo-Arlimusc (1926–1928) encouraged interactions among artists, littérateurs, musicians, and scientists, as did Margaret Anderson's A Little Review a decade before. Contacts with writers Theodore Dreiser and Sherwood Anderson, the latter of whom exhibited paintings in Chicago, helped sustain modernist painter Jerome Blum, whose aspirations met family and public resistance and who found the physical city's predominant grays and browns dispiriting. In later years visual artists met other creative figures, including out-of-town visitors such as Thorton Wilder, Dizzy Gillespie, and Sarah Vaughan, at painter Gertrude Abercrombie's Hyde Park home. Painter and patron Frederick Clay Bartlett's remarkable gift, the Helen Birch Bartlett Memorial Collection (1926), brought to the Art Institute over 20 major works, including Georges Seurat's Sunday Afternoon on the Island of La Grande Jatte (1884–86), which influenced many Chicago artists.

Such organizational and cultural opportunities did not satisfy all the needs of Chicago artists. Clarkson in 1921 listed over 70 who had left for better opportunities elsewhere, and following decades brought similar reports. Yet the ties between art and commerce, encouraged by organizations such as the Chicago Association of Arts and Industries, founded in 1922, far surpassed those in any American city other than New York. A 1925 index of advertising artists and illustrators listed 750. Many lost their jobs in the 1930s, yet that decade created additional links among fine and commercial art, industry, and education. Chicago's Century of Progress Exposition of 1933–34 attracted industrial and interior designers to work on its various buildings and displays and brought commissions to many painters and sculptors, some local. With support from the Association of Arts and Industries and then from Container Corporation of America founder Walter Paepcke, émigré László Moholy-Nagy helped establish the New Bauhaus (1937). Moholy-Nagy drew on his experience at the Bauhaus in Germany to teach students how to infuse such utilitarian tasks as product design with a highly developed aesthetic sensibility rooted in cultivation of their sensory and intellectual faculties.

The federal government played the largest new role in sustaining Chicago artists through the Great Depression years. The Federal Art Project and other agencies employed hundreds and left legacies such as the South Side Community Art Center (1941). Project administrators urged painting of scenes of American life, reinforcing local interest in regionalism, but with a stylistic diversity exemplified by the more than 50 artists presented in J. Z. Jacobson's Art of Today: Chicago, 1933. The immensely popular exhibitions of earlier and contemporary art at the Art Institute held in conjunction with the Century of Progress Exposition demonstrated public interest in a variety of work including modernist art. Concerned by such trends, the conservative Society for Sanity in Art, established by Josephine Hancock Logan in 1936, called for traditional art as represented in the exemplary collection of the Union League Club.

During World War II, enrollment in Chicago's art schools declined (at the School of the Art Institute it dropped 50 percent between 1938 and 1943) as students entered the military. Those who remained learned to respond to wartime needs, for instance by using less fabric, in short supply thanks to military demand, in their fashion design classes. At war's end the GI Bill helped fill the city's colleges, including its art schools, with former soldiers who brought a new level of maturity and intensity to undergraduate education. Enrollments at the School of the Art Institute and elsewhere surpassed earlier highs. The New Bauhaus in 1944 became the Institute of Design, affiliated from 1949 with the Illinois Institute of Technology (IIT). The Institute of Design made Chicago a national center for study of photography. Its socially oriented and rationally grounded design tradition presented an invigorating contrast to expressive and personal approaches more typical at the School of the Art Institute.

Galleries became more relevant to Chicago artists when in the 1950s Allan Frumkin and Fairweather-Hardin brought contemporary art from New York and Europe and showed local work, encouraging dozens of other galleries to do the same. Serious collectors with local interests appeared, including Jory and Joseph Randall Shapiro, who made their collections accessible to artists and led in founding the Museum of Contemporary Art (1967). Other new venues for seeing and showing included the Terra, Smart, and Block museums. The gift of the

Bergman Collection gave the Art Institute a superb surrealist collection. Also important were community venues such as the 57th Street Art Fair, established in 1948 and soon followed by the Old Town Art Fair.

In the 1960s and 1970s, outlying institutions such as the College of DuPage, as well as institutions in or close to the city such as the University of Illinois at Chicago, Roosevelt University, and Columbia College, joined the School of the Art Institute as significant employers of artists, making issues such as a school's part-time faculty benefits important factors. Influential teachers from this period included Kathleen Blackshear, Harry Callahan, Aaron Siskind, George Cohen, Ed Paschke, Ray Yoshida, and Robert Loescher.

Both institutional growth and resistance to it generated artistic energy. In 1947, the Art Institute excluded students from the Chicago and Vicinity show, leading to Exhibition Momentum, which brought renowned artists to jury exhibitions in 1948 and after. Yet distinctions between mainstream and alternatives blurred. Venerable organizations became receptive to a wider range of art, as shown by Katherine Kuh's career. Director of a gallery that showed controversial modernist works in the 1930s, Kuh became the first curator of modern art at the Art Institute the following decade. She later assembled a contemporary collection for First National Bank of Chicago. Ethnographic collections at the Field Museum and the Oriental Institute inspired Leon Golub, Nancy Spero, and others as they challenged both traditional and contemporary practices, leading to the first grouping of Chicago artists to receive national attention, the Monster Roster. Another group to achieve this status was the Hairy Who, first shown in 1966 at the Hyde Park Art Center, founded in 1939 and which under the later leadership of Don Baum and with financial support from Ruth Horowitz championed community arts education and emerging Chicago artists. Critics Franz Schulze and Dennis Adrian helped bring attention to these artists. Writing on Chicago art further benefited from the establishment in 1973 of the New Art Examiner.

The black neighborhood mural movement in the early 1960s built on the African American community's tradition of trading art works for goods and services. Establishment of the DuSable Museum (1961) placed into historical context the work of African American artists such as Archibald Motley, Jr., who graduated from the School of the Art Institute in 1918 and whose paintings memorably documented life in Chicago's Bronzeville. The civil rights movement encouraged Motley to deal more explicitly with racial issues by the 1960s. Opposition to American involvement in Vietnam also generated activist art. In November 1968 the Feigen Gallery exhibited works protesting repression of dissenters during the recent Democratic Convention. Vietnam veterans did not have the immediate impact on the Chicago art community that those from World War II did, but after its establishment in 1996 the Chicago-based National Vietnam Veterans Art Museum displayed their work.

Social activism sparked creation of the multiracial Chicago Mural Group (1970), the Public Art Workshop (1972), and Movimiento Artistico Chicano (1975). Artists' cooperative galleries proliferated, including N.A.M.E. and several with a feminist emphasis, such as ARC and Artemesia, outgrowths of women artists' group the West End Bag, sparked by Ellen Lanyon. Beginning in the 1960s the National Endowment for the Arts and the Illinois Arts Council provided modest but often crucial support for organizations and individual artists.

Chicago continued to export artists. Perhaps the most widely recognized Chicago painter at midcentury, Ivan Albright, left after the city demolished the building that housed his studio. Claes Oldenburg, Red Grooms, Golub, Spero, Martin Puryear, Ellen Lanyon, and many others departed, often in search of better opportunities to exhibit, sell, and receive recognition for their work. Artists who left frequently expressed affection for Chicago, as did sculptor H. C. Westermann, who valued its commercialism and abundance of industrial materials. Others remained, or returned after stints elsewhere, including Jim Nutt, Gladys Nilsson, Kerry James Marshall, and Paschke. The city provided a receptive environment for self-taught artists such as Mr.

Imagination. Artists including Roger Brown, Yoshida, and Karl Wirsum built inspiring collections of unconventional works that they made accessible to others. Novelist Leon Forrest considered visual artists indispensable to the "ideal community" for nurturing his own work, and many Chicago artists thrived on their interactions with local writers, musicians, architects, and performers. The Percent for the Arts Program established in 1978 required 1 percent of the cost of new public buildings be set aside to purchase art for the site. Various gigantic exhibitions such as Art Chicago and Chicago International Art Exposition have given Chicago artists additional exposure and made art from around the world accessible to them.

Arts Funding

Chicago's traditions of arts funding have roots in the business community and civic leadership of the mid-nineteenth century. In the 1860s and '70s, early antecedents of cultural institutions grew from arts programs organized by members of elite clubs. During the same period, theater and music organizations gained strength in ethnic neighborhoods with more grassroots support. The swell of civic support to build the Auditorium Theater in 1886 began a tradition of broad-based backing in addition to bringing together wealthy philanthropists who went on to found other major Chicago cultural institutions. The World's Columbian Exposition in 1893 was pivotal in establishing Chicago as a cosmopolitan, cultural city and brought local, national, and international attention. The virtually concurrent establishment of the Chicago Symphony, Art Institute, and Field Museum went hand in hand with the ambitions of the city's aggressive business developers. More specifically community-based arts efforts included programs in music, literature, and visual arts for immigrants at Hull House, founded in 1889. The establishment of the Chicago Community Trust in 1915 encouraged individual philanthropy, and a Trust survey in the early 1920s showed that culture and education received the largest share.

The mix of corporate, individual, and private foundation grants remained the mainstay of arts funding into the 1960s. During that decade, the establishment of the National Endowment for the Arts and the Illinois Arts Council seeded growth in small and midsize arts organizations. These agencies also encouraged greater community participation and funding of arts programs, commonly awarding matching grants and focusing on community-based and culturally specific organizations. Support for the arts by Chicago city government strengthened in the 1980s and 1990s, spurring corporate and foundation leadership in the funding of arts resources, a development reminiscent of the industrialist backing of the previous century. Chicago became, at the end of the twentieth century, a national model for public-private partnerships in support of the arts.

Arts and Crafts Movement

In the 1890s the principles of the British Arts and Crafts movement found a sympathetic audience in Chicago among art workers, educators, and others involved in progressive cultural and social reforms. Convinced that industrial capitalism had caused the degradation of work and the human spirit, the movement advocated a reunification of art and labor, of artist and artisan. Arts and Crafts societies, guilds, and schools spread "the craftsman ideal" and promoted hand workmanship as a moral regenerative force. Hull House, a social settlement founded by Jane Addams, became the center of the movement. It sponsored a variety of handicraft activities and shops and served as headquarters for the Chicago Arts and Crafts Society, founded in 1897.

Less a style than an approach toward the making of objects, the Arts and Crafts philosophy found tangible expression in the revival of traditional crafts, particularly metalwork, ceramics (art pottery, hand-painted china, architectural terra cotta), stained and cut glass (art glass), furniture, books, and weaving.

A number of small shops specializing in Arts and Crafts goods grew up in the Chicago area. Highly skilled metalsmiths hand wrought silver tableware, trophies, and jewelry at the Kalo Shop, the Jarvie Shop, Petterson Studios, and Chicago Art Silver Shop, creating a distinctive Chicago style perpetuated by the Cellini Shop (Evanston), Mulholland Brothers (Aurora), the Randahl Shop (Park Ridge), and the Tre'O Shop (Evanston).

The Pickard China Company and numerous studios hand painted porcelain. Other small shops crafted leather goods, hand printed books, cut and engraved glass, or made intricate leaded glass windows and light fixtures. Small workshops and large factories turned out straight-lined furniture in the Mission style for thousands of new bungalows.

The city's leading producers of art pottery were primarily engaged in the manufacture of architectural terra cotta. Frank Lloyd Wright and several architects associated with the Prairie School designed Teco ware, a molded art pottery produced at the American Terra Cotta & Ceramic Company's factory near Crystal Lake.

By 1914 these handicrafts industries, as well as the Arts and Crafts movement itself, had reached their peak of popularity and were turning into leisure activities or personal and social therapy.

Cultural institutions

Many of Chicago's arts groups and institutions may be found in clusters. Michigan Avenue might fairly be called the main cultural thoroughfare of Chicago, because most of the major institutions are located on or near it. South of the Loop and east of Michigan Avenue is the Museum Campus (created in the 1990s by relocating part of Lake Shore Drive), which joins the south end of Grant Park to the Adler Planetarium & Astronomy Museum (1930), the John G. Shedd Aquarium (1930), and the Field Museum of Natural History (1893). Several blocks farther north, the Auditorium Theatre (1889) is the site of touring plays, popular concerts, and visiting orchestras and is the home of the Joffrey Ballet, which moved from New York City to Chicago in 1995. A few more blocks north is Symphony Center (formerly Orchestra Hall), home of the Chicago Symphony Orchestra and its training ensemble, the Civic Orchestra of Chicago, as well as a venue for other musical events.

Across the street sits the Art Institute of Chicago, a world-class art museum and school dating to 1893 at its present site; it surveys world art and is notable for its large collection of French Impressionist paintings. Just to the north is the old Chicago Public Library (1897) building, since 1991 the Chicago Cultural Center; graced with marble and mosaic interiors and a large Tiffany stained-glass dome, it provides a variety of spaces for performances and temporary art exhibits. The Cultural Center is on the edge of a burgeoning downtown theatre district, with large venues for touring plays and musicals, more-intimate stages for smaller groups, and the Goodman Theatre, which was founded in the 1920s. East of North Michigan Avenue is the Museum of Contemporary Art (founded 1967), which collects works created after 1945. On the west side of the Loop, the Civic Opera House (1929) on Wacker Drive is the home of Chicago's Lyric Opera.

Another notable cluster of cultural institutions is found in the Hyde Park community on the South Side near the University of Chicago campus. The Museum of Science and Industry opened in 1933 in the heavily restored Palace of Fine Arts from the 1893 World's Columbian Exposition. It houses a five-story Omnimax theatre. The university's Oriental Institute (1931) contains a collection of artifacts from archaeological expeditions to the Middle East and East Asia. The DuSable Museum of African American History (1961) is one of the country's oldest museums devoted to the study of African American life and history. In addition, Robie House (1908–10), owned by the university, is one of the finest examples of Prairie-style architecture.

Chicago's cultural life is by no means concentrated in a few places. Its voluminous libraries, located around the city, also make it a major research centre. After the Great Fire of 1871 destroyed private collections in the city, a gift of books from donors in England was used to create the Chicago Public Library. Philanthropists also established the private Newberry (1887) and John Crerar (1894) libraries, the latter now a part of the University of Chicago. The varied collections of institutions of higher education also help make Chicago one of the country's leading library centres.

There are other specialized institutions scattered throughout the city, including the Chicago History Museum (established 1856; formerly the Chicago Historical Society), which focuses on local and American history. Ethnic diversity and pride are reflected in the many small museums devoted to the art and history of various national groups. Several gallery districts have also developed north and west of the downtown area to showcase the work of artists who have found relatively inexpensive space in scattered neighbourhoods.

Recreation

Tourists and Chicagoans alike are drawn as culture and amusement consumers to the varied and lively leisure life of the city. The slogan "Urbs in Horto" ("City in a Garden"), which has appeared on the official seal of the city since 1837, reflects not only an extensive system of city parks as well as backyard and rooftop gardening but also public institutions dedicated to nature education and recreation. Within the city the Peggy Notebaert Nature Museum of the Chicago Academy of Sciences (1999) is located near the Lincoln Park Zoo (1868), one of the country's few remaining zoos offering free admission, and the West Side's Garfield Park contains one of the nation's largest conservatories (1907). The more-open space of the suburbs is home to other nature retreats, including a second zoological park, the Brookfield Zoo (formally the Chicago Zoological Society). The more than 1,500-acre (600-hectare) Morton Arboretum (1922) in Lisle and the Chicago Botanic Garden (1972) in Glencoe are outstanding open-air museums. Added to these are the belts of county forest preserves.

"Wait till next year!" is the perennial cry of the ever-optimistic Chicago sports fan. The city has produced some championship professional teams over the years notably the Bulls (men's basketball) during the 1990s but, more typically, teams find themselves out of contention at the end of the regular season; the Cubs and White Sox, two of the oldest franchises in Major League Baseball, have made only a handful of World Series appearances between them. Other professional teams include the Bears (gridiron football), Blackhawks (hockey), Fire (football [soccer]), and Sky (women's basketball).

The park district offers many opportunities for nonprofessional athletics of all types, while many local residents find great pleasure as weekend sailors and power boaters on Lake Michigan. In addition, crowds of runners, walkers, and cyclists take advantage of the paths that wind their way through the city's lakefront parkland. Two newer venues, Navy Pier and Millennium Park, have become the most popular lakefront draws for visitors and residents alike. Navy Pier, extensively renovated in the 1990s, boasts amusements, restaurants, theatres, and docking facilities for boat excursions. Millennium Park, built largely over railroad tracks at the northwestern corner of Grant Park and officially opened in 2004, includes fountains, eye-catching sculptures, gardens, a large outdoor concert facility designed by architect Frank Gehry, a restaurant, and an outdoor ice skating rink.

Press and broadcasting

Chicago has always been one of the country's great newspaper towns, but the once-numerous major metropolitan dailies have dwindled to only two: the Chicago Sun-Times and the Chicago Tribune. Another daily, the Chicago Defender, is oriented primarily toward the city's African American community, and Crain's Chicago Business provides economic and financial news. In addition, there are dozens of daily and weekly foreign-language, neighbourhood, and suburban newspapers, including the weekly La Raza, which serves a growing Hispanic population.

Chicago had a central role in the development of both radio and television broadcasting, and it has continued to be a leader in both mediums. The public television station WTTW was one of the country's pioneers in educational programming. There are scores of radio and television stations in the region.

History

The 19th century

Early growth

Chicago's critical location on the water route linking the Great Lakes and the Mississippi River shaped much of its early history. It was populated by a series of native tribes who maintained villages in the forested areas near rivers. Beginning with Father Jacques Marquette and French Canadian explorer Louis Jolliet in 1673, a steady stream of explorers and missionaries passed through or settled in the region, but it was not until 1779 that the first nonnative resident made it his permanent home: Jean-Baptist-Point Du Sable maintained a thriving trading post near the mouth of the Chicago River until 1800, when he moved out of the region. Within a few years the federal government had erected Fort Dearborn to establish a military presence in the area. The garrison was located on the south bank at the river mouth; it was destroyed during the War of 1812 but was rebuilt in 1816. By that time, numerous traders linked the region with international fur markets. Even after Illinois became a state in 1818, however, Chicago remained a small settlement. It was incorporated as a town in 1833 with a population of about 350.

Population growth remained stagnant until the federal government allocated funding that allowed work to begin on the Illinois and Michigan Canal, a vital link between Lake Michigan and the Illinois River. Because the project was to be financed largely by sales of adjacent land, which would benefit from the commerce it brought, the canal helped to fill Chicago with speculators. The boom led to a second incorporation, this time as a city, on March 4, 1837; the population was 4,170. That same year a devastating national economic depression delayed the city's development for several years. Canal construction drew thousands of Irish labourers to the area, when what was supposed to be a simple ditch a few hundred yards long grew into a waterway of some 75 miles (120 km), often cut through solid rock. After the canal opened in 1848, it brought grain and other raw materials to the city, while providing what was then a fast and convenient means of travel to the interior of the state.

Emergence as a transportation hub

Chicago's railway age also began in 1848, when a locomotive named the Pioneer arrived by ship from Buffalo, New York, and went into service for the new Galena and Chicago Union Railroad. The line's 11-mile (18-km) track extended straight west from the city, but its namesake destination, the lead-mining metropolis in the northwest corner of the state, declined in importance before extensions even reached it. Other lines soon extended to the west, including the Chicago, Burlington and Quincy, the Rock Island, and the Illinois Central. The Chicago and Milwaukee line linked the rival ports by rail. In 1852 two separate lines entered from the east and provided direct rail service to the Eastern Seaboard. By the beginning of the 20th century, no fewer than 30 interstate routes fanned out from the city, and the resulting ease in reaching both raw materials and markets contributed to the city's rapid commercial and industrial development. Most important of all, Chicago was the terminus of every one of the railroads; passengers, raw materials, and finished goods all had to be transferred between lines in the city, thus contributing to an extraordinary development of hotels, restaurants, taxicabs, warehouses, rail yards, and trucking companies.

The railroad, along with the telegraph, the grain elevator, agricultural newspapers, and the trading floor of the Chicago Board of Trade, facilitated the collection of commodities from the farm belt, which was rapidly developing to the west. The city soon became the focal point of a "golden funnel" that collected and processed grain, lumber, and meat and then sent them to markets in the eastern United States and Europe. Trade encouraged ancillary industries such as the manufacture of steel rails and railroad equipment, shipbuilding, packaging, and printing, as well as the development of hotels and restaurant facilities. However, nothing at that time personified Chicago industry more than meatpacking and the vast Union Stock Yards on the city's Near Southwest Side.

Conflagration and rebirth

Chicago's growth was unprecedented. The population reached nearly 30,000 in 1850 and was triple that a decade later. Cheap transportation to the outskirts of the city encouraged middle-class dispersal, but poor neighbourhoods near the downtown area were congested; structures there were also built of wood. Serious fires were frequent, but no one could have anticipated the events of the evening of October 8, 1871. Months without rain had parched the city, and a major fire the previous night had exhausted firefighters and damaged equipment. It is not known what happened in the De Koven Street barn of Patrick and Catherine O'Leary, on the city's West Side. Vandals, milk thieves, a drunken neighbour, spontaneous combustion, even (though unlikely) the O'Learys' legendary cow any could have started a blaze there that roared out of control in minutes. Misdirected fire equipment arrived too late, and a steady wind from the southwest carried the flames and blazing debris from block to block. The slums became kindling for the downtown conflagration, where even the supposedly fireproof stone and brick buildings exploded in flames as the destruction swept northward. Only rainfall, the lake, and stretches of unbuilt lots on the North Side finally halted the wave of destruction a full day after it started. The most famous fire in American history claimed about 300 lives, destroyed some 17,450 buildings covering almost 3.5 square miles (9 square km), and caused $200 million in damage. Roughly one-third of the city lay in ruins, and an equal proportion of the population nearly 100,000 people was homeless.

Chicago rebuilt quickly, reached more than a half million residents in 1880, and accomplished construction miracles. As a response to public health concerns, the newly formed Sanitary District of Metropolitan Chicago began work in 1889 on the Chicago Sanitary and Ship Canal, the waterway that when opened in 1900 not only allowed larger vessels to pass through the port of Chicago but also made it possible to reverse the flow of the Chicago River; the improvement in public health once pollutants were carried away from Lake Michigan was dramatic.

Meanwhile, a host of talented architects that included Louis Sullivan, Dankmar Adler, William Holabird, Daniel H. Burnham, John Wellborn Root, and William Le Baron Jenney, who had been attracted to Chicago by the postfire rebuilding opportunities, stayed on in the 1880s to design a new generation of even taller downtown buildings. Department stores and offices crowded into the central area, and industrial growth along the river branches and rail lines was equally phenomenal. Commuter railroads and transit improvements promoted outward residential dispersal of the middle class, a clientele served by a young Frank Lloyd Wright and the emerging "Prairie school" architects. This suburban boom prompted the city to annex some 125 square miles (324 square km) in 1889, which included many adjacent communities and also much open farmland.

Social strains and a world's fair: the city comes of age

That same year two young women, Jane Addams and Ellen Gates Starr, arrived to take up residence in one of the congested slums that had sprung up in the tumbledown West Side of the city. Their Hull House programs in recreation, job training, day care, health care, thrift, workplace safety, and culture combated but did not eradicate rampant unemployment, crime, and other social problems that were endemic in urban tenements. Discontent with living conditions, in turn, helped to fuel outbursts against the low wages, unemployment, monotonous work, and steep production quotas that came with the city's rapid industrialization.

Outbreaks of labour violence became common, and the Chicago experience made the rest of the country fearful that the future would be filled with proletarian strife. Local workers battled police during the nationwide railway strike of 1877. But the Haymarket Riot of 1886 captured the world's attention when police efforts to break up a protest meeting in the Randolph Street produce market were met with a bomb explosion that killed seven policemen and an unknown number of workers. The prolonged trial and the execution of those who were accused of plotting the blast deeply divided the community and the world. Eight years after that, violence once more erupted as workers at the Pullman Palace Car Company on the South Side walked off the job to protest wage cuts that were not matched by rent reductions at George Pullman's model town where most were forced to live.

In 1890 Chicago's population pushed past the one million mark. That year the U.S. Congress granted the city the right to host the World's Columbian Exposition, honouring the 400th anniversary of Christopher Columbus's 1492 arrival in the New World. Delays pushed the opening into 1893. Set in Jackson Park, some 8 miles (13 km) south of downtown along the lakeshore, the event was a spectacular extravaganza that assembled more than a million artifacts representing the world's industrial and cultural progress. Besides enlightening exhibits, performances, and off-site intellectual conferences, the fair offered the Midway Plaisance, a collection of ersatz travel experiences, bazaars, eateries, and rides, the most famous of which was the 255-foot (78-metre) Ferris wheel. The event attracted some 25.8 million visitors during its six-month run.

Chicago since c. 1900

"No little plans"

The fair opened during a financial panic and closed during a deep depression, but the city's recovery four years later was dramatic. Chicago's population surged past two million in 1907 and three million in 1923. The city eagerly adopted every transportation innovation: streetcars moved first by horses, then by means of underground cables, and finally by electricity were supplemented in the 1890s by the first elevated rail lines. However, every transportation innovation seemed to produce only more congestion. The railroads also left their physical mark on the city. Concerns over grade-crossing safety forced the rail lines to construct tall embankments for their tracks, which, in turn, walled off neighbourhoods. The smoke and noise from thousands of freight trains and hundreds of passenger-train arrivals and departures each day saturated the city in gloomy soot and jangled its nerves.

Chicago was well on its way to choking on its growth when architects Daniel H. Burnham and Edward P. Bennett unveiled their 1909 Plan of Chicago. Commissioned by two private commercial organizations, the plan provided a rational transportation-based blueprint for urban growth, notably in the central area. It promised to replace ugliness and congestion with extraordinary beauty and efficiency. Although plans for relocating railroads were ignored, Chicago's city government eagerly adopted ideas for plazas, major thoroughfares that bridged railway tracks, a double-deck street along the river downtown, monumental bridge structures, and the preservation of the lakefront for park purposes inspired by Burnham's now-famous credo "Make no little plans."

The document was never officially adopted by the city council, but it became a shopping list for projects started during the 1920s, including construction of the Michigan Avenue Bridge and the Outer Drive. In 1916 the city completed the 1.5-mile- (2.4-km-) long Municipal (later Navy) Pier as a combination shipping warehouse and public recreation retreat. But the city, under the leadership of Mayor William Hale ("Big Bill") Thompson, went into debt far beyond its ability to repay, and the double-deck Wacker Drive and Outer Drive Bridge improvements remained unfinished at the onset of the Great Depression.

Chicago became notorious during the Prohibition years of the "Roaring" 1920s as a wide-open town, gaining a reputation for corruption, gangsterism, and intermittent mayhem. Al Capone, John Dillinger, and the St. Valentine's Day Massacre became bywords worldwide. Furthermore, the city government was virtually insolvent years before the 1929 stock market crash. Republican Thompson was defeated by Democrat Anton Cermak in 1931, the first of a long string of Democratic mayors. Cermak, however, fell two years later to an assassin's bullet intended for U.S. President-elect Franklin D. Roosevelt, who was visiting the city.

The new mayor, Edward J. Kelly, gladly accepted federal relief funds that employed thousands on projects that completed the Outer Drive Bridge, built the State Street subway, and constructed hundreds of miles of streets, sewers, sidewalks, and curbs. Workers for other relief projects painted murals in post offices and schools, collected sources for historical research, and provided free music. Chicago's WPA Federal Theatre created Swing Mikado, which later enjoyed success on Broadway, and also developed new techniques of improvisational comedy and puppetry. In 1933–34 Chicago played host to its second world's fair, the Century of Progress Exposition, organized to mark the centennial of the town charter. Conceived initially to displace the Capone crime era from the city's image, the fair turned into a celebration of technology as the saviour of the country's economy. Its Art Deco–style architecture and brilliant colours were a lure for tens of millions of visitors during its two-year run.

Decline and confrontation

World War II placed Chicago in a strategic production role because of its diverse industrial base, and the city's economy boomed. In addition, the nearby Great Lakes Naval Training Center and Fort Sheridan were major induction and basic-training facilities, and Northwestern University operated the country's largest naval midshipmen's school. Thousands of naval pilots also passed through Glenview Naval Air Station, receiving flight instruction on two aircraft carriers on the lake that were converted from old passenger vessels. As the country's rail hub, Chicago hosted traveling military personnel in four Chicago servicemen's centres; one of them, the historic Auditorium Building, not only served 24 million meals by the war's end but also saw its magnificent stage used as a bowling alley.

The postwar years began a period of many adjustments. In 1947 Mayor Kelly was replaced by a reform-oriented businessman named Martin Kennelly, whose eight years in office ended with the election of Richard J. Daley in an intra-party coup. Chicago reached its population peak of 3.62 million in 1950, but by that time there were already signs of impending industrial decline. In addition, the city's social fabric was changing. Chicago went through many difficult years of increasing racial tensions, as its expanding African American community sought to escape the boundaries of segregated neighbourhoods. Some efforts to achieve this were peaceful, such as the crusade that brought civil rights leader Martin Luther King, Jr., to Chicago in 1966. However, black frustrations also spilled over into violence, including riots in the summer of 1967 and even larger ones following King's assassination (in Memphis, Tennessee) in 1968. Whites generally responded by leaving the city in increasing numbers for the suburbs.

The bloody confrontation that erupted between anti-Vietnam War protesters (and other demonstrators) and police at the 1968 Democratic National Convention in Chicago focused negative attention on the city and the last major old-fashioned big-city political machine in the country. However, the growing difficulties and uncertainties of the postwar era that, essentially, came to a head at the convention help explain why so many Chicagoans held on for so long to the Democratic machine, especially as it developed under Daley. His leadership gave them jobs, representation by nationality, and, most important, some sense of predictability in a changing world.

Renewal

Although some of Chicago's neighbourhoods decayed and much of its industry moved either to the suburbs, out of state, or overseas, the city's central area began to revive in the late 1950s under Daley's leadership. The John Hancock Building, the Sears (now Willis) Tower, and dozens of other new office structures in the Loop and Near North areas, as well as the emergence of O'Hare International Airport as the country's air hub, provided enticements for attracting corporate headquarters. By the mid-1970s the downtown office revival was beginning to produce the first signs of gentrification in nearby neighbourhoods. The political upheaval that followed Daley's death in 1976 drew headlines away from the nascent downtown revival. The initiation of Chicagofest, a music and food extravaganza that was later transformed into the Taste of Chicago, signaled the beginning of what has been a continuing city effort to lure suburban leisure spending back to the city through a series of outdoor special events.

In 1989 Daley's son, Richard M. Daley, took office as mayor and placed even more emphasis on attracting corporate headquarters, trade, tourism, and the convention business. The influx of new residents to downtown, as well as growing Hispanic and other ethnic communities, brought a halt to half a century of population decline, and Chicagoans numbered some 2.8 million by the early 21st century. Two events held in Chicago in the 1990s several opening matches of the 1994 World Cup football (soccer) finals and the 1996 Democratic National Convention were great successes for the city and garnered it considerable national and international notice. In 2007, shortly after Daley was reelected to his fifth (and fourth full) term as mayor (his first had been for two years), the city was selected as the U.S. entry for hosting the 2016 Olympic Summer Games; however, it was eliminated in the first round of voting by the International Olympic Committee. (Rio de Janeiro was chosen in the third round.)

The second Daley era began drawing to a close when the mayor announced in September 2010 that he would not seek reelection to a seventh term, and a mayoral election was called for February 22, 2011. An initially wide field of hopefuls was ultimately winnowed to six candidates. The front-runner was Rahm Emanuel, who stepped down from his position as White House chief of staff under Pres. Barack Obama in order to run for Chicago mayor. Emanuel won the election and took office on May 16. His first term was characterized in part by a controversial decision to close dozens of public schools. In his 2015 bid for reelection, Emanuel failed to win a majority in the first round of voting in February and faced his nearest challenger, Jesús ("Chuy") García, a longtime public servant, in the city's first-ever mayoral runoff election. Emanuel was victorious, however, in the April contest.

Creativity, a fascinating mix of cultures, bold new buildings, a vital economy, and the dichotomy between wealth and poverty continue to mark life in Chicago. While it deservedly celebrates a rich cultural past, Chicago remains the innovative cultural centre of the Midwest. Much as it did more than a century ago, the city continues to attract talented young artists, musicians, actors, and writers from throughout the region.

Travel and Tlourism

Things to Do

The quintessential American city stuffed with things to do, Chicago offers world-class culture with zero attitude. From Grant Park, the skyline is awe-inspiring, while the attractions of the nearby Museum Campus draw visitors and locals alike. Serious shoppers head for the high-fashion boutiques and multilevel malls along the Magnificent Mile, but the tree-lined streets of the Gold Coast and walking trails along the Lake Michigan shoreline offer a respite from the crowds. A rattling El ride through the heart of the Loop brings the city's booming business district up close and personal.

Things to See: For an overview of Chicago's iconic cityscape, head for the top of the Willis (Sears) Tower or the John Hancock Center. Admire American Gothic and other masterpieces at the Art Institute, then get a waterfront view of the city's past and present on a Chicago Architecture Foundation boat tour. Traveling with kids? Stroll Lincoln Park Zoo (for free!) or spend a day exploring the U-505 submarine and other wonders of the Museum of Science and Industry.

Active Pursuits: Explore the miles-long path that hugs the Lake Michigan coastline, then rent a bike or join a pickup volleyball game at sprawling North Avenue Beach. Culturally minded? Take a sculpture-spotting stroll through the Loop to admire works by Picasso and Miró, and walk through the wildly popular, bean-shaped Cloud Gate. Baseball fans can pay homage to one of the last of the old-time ballparks, Wrigley Field; cheer on the Cubbies from the raucous bleachers, or check out the view from the field on a behind-the-scenes tour.

Restaurants & Dining: From haute to down-home, Chicago has restaurants to suit all tastes. Chef Grant Achatz redefined fine dining at Alinea, while his fellow superstar chef Tony Mantuano at Spiaggia gets global raves. Explore the city's ethnic diversity in Greektown and at Mexican mainstay Frontera Grill. For gut-busting satisfaction, chow down on Chicago-style deep-dish pizza at Gino's East or the original Pizzeria Uno.

Nightlife & Entertainment: The Goodman Theatre and Chicago Shakespeare Theatre are the heavy-hitters of Chicago's vibrant theater scene. Classical superstars take the stage at the Lyric Opera and Chicago Symphony Orchestra, while Second City and iO continue the city's legacy of improv comedy. Catch top pop acts at venues such as the Chicago Theatre, or head to grungy-cool Wicker Park to hear up-and-coming bands.

The Best Museums in Chicago

Art Institute of Chicago: A must-see for art lovers, the Art Institute manages to combine blockbuster exhibits with smaller, uncrowded spaces for private meditation. Internationally known for its French Impressionist collection, the Art Institute can also transport you to Renaissance Italy, ancient China, or the world of the Old Masters. The dazzling, light-filled Modern Wing, added in 2009, has also given the museum's 20th-century modern art collection the setting it deserves.

Field Museum of Natural History: The grand neoclassical entrance hall will make you feel as if you've entered somewhere important, a sense of drama only enhanced by the towering figure of Sue, the largest *Tyrannosaurus* rex skeleton ever uncovered. The Field can easily entertain for an entire day. Exhibits include ancient Egyptian mummies, a full-size Maori Meeting House, and stuffed figures of the notorious man-eating lions of Tsavo.

<u>John G. Shedd Aquarium</u>: Sure, you'll find plenty of tanks filled with exotic fish, but the Shedd is also home to some wonderful large-scale re-creations of natural habitats. Stroll through Wild Reef, and you'll see sharks swim overhead. The lovely Oceanarium, where you can watch a dolphin show, features floor-to-ceiling windows; you'll feel as if you're sitting outdoors, even on the chilliest Chicago day.

<u>Museum of Science and Industry</u>: Families can easily spend an entire day at this sprawling museum and still not see everything. Although the exhibits promote scientific knowledge, most have an interactive element that keeps kids engaged. But it's not all computers and technology. Some of the classic exhibits the underground re-creation of the coal mine and the World War II German U-boat have been drawing visitors for generations.

<u>Frank Lloyd Wright Home and Studio</u>: The Midwest's greatest architect started out in the Chicago suburb of Oak Park, and his house now a museum with guided tours   gives a firsthand look at how his ideas developed and influenced American architecture. The surrounding neighborhood, where Wright's Prairie-style homes sit side by side with rambling Victorian villas, is an eye-opening lesson in architectural history.

The Best Nightlife in Chicago

<u>Getting the Blues</u>: Here, in the world capital of the blues, you've got your pick of places to feel them, from the touristy but lively atmosphere of <u>Kingston Mines</u> in Lincoln Park, where musicians perform continuously on two stages, to the roadhouse feel of <u>Buddy Guy's Legends</u>, where musicians in town while on tour have been known to play impromptu sets.

<u>Taking in a Show</u>: The stage lights rarely go dark on one of the country's busiest theater scenes. Chicago is home to a downtown Broadway-style district anchored by beautifully restored historic theaters, the nationally known <u>Goodman Theatre</u>, and, on nearby <u>Navy Pier</u>, the city's resident <u>Shakespeare troupe</u>. Beyond downtown,

you'll find a number of innovative independent companies where future stars get their big breaks and the pure love of theater makes up for the low budgets.

Experiencing Cool Jazz at the Green Mill: This atmospheric Uptown jazz club is the place to go to soak up smooth sounds from some of the hottest up-and-coming performers on the jazz scene, while the club itself is a living museum of 1930s Chicago. The Sunday night "Poetry Slam" is a big crowd-pleaser.

Watching Improv Come Alive: Chicago is a comedy breeding ground, having launched the careers of John Belushi, Bill Murray, Mike Myers, and Tina Fey through improv and sketch-comedy hotspots such as Second City and iO. The shows may soar or crash, but you just might catch one of comedy's newest stars.

Best Dining Bets in Chicago

Best Splurge: The standard-bearer for Chicago's reinvention as a culinary leader is Alinea, where chef Grant Achatz astounds and delights professional critics and amateur foodies with his ability to transform familiar food into unexpected shapes, textures, and presentations.

Best View: Forty stories above Chicago, Everest, in the heart of the Loop, astounds with a spectacular view   and food to match. The panoramas are equally awe-inspiring at the Signature Room at the 95th, which is perched on the 95th floor of the John Hancock Center, the city's second-tallest building. Closer to earth, diners on the patio at Greektown's Athena get a panoramic view of the city skyline.

Best Spot for a Romantic Dinner: Secluded North Pond is an Arts and Crafts-style retreat with a postcard-perfect setting in Lincoln Park. Not only does it boast a dramatic vista of the Gold Coast skyline, but the restaurant's out-of-the-way locale also requires diners to begin and end their meals with an idyllic stroll through the park.

Best Cheap Eats: It's hard to find a dining bargain downtown, but foodlife, inside the Water Tower Place shopping center, offers affordable lunch and dinner options in the heart of North Michigan Avenue's shopping district. Yes, it's a food court, but there are no chain fast-food stalls here: Instead you'll find a variety of made-to-order choices, from stir fry and burgers to fresh salads and pastas. In Lincoln Park and Wicker Park, cash-strapped 20-somethings and families head to Penny's Noodle Shop for delicious, low-priced Asian noodle dishes and soups.

Best for Kids: Going out for deep-dish pizza is pretty much a requirement for any family visiting Chicago. Gino's East and the original Pizzeria Uno have been around for decades, and they're still serving up authentic versions of the city's gooey, gut-busting specialty. For something different from the usual fast food, try Wishbone in the West Loop, a family-owned spot specializing in Southern food with a casual vibe and plenty of mix-and-match menu options for fussy eaters.

Best American Cuisine: It's no longer the see-and-be-seen spot it was when it first opened, but mk is actually better now that the crowds have moved on, serving up accessible twists on classic American dishes in a space that is both comfortable and sophisticated.

Best French Cuisine: An updated take on the bistro experience, Bistronomicoffers classic French dishes in a fresh, modern setting, just a few blocks from the Magnificent Mile. Convivial Mon Ami Gabi re-creates the look and feel of a Parisian cafe, steps from Lincoln Park Zoo and the lakefront.

Best Italian Cuisine: Even without the glamorous view of the Magnificent Mile, ultra-elegant Spiaggia would draw diners with its gourmet versions of classic Italian cuisine. For a more casual atmosphere, it's hard to beat Mia Francesca in Lincoln Park, or its sister restaurant, Francesca's on Chestnut, just off the Magnificent Mile. Both are bustling, Americanized twists on classic trattoria dining, where the fresh, seasonal pastas are the main draw.

Best Steakhouse: Legendary Chicago restaurateur Arnie Morton no longer prowls the dining room, but <u>Morton's</u> remains the king of the city's old-guard steakhouses, serving up gargantuan wet-aged steaks and baked potatoes. <u>Gene & Georgetti</u> is another blast from the past, a long-time hangout for the city's movers and shakers that's barely changed since it opened in 1941   and that's exactly why the regulars like it. And we'd be remiss not to mention <u>Gibsons Bar & Steakhouse</u> which is the kind of place to live large (literally). The portions are enormous, so you're encouraged to share, which only adds to the party atmosphere.

Best Pretheater Dinner: A longtime local favorite in the Loop, the <u>Italian Village</u>   three restaurants run by one family under one roof knows how to get its clientele seated and fed in time for a show. For Chicago Symphony Orchestra audiences, <u>Rhapsody</u> is conveniently located in the Symphony Center building. If you're seeing a play in Lincoln Park, stop first for tasty tapas and pitchers of sangria at <u>Café Ba-Ba-Reeba</u>!

The Best Shopping in Chicago

<u>ArchiCenter Shop</u>: Looking for unique, well-designed souvenirs? This store, run by the Chicago Architecture Foundation, should be your first stop. You'll find Frank Lloyd Wright bookmarks, puzzles of the Chicago skyline, picture frames with patterns designed by famed local architect Louis Sullivan, and a great selection of Chicago history books.

<u>The T-Shirt Deli</u>: Got a soft spot for those cheesy 1970s "Foxy Lady" T-shirts? Head to the T-Shirt Deli, where the staff will customize shirts while you wait. Come up with your own message, or browse the hundreds of in-stock iron-on decals (everything from Gary Coleman to Hello Kitty). And just like at a real deli, your purchase is wrapped in white paper and served with a bag of potato chips.

<u>Architectural Artifacts, Inc.</u>: This vast warehouse of material salvaged from historic buildings is a home renovator's dream. Although it's far off the usual tourist route, design buffs will find it well worth the trip

the enormous inventory includes fireplace mantels, stained glass windows, and garden sculptures. The owners display pieces of particular historic value in an attached museum.

Best Hotel Bets in Chicago

Best Splurge: The <u>Waldorf Astoria Chicago</u>, steps from Barneys New York and Prada on the Gold Coast, fits right in with its swanky neighborhood. King rooms come with fireplaces, Italian luxury linens, and extra-large soaking tubs; guests can lounge at the spa, or take advantage of the hotel's fleet of Lexus automobiles to head beyond downtown.

Best Bang for Your Buck: The <u>Hampton Inn & Suites</u> not only offers consistently lower rates than other hotels in centrally located River North, it's also more stylish than the name implies, with Deco-style touches in the lobby and common rooms. What really sets it apart, though, are the amenities that come with those reasonable rates: an indoor pool with hot tub, rooftop deck, and a free hot breakfast buffet.

Best Historic Hotels: <u>The Drake Hotel</u> is Chicago's original luxury hotel, and walking into its grand, formal lobby is like stepping back into the 19th century, especially if you settle down for afternoon tea in the elegant Palm Court. The comfortable rooms don't have quite as much character, but those facing north offer only-in-Chicago views of Lake Michigan and Lake Shore Drive. To experience Chicago <u>architectural history</u> first-hand, book a room at the <u>Hotel Burnham</u>, a complete rehab of the revered Reliance Building, one of the world's first glass-walled skyscrapers.

Best for Business Travelers: Virtually every hotel in Chicago qualifies, but the <u>Swissôtel Chicago</u> combines extensive business services with stunning views from all rooms. Traveler-friendly amenities include generously sized desks and ergonomic chairs in each room, and the light-filled penthouse fitness center allows you to admire the city while working out.

Best Service: The attention to detail, regal pampering, and well-connected concierges at both the <u>Ritz-Carlton</u> and the <u>Four Seasons</u> make them the hotels of choice for travelers who want to feel like royalty.

Most Romantic: For a splurge, the <u>Peninsula</u> pampers couples with luxurious rooms and top-notch amenities, including massages in the onsite spa and an outdoor terrace for lounging; the dimly lit, sexy lobby bar makes a good spot for a nightcap, especially if you snag a spot by the fireplace. For a cozier getaway, try the <u>Talbott Hotel</u>, which is centrally located but tucked away from the crowds. Book the hotel's Romance Package, and you'll get a set of monogrammed bathrobes, as well as a late-afternoon checkout.

Best Views: Almost every hotel in town has rooms with great views and others that look straight into neighboring offices. The <u>Swissôtel</u> and the <u>Park Hyatt Chicago</u> are both set apart from surrounding buildings, giving their rooms unobstructed views across the city (the higher the room, the more you'll see). For a distinctly urban vista, <u>The Wit Hotel</u> looks out over the Loop's busy El tracks; its rooftop lounge is the perfect place to admire the city lights by night.

Best for Families: With every room a suite, the <u>Embassy Suites</u> and <u>Homewood Suites</u> are ideal for families looking for a little more space than the typical hotel room provides (units at Homewood Suites also include a full kitchen, so parents can save money by preparing their own meals). Both have indoor pools, so the kids can splash around no matter what the weather, and offer a free hot breakfast buffet.

Best Hotel Pool: With its floor-to-ceiling windows overlooking Michigan Avenue, the pool at the <u>Peninsula Chicago</u> is a bright, stylish oasis flooded with natural light. But for historic charm, it's hard to beat the Spanish-styled junior Olympic-size pool at the <u>InterContinental Chicago</u>. Considered an engineering marvel when it was constructed in 1929, it was a favorite training spot for Olympic gold-medal swimmer (and later *Tarzan* star) Johnny Weissmuller.

Best Off-the-Beaten-Path Hotels: The <u>City Suites Hotel</u>, the <u>Majestic Hotel</u>, and the <u>Best Western Hawthorne Terrace</u>, located in residential <u>North Side neighborhoods</u>, have a more personal feel than many downtown hotels. They're also convenient to public transportation.

Best Free Things to Do in Chicago

<u>Exploring Millennium Park</u>: This downtown park, carved out of the northwest corner of Grant Park, is one of the city's best spots for strolling, hanging out, and people-watching. (*Bonus:* It's an easy walk from downtown hotels.) While the Pritzker Music Pavilion, designed by Frank Gehry, is the highest-profile attraction, the park's two main sculptures have quickly become local favorites. *Cloud Gate,* by British sculptor Anish Kapoor, looks like a giant silver kidney bean; watch your reflection bend and distort as you walk around and underneath. The *Crown Fountain,* designed by Spanish sculptor Jaume Plensa, is framed by two giant video screens that project faces of ordinary Chicagoans. It looks a little creepy at first, but watch the kids splashing in the shallow water and you'll soon realize that this is public art at its best.

<u>Bonding with the Animals at Lincoln Park Zoo</u>: You have no excuse not to visit: Lincoln Park Zoo is open 365 days a year and astonishingly remains completely free, despite many recent upgrades. Occupying a prime spot of <u>Lincoln Park</u> close to the lakefront, the zoo is small enough to explore in an afternoon and varied enough to make you feel as though you've traveled around the world. For families, this is a don't-miss stop.

<u>Listening to Music Under the Stars</u>: Summer is prime time for live music and often you won't have to pay a dime. The Grant Park Music Festival presents free classical concerts from June through August in Millennium Park. A few blocks south, you'll find the outdoor dance floor that's home to Chicago SummerDance, where you can learn new dance moves and swing to a variety of live acts on Thursday through Sunday nights. The summer also brings a range of large-scale music festivals from Blues Fest to a rock-'n'-roll-themed Fourth of July

concert but the Grant Park classical concerts are considerably less crowded (and far more civilized).

Discovering Future Masterpieces: Chicago's vibrant contemporary art scene is divided between two different neighborhoods. The original, River North, is still home to many of the city's best-known galleries and is within walking distance from downtown hotels. The West Loop houses newer galleries with, overall, a younger perspective in freshly renovated lofts. You don't need to be a serious collector to browse; just bring an open mind.

The Best Authentic Experiences in Chicago

Shopping the Town: Michigan Avenue is often touted as a shopper'sparadise, thanks to its lineup of big-name designer boutiques and multilevel high-end shopping malls. But that's all stuff you can find in any other big city. For more distinctive items, head to Chicago's residential districts, where trendy independent clothing boutiques sit next to eclectic home design stores filled with one-of-a-kind treasures. The home decor shops along Armitage Avenue cater to stylish young families with plenty of spending money, while Wicker Park and Bucktown attract edgy fashionistas with a range of funky clothing shops. Southport Avenue (near Wrigley Field) and West Division Street (south of Wicker Park) are the newest cool shopping meccas with no nametag-wearing conventioneers in sight.

Soaking up Sun at Wrigley Field: It's a Chicago tradition to play hooky for an afternoon, sit in the bleachers at this historic baseball park, and watch the Cubbies try to hit 'em onto Waveland Avenue. Note that the Cubs sell out almost every game; your best bet is to buy tickets for a weekday afternoon (although you'll often find season ticket holders selling seats at face value in front of Wrigley right before a game). Even if you can't get in, you can still soak in the atmosphere at one of the neighborhood's many watering holes.

Playing in the Sand: If you're staying at a downtown hotel, you can hit the sands of Chicago's urban beaches almost as quickly as your elevator gets you to the lobby. Oak Street Beach (at Michigan Ave. and Lake Shore Dr.) is mostly for posing. North Avenue Beach, a little farther north along the lakefront path, is home to weekend volleyball games, family beach outings, and a whole lot of eye candy. You probably won't do any swimming (even in the middle of summer, the water's frigid), but either beach makes a great place to hang out with a picnic and a book on a warm afternoon.

Raising a Glass (or a Coffee Cup): Chicago has its share of trendy lounges that serve overpriced specialty martinis, but the heart of the city's nightlife remains the neighborhood taverns. These are the places you can soak in a convivial atmosphere without attitude or self-consciously flashy decor, but also have a conversation without being drowned out by the hoots and hollers of drunken frat boys (although there are plenty of bars catering to that particular demographic). Favorite local hangouts include Celtic Crossings in River North, Miller's Pub in the Loop, and the Map Room in Bucktown. If you prefer to keep things nonalcoholic, grab coffee and dessert at the 3rd Coast on the Gold Coast or Uncommon Ground in Wrigleyville.

Hotels

Downtown Chicago is packed with hotels, thanks to the city's position as the business center of the Midwest. The majority are tucked amid the high-rises of the Loop and North Michigan Avenue, so staying here offers the pros and cons of any urban destination: Your room may look out onto a stunning cityscape, or no farther than the building next door. Lake Michigan views are highly prized and therefore command the highest prices. Although every hotel caters to business travelers, this is not a city where luxury hotels have dibs on all the prime real estate; casual, family-friendly properties are scattered throughout downtown. Affordable rooms, unfortunately, aren't so easy to find: Chicago hotels are among the most expensive in the country.

The Big Picture For the most part, Chicago hotels offer a quintessential urban experience: Rooms come with views of surrounding skyscrapers, and the bustle of city life hits you as soon as you step outside the lobby doors. Every major hotel chain is represented here, from the traditionally luxe Ritz-Carlton and Peninsula to the more casual, family-focused Embassy Suites or Best Western River North. But many hotels here have their own unique character, from the industrial-chic look of the Dana Hotel and Spa to the vibrant in-room art at the Hotel Indigo.

Chicago has its share of places that tout themselves as "boutique" hotels, such as the Hotel Felix and The James Chicago, but these aren't quite the same as their New York, Miami, or Los Angeles counterparts; the so-called beautiful people who frequent these spots on the coasts aren't likely to stop off in Chicago. No matter where you stay in town, you'll likely find that your fellow guests are business travelers or vacationing families, though the boutiques attract a generally younger crowd.

A note about smoking: A number of Chicago hotels, such as The Drake Hotel and the Renaissance Chicago, are completely nonsmoking. If you want to make sure you can light up in your room, check the hotel's policy when making your reservation.

Reservation Services The Chicago Convention & Tourism Bureau's website (www.choosechicago.com) allows you to book hotels as well as complete travel packages. Check out the "Immersion Weekends," trips planned around a particular theme (such as fashion or museums) that include behind-the-scenes tours and meals at distinctive local restaurants. For a free copy of the annual *Illinois Hotel-Motel Directory,* which also provides information about weekend packages, call the Illinois Bureau of Tourism at tel. 800/2-CONNECT [226-6632].

Alternative Accommodations If you'd prefer to stay in a private home, a centralized reservations service called At Home Inn Chicago, P.O. Box 14088, Chicago, IL 60614 (tel. 800/375-7084 or 312/640-1050; fax 312/640-1012; www.athomeinnchicago.com), lists more than 70 accommodations in the city. Options range from high-rise and loft apartments to guest rooms carved from a former private club on the

40th floor of a Loop office building. Most lie within 3 miles of downtown (many are located in the Gold Coast, Old Town, and Lincoln Park neighborhoods) and will run you about $150 to $300 per night for apartments, and as low as $105 for guest rooms in private homes. Most require a minimum stay of 2 or 3 nights.

A group of local B&B owners has formed the Chicago Bed and Breakfast Association, with a website that links to various properties throughout the city: www.chicago-bed-breakfast.com.

What You'll Really Pay

Chicago hotel rates vary widely throughout the year, making it difficult to pin down the average price for any given property. For each hotel listed, I've provided a range of rates that reflect the city's seasonal price fluctuations (cheaper in the winter, more expensive in the summer). The highest rate, known as the rack rate, is the maximum a hotel charges.

You can typically find discounts of up to 20% for rooms when booking through websites such as hotels.com or expedia.com. The hotels' own websites are also a good place to check for specials. During slow times, it's not impossible to obtain a room at an expensive property for the same rate as a more moderate one. Rack rates at the W Chicago City Center start at $279 but in March 2011, just a cursory search of the usual Web discount sites revealed that the going rate was actually closer to $179. *Note:* Quoted rates do not include Chicago's hefty hotel tax; at 14.9%, it can add significantly to the cost of your stay.

Getting the Best Deal Because Chicago's hospitality industry caters first and foremost to the business traveler, rates tend to be higher during the week. The city's slow season is from January to March, when outsiders steer clear of the cold and the threat of being snowed in at O'Hare. If you're not doing a lot of outdoor sightseeing, it's a great time to take advantage of the lowest room rates of the year.

Hotels charge premium prices during major conventions, most notably the International Home & Housewares Show in early March and the

Restaurant Show in late May. Other conventions gobble up desirable rooms periodically throughout the year.

The best rates tend to show up on the hotels' websites, which often tout special deals. The only downside to booking online is that you often can't be sure what kind of room you're getting (at older properties in particular, room sizes can vary widely, as can the views). Follow up with a call to the hotel if you want to make sure your windows don't look out on an alley.

A local service, Hot Rooms (tel. 800/468-3500 or 773/468-7666; www.hotrooms.com), offers discounts of 25% to 50% off standard rates at more than 30 downtown hotels. (The rates here aren't always cheaper than the hotels' own websites, but it's worth checking out.) The 24-hour service is free, but if you cancel a reservation, you're assessed a $25 fee.

Most hotels offer discounts of roughly 10% to individuals who are visiting Chicago on business. To qualify for this rate, your company usually must have an account on file at the hotel. In some cases, however, you may be required only to present some perfunctory proof of your commercial status, such as a business card or an official letterhead, to receive the discount. It never hurts to ask.

Chicago Hotels Go Green

With their large-scale heating and cooling costs not to mention all those loads of laundry Chicago's hotels suck up a considerable amount of energy. Now the city's hospitality industry is taking a leading role in lessening that environmental footprint. About two dozen local hotels have signed up for a city-wide Green Hotels Initiative, signaling their commitment to recycling and energy conservation.

Hotel Allegro, Hotel Burnham, Hotel Monaco, and Hotel Palomar all part of the Kimpton hotel chain print all material on recycled paper using soy-based inks. Though all three hotels are located in historic buildings, they've been fitted with energy-efficient lighting and air-conditioning systems.

At the Talbott Hotel, automatic sensors adjust the lighting, heating, and air-conditioning in low-traffic areas when they're not in use, and unused in-room soaps and shampoos are donated to a charity that recycles them for the needy. The hotel also purchases wind energy credits to offset 100% of the property's carbon footprint.

The InterContinental Chicago was the first hotel in the city to receive an Energy Star rating from the Environmental Protection Agency, thanks to its use of water-conserving toilets and sinks and motion-sensitive thermostats in the guest rooms (which lower the heat or air-conditioning when there's no one inside).

Then there's the Hotel Felix, the first hotel in the city to be built from the ground up with environmentally sensitive practices in mind. Sustainable or recycled materials were used throughout the property, from the flooring to the bedding. Guests who arrive in a hybrid car can even park free.

Family-Friendly Hotels in Chicago

Chicago has plenty of options for families on the go. At the south end of the Loop, the Hilton Chicago has lots of public space for wandering, and many of the rooms come with two bathrooms. Another bonus: Both the Field Museum and the Shedd Aquarium are within walking distance. At the north end of the Loop near the intersection of Lake Michigan and the Chicago River, the Swissôtel Chicagooffers Kids' Suites filled with kid-sized furniture, DVDs, stuffed animals, and coloring books.

In River North, the Hampton Inn & Suites keeps the kids in a good mood with a pool, Nintendo, free breakfast, and proximity to the Hard Rock Cafe and the Rainforest Cafe. The Best Western River North Hotel won't win any prizes for its no-frills decor, but it's close to both Michigan Avenue and a dozen family-friendly restaurants. The indoor pool and outdoor deck with great city views are other big draws.

When you want a little extra room to spread out, both <u>Homewood Suites</u> and <u>Embassy Suites</u> make traveling en masse a little easier with separate bedrooms and kitchenettes (so you can save money on food). Both offer free breakfast buffets and have indoor pools.

Of course, luxury hotels can afford to be friendly to all of their guests. At the <u>Four Seasons Hotel</u>, kids are indulged with little robes, balloon animals, Nintendo, and milk and cookies; the hotel also has a wonderful pool. The concierge at the <u>Ritz-Carlton Chicago</u> keeps a stash of toys and games for younger guests to borrow, and kids' menu items are available 24 hours; the hotel even provides a special gift pack just for teenage guests. The upscale <u>Westin Chicago River North</u> also caters to families with baby accessories and programs for older kids, respectively.

The Best Luxury Hotels in Chicago

<u>The Waldorf Astoria</u>: The Parisian-style exterior exudes Old World glamour, but inside, the Waldorf Astoria is all about sleek, streamlined luxury. The guest rooms are some of the biggest in town, and include bonuses such as fireplaces and furnished terraces. The Gold Coast location removed from the traffic of downtown adds to the feeling of an urban retreat.

<u>Park Hyatt</u>: If the thought of overstuffed couches and thick brocade curtains makes you wince, this is the hotel for you. With its focus on modern design and clean lines, the Park Hyatt feels like one of those cool urban spaces featured in *Architectural Digest.* The coolest feature? Moveable bathroom walls that allow you to soak in the view while you lounge in the tub.

<u>Peninsula</u>: Inspired by the elegance of 1920s Shanghai and Hong Kong, the Chicago outpost of this Asian chain is a seamless blend of classic and modern. The grand public spaces may be a throwback to the past, but the hotel's amenities are ultramodern. The top-notch gym, spa, and indoor swimming pool (filled with natural light) make the Peninsula a must for fitness fanatics.

The Ritz-Carlton Chicago: Appropriately enough in this skyscraper-packed city, some of the best hotels perch far above the sidewalk. Located above the Water Tower Place shopping center, the Ritz has one of the most welcoming lobbies in town, with light streaming through the windows, masses of fresh flowers, and bird's-eye views of the city. The elegant guest rooms are decorated in Art Deco—inspired shades of silver, black, and gold, and the staff prides itself on granting every wish.

Trump International Hotel & Tower: Want to make-believe you've got your own *pied-à-terre* in the heart of downtown? This is the place to live out your fantasy the contemporary-cool rooms are actually studio apartments with full kitchens, plenty of space to lounge, and killer views of the skyline.

The Best Mid-Range Hotels in Chicago

Hotel Allegro Chicago: Its prime Loop location and stylish decor make the Allegro an appealing home base for visitors in search of an urban getaway. Rooms are compact but cheerful, and you can mingle with other guests at the complimentary evening wine reception in the lobby.

Hampton Inn & Suites Chicago Downtown: Located in a busy neighborhood full of restaurants and nightlife, the Hampton Inn feels more expensive than it is. The rooms have an upscale urban look, and the indoor pool is a draw for families. The hotel's hot breakfast buffet, included in the room rates and served in an attractive second-floor lounge, puts the standard coffee-and-doughnut spread at other motels to shame.

Red Roof Inn: This high-rise version of the roadside motel is your best bet for the cheapest rates downtown. The rooms don't have much in the way of style (or natural light), and the bathrooms, though spotless, are a little cramped, but it fits the bill if you want a central location and plan on using your hotel as a place to sleep rather than hang out.

<u>Majestic Hotel</u>: A bit off the beaten path, this neighborhood hotel is tucked away on a residential street just a short walk from Wrigley Field and the lakefront. You won't find lots of fancy amenities, but the atmosphere here has the personal touch of a B&B. Rates include continental breakfast and afternoon tea in the lobby.

Things to See

From the bustle of the Loop on a weekday morning to the tranquility of Lake Michigan on a cool fall afternoon, Chicago is an experience in contrasts. Its cultural offerings and historic attractions draw seasoned international travelers, but the city's mix of family-friendly museums, beautiful parks, and iconic skyscrapers also attract vacationers of all ages. The fun and the challenge is to fit everything in one trip. You can put together a full itinerary each day and still have plenty left over for your next visit.

What you see will depend on your interests and stamina. The city's museums alone could keep you busy for at least a week. (If you don't have that much time, the top three exhibits that shouldn't be missed are the Impressionist masterpieces at the Art Institute of Chicago; Sue, the biggest *Tyrannosaurus rex* fossil ever discovered, at the Field Museum of Natural History; and the U-505 submarine at the Museum of Science and Industry). Come summertime, a stroll through picturesque Lincoln Park Zoo on the Near North Side is the perfect way to spend an afternoon; the setting makes it worth visiting even if you don't have kids along. (*Added bonus:* It's free!)

From a traveler's perspective, visiting Chicago is especially hassle-free because the majority of the places you'll want to see are in or near downtown, making it easy to plan your day and get from place to place. And because this is a town with a thriving tourist economy, you have plenty of guided sightseeing options: walking tours of famous architecture, boat cruises on Lake Michigan, and even bus tours of notorious gangster sites. If you're lucky enough to visit when the weather's nice, you can join the locals at the parks and the beaches along Lake Michigan.

Extensive public transportation makes it simple to reach almost every tourist destination, but some of your best memories of Chicago may come from simply strolling along the sidewalks. Chicago's neighborhoods have their own distinct styles and looks, and you'll have a more memorable experience if you don't limit yourself solely to the prime tourist spots. And if you *really* want to talk about da Bears or da Cubs, chances are, you'll find someone who's more than happy to join in.

Exploring the 'Burbs in Chicago

Oak Park

Architecture and literary buffs alike make pilgrimages to Oak Park, a nearby suburb on the western border of the city that is easily accessible by car or train. Bookworms flock here to see the town where Ernest Hemingway was born and grew up, while others come to catch a glimpse of the Frank Lloyd Wright-designed homes that line the well-maintained streets.

Getting There

By Car Oak Park is 10 miles due west of downtown Chicago. By car, take the Eisenhower Expressway (I-290) west to Harlem Avenue (Ill. 43) and exit north. Continue on Harlem north to Lake Street. Take a right on Lake Street and continue to Forest Avenue. Turn left here, and immediately on your right you'll see the Oak Park Visitor Center .

By Public Transportation Take the Green Line west to the Harlem stop, roughly a 25-minute ride from downtown. Exit the station onto Harlem Avenue, and proceed north to Lake Street. Take a right on Lake Street, follow it to Forest Avenue, and then turn left to the Oak Park Visitor Center .

By Tour The Chicago Architecture Foundation regularly runs guided tours from downtown Chicago to Oak Park.

Visitor Information The Oak Park Visitor Center, 158 Forest Ave. (tel. 888/OAK-PARK [625-7275]; www.visitoakpark.com), is open daily from 10am to 5pm April through October, and from 10am to 4pm November through March. Stop here for an orientation, maps, and guidebooks. There's a city-operated parking lot next door. The heart of the historic district and the Frank Lloyd Wright Home and Studio are only a few blocks away.

An extensive tour of Oak Park's historic district leaves from the Ginkgo Tree Bookshop, 951 Chicago Ave., on weekends from 11am to 3:30pm (exact departure times vary, depending on how many people show up). The tour lasts 1 hour and costs $15 for adults, $12 for seniors and children ages 4 to 17 (free for children 3 and under). If you can't make it to Oak Park on the weekend, you can follow a self-guided map and audiocassette tour of the historic district for the same price; the audio tour is available at the Ginkgo Tree Bookshop from 10am to 3:30pm. In addition to homes designed by Wright, you will see work by several of his disciples, as well as some charming examples of the Victorian styling that he so disdained. A more detailed map, *Architectural Guide Map of Oak Park and River Forest,* includes text and photos of all 80 sites of interest in Oak Park and neighboring River Forest.

The North Shore

Between Chicago and the state border of Wisconsin is one of the nation's most affluent residential areas, a swath of suburbia known as the North Shore. Although towns farther west like to co-opt the name for its prestige, the North Shore proper extends from Evanston, Chicago's nearest neighbor to the north, along the lakefront to tony Lake Forest, originally built as a resort for Chicago's aristocracy. Dotted with idyllic, picture-perfect towns such as Kenilworth, Glencoe, and Winnetka, this area has long attracted filmmakers such as Robert Redford, who filmed *Ordinary People* in Lake Forest, and the North Shore's own John Hughes, who shot most of his popular coming-of-age comedies (*Sixteen Candles, Ferris Bueller's Day Off, Home Alone,* and so on) here.

Although a Metra train line extends to Lake Forest and neighboring Lake Bluff, I highly recommend that you rent a car and drive north along Sheridan Road, which winds its leisurely way through many of these communities, past palatial homes and mansions designed in a startling array of architectural styles. Aside from Lake Shore Drive in Chicago, you won't find a more impressive stretch of roadway in the entire metropolitan area.

Exploring Evanston Despite being frequented by Chicagoans, Evanston, the city's oldest suburb, retains an identity all its own. A unique hybrid of sensibilities, it manages to combine the tranquillity of suburban life with a highly cultured, urban charm. It's great fun to wander amid the shops and cafes in its downtown area or along funky Dempster Street at its southern end. The beautiful lakefront campus of Northwestern University (tel. 847/491-3741; www.northwestern.edu) is here, and many of its buildings such as Alice Millar Chapel, with its sublime stained-glass facade, and the Mary and Leigh Block Gallery, a fine-arts haven that offers a top-notch collection and intriguing temporary exhibitions are well worth several hours of exploration.

Evanston was also the home of Frances Willard, founder of the Women's Christian Temperance Union (WCTU). The Francis Willard House Museum, 1730 Chicago Ave. (tel. 847/328-7500; www.franceswillardhouse.org), is open to visitors on the first and third Sundays of every month from 1 to 4pm ($10 adults, $5 children 12 and under). Nine of the 17 rooms in this old Victorian "Rest Cottage" (as Willard called it) have been converted into a museum of period furnishings and temperance memorabilia. Among her personal effects is the bicycle she affectionately called "Gladys" and learned to ride late in life, in the process spurring women across the country to do the same. The headquarters of the WCTU are still on-site.

Tucked away in north Evanston, a few miles from the Northwestern campus, is the unusual and informative Mitchell Museum of the American Indian, 2600 Central Park Ave. (tel. 847/475-1030; www.mitchellmuseum.org). The collection ranges from stoneware tools and weapons to the work of contemporary Native-American artists. The museum is open Tuesday through Saturday from 10am to 5pm (Thurs until 8pm), and Sunday from noon to 4pm. It's closed on holidays and during the last 2 weeks of August. Admission is $5 for adults, $2.50 for seniors and children. Call in advance to arrange a volunteer-led tour.

For a bit of serenity, head to <u>Grosse Point Lighthouse and Maritime Museum</u>,2601 Sheridan Rd. (tel. 847/328-6961; www.grossepointlighthouse.net), a historic lighthouse built in 1873, when Lake Michigan still teemed with cargo-laden ships. Tours of the lighthouse, situated in a nature center, take place on weekends from June to September at 2, 3, and 4pm ($6 adults, $3 children 8-12; children 7 and under not admitted, for safety reasons). The adjacent Lighthouse Beach is a favorite spot for local families during the summer. If you're here between Memorial Day and Labor Day, you'll have to pay to frolic on the sand ($7 adults, $5 children 1-11), but it's a great place for a (free) stroll on a sunny spring or fall day.

The North & Northwest Suburbs

The North Shore is only one slice of life north of Chicago. To its west lies a sprawling thicket of old and new suburbs, from the bucolic environs of equestrian-minded <u>Barrington</u> and its ring of smaller satellite communities in the far northwest, to near-northwest shopping mecca <u>Schaumburg</u>, home to the gigantic Woodfield Mall. While Woodfield attracts a steady stream of dedicated shoppers allowing it to tout its status as one of the top tourist destinations in Illinois it's not that distinctive; you'll find most of the same stores at your local megamall back home.

A more pastoral option for visitors with time on their hands might be a day trip to the <u>historic village of Long Grove</u>, about 30 miles northwest of Chicago. Settled in the 1840s by German immigrants and pioneers traveling west from New England, Long Grove has assiduously preserved its old-fashioned character. Set amid 500 acres of oak- and hickory-tree groves, the village maintains nearly 100 specialty stores, galleries, and restaurants, many of which are in former smithies, wheelwright barns, and century-old residences. (Don't skip the <u>Long Grove Confectionery Company</u>, a local institution.) By village ordinance, all new buildings constructed in the shopping district must conform to the architecture of the early 1900s. The village schedules several cultural and entertainment events, festivals, and art fairs throughout the year. The biggest and best is the annual <u>Strawberry Festival</u>, held during the last weekend in June. Call the village's information center or check the town's website (tel. 847/634-0888; www.longgroveonline.com) for updates on coming events. To get there from the Chicago Loop, take the I-94 tollway (also known as the Kennedy Expwy.) north until it separates at I-90, another tollway that runs northwest. Follow I-90 until you reach Rte. 53, and drive north on 53 until it dead-ends at Lake-Cook Road. Take the west exit off 53, and follow Lake-Cook Road to Hicks Road. Turn right on Hicks Road and then left on Old McHenry Road, which will take you right into the center of town.

The Western Suburbs

So many corporations have taken to locating their offices beyond the city limits that today more people work in the suburbs than commute into Chicago. Much of the suburban sprawl in counties such as DuPage and Kane consists of seas of aluminum-sided houses that seem to sprout from cornfields overnight. But there are also some lovely older towns, such as upscale <u>Hinsdale</u> and, much farther west, the quaint tandem of <u>St. Charles and Geneva</u>, which lie across the Fox River from each other. Perhaps there is no more fitting symbol of this booming area than the city of <u>Naperville</u>. A historic, formerly rural community with a Main Street U.S.A. downtown district worthy of Norman Rockwell, Naperville has exploded from a population of about 30,000 residents in the early 1970s to approximately 145,000 today which makes it the third-largest municipality in the state. Naperville maintains a collection of 19th-century buildings in an outdoor setting known as Naper Settlement, and its river walk is the envy of neighboring village councils. But much of its yesteryear charm seems to be disappearing bit by bit as new subdivisions and strip malls ooze forth across the prairie.

In & Around the Loop

The heart of the Loop is Chicago's business center, where you'll find some of the city's most famous early skyscrapers, the Chicago Board of Trade (the world's largest commodities, futures, and options exchange), and the Sears Tower (officially renamed the Willis Tower, though Chicagoans still refer to the landmark high-rise by its original name). If you're looking for an authentic big-city experience, wander the area on a weekday, when commuters are rushing to catch trains and businesspeople are hustling to get to work. The Loop is also home to one of the city's top museums, the Art Institute of Chicago, as well as a number of cultural institutions including the Symphony Center (home of the Chicago Symphony Orchestra), the Auditorium Theatre, the Civic Opera House, the Goodman Theatre, and two fabulously restored historic theaters along Randolph Street. On the eastern edge of the Loop in Grant Park, three popular museums are conveniently located within a quick stroll of each other on the landscaped Museum Campus. Busy Lake Shore Drive, which brings cars zipping past the Museum Campus, was actually rerouted a few years ago to make the area easier to navigate for pedestrians.

Walker's Warning While Chicago is a great city to explore on foot, Lake Shore Drive is no place for pedestrians. People have been seriously injured and even killed attempting to dodge traffic on the busy road. Near Grant Park, cross only in crosswalks at Jackson Boulevard or Randolph, East Monroe, or East Balbo drives, or by using the underpass on the Museum Campus. North of the river, use underpasses or bridges at East Ohio Street, Chicago Avenue, Oak Street, and North Avenue.

The Loop Sculpture Tour

Grand monuments, statues, and contemporary sculptures are scattered in parks throughout Chicago, but the concentration of public art within the Loop and nearby Grant Park is worth noting. The best known of these works are by 20th-century artists including Picasso, Chagall, Miró, Calder, Moore, and Oldenburg. The newest addition is the massive elliptical sculpture Cloud Gate (known as "The Bean" because it looks like a giant silver kidney bean) by British artist Anish Kapoor. The sculpture, in Millennium Park, was Kapoor's first public commission in the U.S.

A free brochure, The Chicago Public Art Guide (available at the Chicago Cultural Center, 78 E. Washington St.), can help steer you toward the best examples of monumental public art. You can also conduct a self-guided tour of the city's best public sculptures by following "The Loop Sculpture Tour" map.

The single most famous sculpture in Chicago is Pablo Picasso's Untitled, located in Daley Plaza and constructed out of Cor-Ten steel, the same gracefully rusting material used on the exterior of the Daley Center behind it. Viewed from various perspectives, its enigmatic shape suggests a woman, bird, or dog; the artist himself never discussed its inspiration or meaning. Perhaps because it was the first monumental modern sculpture in Chicago's conservative business center, its installation in 1967 was met with hoots and heckles, but today "The Picasso" enjoys semiofficial status as the logo of modern Chicago. It is by far the city's most popular photo opportunity among visiting tourists. At noon on weekdays during warm weather, you'll likely find a dance troupe, musical group, or visual-arts exhibition here as part of the city's long-running "Under the Picasso" multicultural program. Call tel. 312/346-3278 for event information.

Grant Park & Millennium Park

Thanks to architect Daniel Burnham and his coterie of visionary civic planners who drafted the revolutionary 1909 Plan of Chicago the city boasts a wide-open lakefront park system unrivaled by most major metropolises. Modeled after the gardens at Versailles, Grant Park (tel. 312/742-PLAY [7529]; www.chicagoparkdistrict.com) is Chicago's front yard, composed of giant lawns segmented by allées of trees, plantings, and paths, and pieced together by major roadways and a network of railroad tracks. Incredibly, the entire expanse was created from sandbars, landfill, and debris from the Great Chicago Fire; the original shoreline extended all the way to Michigan Avenue. A few museums are spread out inside the park, but most of the space is wide open (a legacy of mail-order magnate Aaron Montgomery Ward's late-19th-c. campaign to limit municipal buildings).

The northwest corner of Grant Park (bordered by Michigan Ave. and Randolph St.) is the site of Millennium Park, one of the city's grandest public works projects. Who cares that the park cost hundreds of millions more than it was supposed to, or the fact that it finally opened a full 4 years after the actual millennium? It's a winning combination of beautiful landscaping, elegant architecture (the classically inspired peristyle), and public entertainment spaces (including an ice rink and theater). The park's centerpiece is the dramatic Frank Gehry-designed Pritzker Music Pavilion, featuring massive curved ribbons of steel.

The Grant Park Symphony Orchestra and Chorus stages a popular series of free outdoor classical music concerts here most Wednesday through Sunday evenings in the summer. For a schedule of concert times and dates, contact the Grant Park Music Festival (tel. 312/742-7638; www.grantparkmusicfestival.com). Two public artworks well worth checking out are the kidney bean-shaped sculpture Cloud Gate and the Crown Fountain, where children splash in the shallow water between giant faces projected on video screens. Free walking tours of the park are offered daily from May through October at 11:30am and 1pm, starting at the park's Welcome Center, 201 E. Randolph St. (tel. 312/742-1168; www.millenniumpark.org).

During the summer, a variety of music and food festivals take over central Grant Park. Annual events that draw big crowds include a blues music festival (in June) and a jazz festival (Labor Day). The Taste of Chicago (tel. 312/744-3315; www.cityofchicago.org/specialevents) is purportedly the largest food festival in the world, with attendance estimated at 3.5 million people during the 10 days leading up to the

4th of July. Local restaurants serve up more ribs, pizza, hot dogs, and beer than you'd ever want to see, let alone eat.

Head south to the lake via Congress Parkway, and you'll find Buckingham Fountain, the baroque centerpiece of Grant Park, composed of pink Georgia marble and patterned after but twice the size of the Latona Fountain at Versailles, with adjoining esplanades beautified by rose gardens in season. From April through October, the fountain spurts columns of water up to 150 feet in the air every hour on the hour, and beginning at 4pm, a whirl of colored lights and dramatic music amps up the drama. The fountain shuts down at 11pm; concession areas and bathrooms are available on the plaza.

Sculptures and monuments stand throughout the park, including a sculpture of two Native Americans on horseback, The Bowman and the Spearman (at Congress Pkwy. and Michigan Ave.), which was installed in 1928 and has become the park's trademark. Also here are likenesses of Copernicus, Columbus, and Lincoln, the latter by the great American sculptor Augustus Saint-Gaudens, located on Congress Parkway between Michigan Avenue and Columbus Drive. On the western edge of the park, at Adams Street, is the Art Institute , and at the southern tip, in the area known as the Museum Campus, are the Field Museum of Natural History, the Adler Planetarium, and the Shedd Aquarium.

To get to Grant Park, take bus no. 3, 4, 6, 146, or 151. If you want to take the subway/El, get off at any stop in the Loop along State or Wabash streets, and walk east.

The Grant Park Museum Campus's Big Three With terraced gardens and broad walkways, the Museum Campus at the southern end of Grant Park makes it easy for pedestrians to visit three of the city's most beloved institutions: the Field Museum of Natural History, Shedd Aquarium, and Adler Planetarium. To get to the Museum Campus from the Loop, walk south on Michigan Avenue to East Balbo Drive. Head east on Balbo, across Grant Park, then trek south along the lakeshore path to the museums (about a 15-min. walk). Or follow 11th

Street east from South Michigan Avenue, which takes you across a walkway spanning the Metra train tracks. Cross Columbus Drive, and then pick up the path that will take you under Lake Shore Drive and into the Museum Campus. The CTA no. 146 bus will take you from downtown to all three of these attractions; it also stops at the Roosevelt El stop on the Red Line. Call tel. 312/836-7000 (from any city or suburban area code) for the stop locations and schedule.

A large indoor parking lot is accessible from Lake Shore Drive southbound; you can park there for $16 for up to 4 hours, $19 all day. Be aware that there is no public parking during Chicago Bears games in the fall; Soldier Field is next to the Museum Campus, and football fans get first dibs on all the surrounding parking spaces.

Along South Michigan Avenue

The high-fashion boutiques may be clustered along the Magnificent Mile, but aesthetically, Chicago's grandest stretch of boulevard is still the stretch of Michigan Avenue that runs south of the river. Running from the Michigan Avenue Bridge all the way down to the Field Museum, it serves as the boundary between Grant Park on one side and the Loop on the other. A stroll along this boulevard in any season offers both visual and cultural treats. Particularly impressive is the great wall of buildings from Randolph Street south to Congress Parkway (beginning with the Chicago Cultural Center and terminating at the Auditorium Building) that architecture buffs refer to as the "Michigan Avenue Cliff."

Photo Op For a great photo op, walk on Randolph Street toward the lake in the morning. The sun, rising in the east over the lake, hits the cliff of buildings along South Michigan Avenue, giving you the perfect backdrop for an only-in-Chicago picture.

Special-Interest Sightseeing

Obama's Chicago

For years, Chicago's biggest hometown celebrity was Oprah Winfrey (despite the fact that she's rarely seen out and about, preferring to spend her free time at her sprawling California estate). These days, she's been replaced by another big O President Barack Obama. Though his primary residence is now a certain White House in Washington, D.C., the First Couple still own a home here and maintain strong local ties.

Tourists from around the world make pilgrimages to the Obamas' house at 5046 S. Greenwood Ave. on the city's South Side. You can get a glimpse of the home from a distance, but you won't see much; the whole block is closed to passersby for security reasons. However, the surrounding neighborhood of Kenwood with its lovingly restored historic mansions as well as adjacent Hyde Park, are well worth a stroll. After visiting the campus of the University of Chicago where President Obama once taught constitutional law you can browse the stacks at the Seminary Co-op Bookstore (pictured at right), where he was a regular.

Chicago-based fashion maven Ikram Goldman helped cultivate Michelle Obama's sense of style. For a first-lady-worthy makeover, head to her boutique, Ikram, which stocks pieces by up-and-coming and off-the-radar designers.

For dinners out, the Obamas have often eaten at the upscale Mexican restaurant Topolobampo. Another favorite for special occasions is Spiaggia, one of the best Italian restaurants in the country and among the most expensive. To celebrate their first Valentine's Day as first couple, the Obamas chose Table Fifty-Two, an unassuming spot that gives classic Southern dishes an upscale twist. Not only is the restaurant's owner, Art Smith, a friend and former South Side neighbor, but he also happens to be Oprah's former personal chef.

For more casual meals in Hyde Park, the Obamas were regulars at Italian Fiesta Pizzeria, 1400 E. 47th St. (tel. 773/684-2222; italianfiestapizzeria.com), a family-owned restaurant that was also a favorite of Michelle and her parents when she was growing up. Barack has also mentioned the Valois Cafeteria, 1518 E. 53rd St. (tel. 773/667-0647; www.valoisrestaurant.com), a no-frills, old-school neighborhood landmark, as his top breakfast spot in the city. For family outings on the North Side, the Obamas liked to stop in at R. J. Grunts, 2056 N. Lincoln Park West (tel. 773/929-5363; www.rjgruntschicago.com), known for its all-American lineup of burgers and Tex-Mex specialties, as well as its enormous salad bar. An added bonus for kids: It's right across the street from Lincoln Park Zoo.

North of the Loop in Chicago

Most of these sights are either on the Magnificent Mile (North Michigan Ave.) and its surrounding blocks or close by on the Near North Side.

A River Runs Through It

The Chicago River remains one of the most visible of the city's major physical features. It's spanned by more movable bridges within the city limits (52 at last count) than any other city in the world. An almost-mystical moment occurs downtown when all the bridges spanning the main and south branches connecting the Loop to both the Near West Side and the Near North Side are raised, allowing for the passage of some ship, barge, or contingent of high-masted sailboats. The Chicago River has long outlived the critical commercial function that it once performed. Most of the remaining millworks that occupy its banks no longer depend on the river alone for the transport of their materials, raw and finished.

The river's main function today is to serve as a fluvial conduit for sewage, which, owing to an engineering feat that reversed its flow inland in 1900, no longer pollutes the waters of Lake Michigan. Recently, Chicagoans have begun to discover other roles for the river, including water cruises, park areas, cafes, public art installations, and a riverside bike path that connects to the lakefront route near Wacker Drive. Actually, today's developers aren't the first to wonder why the river couldn't be Chicago's Seine. A look at the early-20th-century

Beaux Arts balustrades lining the river along Wacker Drive, complete with comfortably spaced benches and Parisian-style bridge houses, shows that Chicago architect and urban planner Daniel Burnham knew full well what a treasure the city had.

Rock Around the World

The impressive Gothic Tribune Tower, just north of the Chicago River on the east side of Michigan Avenue, is home to the *Chicago Tribune* newspaper. It's also notable for an array of architectural fragments jutting out from the exterior. The newspaper's notoriously despotic publisher, Robert R. McCormick, started the collection shortly after the building's completion in 1925, gathering pieces during his world travels. *Tribune* correspondents then began supplying building fragments that they acquired on assignment. Each one now bears the name of the structure and the country from whence it came. There are 138 pieces in all, including chunks and shards from the Great Wall of China; the Taj Mahal; the White House; the Arc de Triomphe; the Berlin Wall; the Roman Colosseum; London's Houses of Parliament; the Great Pyramid of Cheops in Giza, Egypt; and the original tomb of Abraham Lincoln in Springfield, Illinois.

Museums in Chicago

Museums for Less If you're planning on visiting lots of Chicago museums, you should invest in a CityPass, a prepaid ticket that gets you into the biggest attractions (the Art Institute, Field Museum of Natural History, Shedd Aquarium, Adler Planetarium, Museum of Science and Industry, and Hancock Observatory). The cost at press time was $76 for adults and $59 for children, which is about 50% cheaper than paying all the museums' individual admission fees. You can buy a CityPass at many museums or purchase one online before you get to town (www.citypass.com).

Museums for Free: The following museums have free admission: Chicago Cultural Center, Garfield Park Conservatory, David and Alfred Smart Museum of Art, Jane Addams Hull-House Museum, Lincoln Park

Conservatory, Lincoln Park Zoo, National Museum of Mexican Art, Museum of Contemporary Photography, and Newberry Library.

Architectural Highlights

Historic Homes of Prairie Avenue

Prairie Avenue, south of the Loop, was the city's first "Millionaire's Row," and its most famous address is Glessner House, 1800 S. Prairie Ave. (tel. 312/326-1480; www.glessnerhouse.org). A must-see for anyone interested in architectural history, and the only surviving Chicago building designed by Boston architect Henry Hobson Richardson, the 1886 structure represented a dramatic shift from traditional Victorian architecture (and inspired a young Frank Lloyd Wright).

The imposing granite exterior gives the home a forbidding air. (Railway magnate George Pullman, who lived nearby, complained, "I do not know what I have ever done to have that thing staring me in the face every time I go out my door.") But step inside, and the home turns out to be a welcoming, cozy retreat, filled with Arts and Crafts furnishings. Visits are by guided tour only; tours begin at 1 and 3pm Wednesday through Sunday (except major holidays) on a first-come, first-served basis (advance reservations are taken only for groups of 10 or more). Tours cost $10 for adults, $9 for students and seniors, and $6 for children 5 to 12.

A visit to Glessner House can also be combined with a tour of the nearby Clarke House Museum, a Greek Revival home that's the oldest surviving house in the city; tours are given at noon and 2pm. Combination tickets for both Glessner House and Clarke House cost $15 for adults, $12 student and seniors, and $8 for children 5 to 12. Admission for all tours is free on Wednesday.

To get to Prairie Avenue, catch the no. 1, 3, or 4 bus from Michigan Avenue at Jackson Boulevard; get off at 18th Street and walk 2 blocks east.

Wright's Oak Park

Oak Park has the highest concentration of Frank Lloyd Wright-designed and -built houses or buildings anywhere. People come here to marvel at the work of a man who saw his life as a twofold mission: to wage a single-handed battle against excessively ornamental architecture (Victorian, in particular), and to create in its place a new form that would be, at the same time, functional, appropriate to its natural setting, and stimulating to the imagination.

Not everyone who comes to Oak Park shares Wright's architectural philosophy, but scholars and enthusiasts admire him for being consistently true to his vision, out of which emerged a unique and genuinely American architectural statement. The reason for Wright's success could stem from the fact that he was a living exemplar of a quintessential American type. In a deep sense, he embodied the ideal of the self-made and self-sufficient individual who had survived, even thrived, in the frontier society qualities that he expressed in his almost-puritanical insistence that each spatial or structural form in his buildings serve some useful purpose. He was also an aesthete in Emersonian fashion, deriving his idea of beauty from natural environments, where apparent simplicity often belies a subtle complexity.

The three principal ingredients of a tour of Wright-designed structures in Oak Park are the Frank Lloyd Wright Home and Studio Tour, the Unity Temple Tour, and a walking tour guided or self-guided to view the exteriors of homes throughout the neighborhood that were built by the architect. Oak Park has 25 homes and buildings by Wright, constructed between 1892 and 1913, which constitute the core output of his Prairie School period.

More Frank Lloyd Wright Homes In addition to Robie House, several of Wright's earlier works, still privately owned, dot the streets of Hyde Park. They include the Heller House, 5132 S. Woodlawn Ave. (1897); the Blossom House, 1332 E. 49th St. (1882); and the McArthur House,

4852 S. Kenwood Ave. (1892). *Note:* These houses are not open to the public, so they can only be admired from the outside.

The Wright Stuff in the Gold Coast Architecture junkies may want to visit the Charnley-Persky House, 1365 N. Astor St., in the Gold Coast (tel. 312/915-0105 or 312/573-1365; www.charnleyhouse.org), designed by Frank Lloyd Wright and Louis Sullivan in 1891. Sullivan was Frank Lloyd Wright's architectural mentor, and although Wright was a junior draftsman on this project, Sullivan allowed him to become involved in the design process. The result is an important landmark in modern architecture that rejected Victorian details and embraced symmetry and simplicity. Free 45-minute tours of the interior are given on Wednesday at noon. A 90-minute tour of the home and the surrounding neighborhood is offered Saturdays at 10am year-round ($10); an additional tour is given at noon April through November. Reservations are not accepted.

The Wright Plus Tour Die-hard fans of the architect will want to be in town on the third Saturday in May for the annual Wright Plus Tour. The public can tour several Frank Lloyd Wright-designed homes and other notable Oak Park buildings, in both the Prairie School and Victorian styles, in addition to Wright's home, his studio, and the Unity Temple. The tour includes 10 buildings in all. Tickets, which go for $100, go on sale March 1 and can sell out by mid-April. Call the Frank Lloyd Wright Home and Studio (tel. 708/848-1976; www.gowright.org) for details and ticket information.

Especially for Kids

Downtown Playgrounds
As anyone who's traveled with little kids well knows, children can take only so much museum-going. Sometimes they have to let loose and run around luckily, there are playgrounds tucked away in unassuming spots, as long as you know where to look. The Seneca Playlot, 228 E. Chicago Ave., is directly east of the Chicago Water Works Visitor Center and across the street from Water Tower Place mall. The play

structures are mostly low-to-the-ground, making it a good choice for toddlers. Walk a few blocks east and you'll come to Lake Shore Park, 808 N. Lake Shore Dr., which has a good assortment of slides and climbing equipment. As an added bonus, you'll enjoy views of the lake. An adjoining athletic field has a running track and plenty of space for impromptu soccer or football games. Occupying a large corner lot on the ritzy Gold Coast, Goudy Square Park, at the corner of Astor and Goethe streets, is a tranquil oasis surrounded by high-rises. There are three separate play areas, along with plenty of benches for parents to lounge.

Lincoln Park Attractions

Lincoln Park is the city's largest park, and certainly one of the longest. Straight and narrow, the park begins at North Avenue and follows the shoreline of Lake Michigan north for several miles. Within its 1,200 acres are a world-class zoo; half a dozen beaches; a botanical conservatory; two excellent museums; a golf course; and the meadows, formal gardens, sporting fields, and tennis courts typical of urban parks. To get to the park, take bus no. 22, 145, 146, 147, 151, or 156.

The park, named after Abraham Lincoln, is home to the statue of the standing Abraham Lincoln (just north of the North Ave. and State St. intersection), one of the city's two Lincoln statues by Augustus Saint-Gaudens (the seated Lincoln is in Grant Park). Saint-Gaudens also designed the Bates Fountain near the conservatory.

A Great View After a visit to Lincoln Park Zoo or the Peggy Notebaert Nature Museum, take a quick stroll along the south side of Fullerton Avenue toward the lakefront. Standing on the bridge that runs over the lagoon (just before you get to Lake Shore Dr.), you'll have a great view of the Chicago skyline and Lincoln Park behind you an excellent backdrop for family souvenir photos. This path can get very crowded with bikers and runners on summer weekends, so this photo op works best during the week. You'll also get good pictures if you continue on to Lake Michigan.

Exploring Hyde Park in Chicago

Hyde Park, south of the Loop, is the birthplace of atomic fission, home to the University of Chicago and the popular Museum of Science and Industry, and definitely worth a trip. It's gotten an added boost of publicity ever since a certain former resident, Barack Obama, came to national prominence. The Obamas are such fans of the area that they've kept their house here. Allow at least half a day to explore the University of Chicago campus and surrounding neighborhood (one of Chicago's most successfully integrated). If you want to explore a museum or two as well, plan on a full day.

Some Hyde Park History

When Hyde Park was settled in 1850, it became Chicago's first suburb. A hundred years later, in the 1950s, it added another first to its impressive résumé, one that the current neighborhood is not particularly proud of: an urban-renewal plan. At the time, a certain amount of old commercial and housing stock just the kind of buildings that would be prized today was demolished rather than rehabilitated and replaced by projects and small shopping malls that actually make some corners of Hyde Park look more like a post-World War II suburb than an urban neighborhood.

What Hyde Park can be proud of is that, in racially divided Chicago, this neighborhood has found an alternative vision. As Southern blacks began to migrate to Chicago's South Side during World War I, many whites fled. But most whites here, especially those who wanted to stay near the university, chose integration as the only realistic strategy to preserve their neighborhood. The 2000 census proved that integration still works: About 40% of the residents are white and 37% are black; there is also a significant Asian population. Hyde Park is decidedly middle class, with pockets of affluence that reflect the early-20th-century period when the well-to-do moved here to escape the decline of Prairie Avenue. A well-known black resident from the area is the late Elijah Muhammad, and numerous Nation of Islam families continue to worship in a mosque, formerly a Greek Orthodox cathedral, that is one of the neighborhood's architectural landmarks. Surrounding this unusual enclave, however, are many marginal blocks where poverty and slum housing abound. For all its nobility, Hyde Park's achievement in integration merely emphasizes that socioeconomic differences are even more unwieldy than racial ones.

The University of Chicago is widely hailed as one of the more intellectually exciting institutions of higher learning in the country and has been home to some 73 Nobel laureates, including physicist Enrico Fermi, novelist Saul Bellow, and economist Milton Friedman. (Almost one-third of all the Nobel Prizes in Economics have gone to University of Chicago professors, twice as many as any other institution.) Another long-time faculty member was English professor Norman Maclean, author of *A River Runs Through It.* Though they may joke about the school's staid social life, U of C undergrads take pride in their school's nerdy reputation.

The year the university opened its doors in 1892 was a big one for Hyde Park, but 1893 was even bigger. In that year, Chicago, chosen over other cities in a competitive international field, played host to the World's Columbian Exposition, commemorating the 400th anniversary of Columbus's arrival in America. To create a fairground, the landscape architect Frederick Law Olmsted was enlisted to fill in the marshlands along Hyde Park's lakefront and link what was to become Jackson Park to existing Washington Park on the neighborhood's western boundary with a narrow concourse called the Midway Plaisance.

On the resulting 650 acres at a cost of $30 million 12 exhibit palaces, 57 buildings devoted to U.S. states and foreign governments, and dozens of smaller structures were constructed under the supervision of architect Daniel Burnham. Most of the buildings followed Burnham's preference for the Classical Revival style and white stucco exteriors. With the innovation of outdoor electric lighting, the sparkling result was the "White City," which attracted 27 million visitors in a single season, from May 1 to October 31, 1893. The exposition sponsors, in that brief time, had remarkably recovered their investment, but within a few short years of the fair's closing, vandalism and fire destroyed most of its buildings. Only the Palace of Fine Arts, occupying the eastern tip of the midway, survives to this day, and it now houses the Museum of Science and Industry. (For more on the behind-the-scenes drama at the Exposition, read *The Devil in the White City,* by Erik Larson, a nonfiction history book that reads like a thriller.)

Did You Know? The world's first Ferris wheel was built on Hyde Park's midway during the World's Columbian Exposition in 1893. It was eventually dynamited and sold for scrap metal.

Getting There

From the Loop, the ride to Hyde Park on the no. 6 Jeffrey Express bus takes about 30 minutes. The bus originates on Wacker Drive, travels south along State Street, and ultimately follows Lake Shore Drive to Hyde Park. The bus runs daily from early morning to late evening, with departures about every 5 minutes on weekdays and every 10 minutes on weekends and holidays. The southbound express bus fare adds a surcharge of 25¢ to the normal fare of $2.25 (there's no surcharge if you use a CTA transit card). The no. 1 local bus originates at Union Station on Jackson Boulevard and Canal Street and takes about an hour.

For a faster trip, take the Metra Electric train on the South Chicago line, which goes from downtown to Hyde Park in about 15 minutes. Trains run every hour (more frequently during rush hour) Monday through Saturday from 5:15am to 12:50am, and every 30 to 90 minutes on Sunday and holidays from 5am to 12:55am. Downtown stations are at Randolph Street and Michigan Avenue, Van Buren Street and Michigan Avenue, and Roosevelt Road and Michigan Avenue (near the Museum Campus in Grant Park). Printed schedules are available at the stations. The fare is approximately $2.50 each way.

For CTA bus and Metra train information, call tel. 312/836-7000, or visit www.transitchicago.com or www.metrarail.com.

For taxis, dial tel. 312/TAXI-CAB (829-4222) for Yellow Cab or tel. 312/CHECKER (243-2537) for Checker. The one-way fare from downtown is around $15 to $20.

A Suggested Itinerary

A long 1-day itinerary for Hyde Park should include the following: a walk through the University of Chicago campus (including a stroll along the Midway Plaisance); a visit to the Museum of Science and Industry (for families), Frank Lloyd Wright's Robie House, or one of the other local museums; and lunch or dinner in the neighborhood's commercial center.

Hyde Park Bites

When you're ready to take a break, Hyde Park has an eclectic selection of restaurants. As in any university town, you'll find plenty of affordable, student-friendly hangouts. The most famous University of Chicago gathering spot is Jimmy's Woodlawn Tap, 1172 E. 55th St. (tel. 773/643-5516). This 50-year-old bar and grill doesn't offer much in the way of atmosphere, but the hamburgers and sandwiches are cheap, and the person sitting next to you might just be a Nobel Prize-winning professor. Another casual spot near campus is Medici, 1327 E. 57th St. (tel. 773/667-7394;www.medici57.com), where a few generations' worth of students have carved their names into the tables while chowing down on pizza, the house specialty. About a block from the main Hyde Park Metra station you'll find La Petite Folie, 1504 E. 55th St. (tel. 773/493-1394; www.lapetitefolie.com), a French bistro that offers a refined escape from student life.

Exploring the University of Chicago

Walking around the Gothic spires of the University of Chicago campus is bound to conjure up images of the cloistered academic life. Allow about an hour to stroll through the grassy quads and dramatic stone buildings. (If the weather's nice, do as the students do, and chill out for a while on the grass.) If you're visiting on a weekday, your first stop should be the university's Visitors Information Desk (tel. 773/702-9739), on the first floor of Ida Noyes Hall, 1212 E. 59th St., where you can pick up campus maps and get information on university events. The center is open Monday through Friday from 10am to 7pm. If you stop by on a weekend when the Visitors Information Desk is closed, you can get the scoop on campus events at the Reynolds Clubhouse student center (tel. 773/702-8787).

Start your tour at the Henry Moore statue, *Nuclear Energy,* on South Ellis Avenue between 56th and 57th streets. It's next to the Regenstein Library, which marks the site of the old Stagg Field, where, on December 2, 1942, the world's first sustained nuclear reaction was achieved in a basement laboratory below the field. Then turn left and follow 57th Street until you reach the grand stone Hull Gate; walk straight to reach the main quad, or turn left through the column-lined arcade to reach Hutchinson Court (designed by John Olmsted, son of revered landscape designer Frederick Law Olmsted). The Reynolds Clubhouse, the university's main student center, is here; you can take a break at the C-Shop cafe or settle down at a table at Hutchinson Commons. The dining room and hangout right next to the cafe will bring to mind the grand dining halls of Oxford and Cambridge.

Other worthy spots on campus include the charming, intimate Bond Chapel, behind Swift Hall on the main quad, and the blocks-long Midway Plaisance, a wide stretch of green that was the site of carnival sideshow attractions during the World's Columbian Exposition in 1893. (Ever since, the term *midway* has referred to carnivals in general.)

The Seminary Co-op Bookstore, 5757 S. University Ave. (tel. 773/752-4381; www.semcoop.com), is a treasure trove of academic and scholarly books. Its selection of more than 100,000 titles has won it an international reputation as "the best bookstore west of Blackwell's in Oxford." It's open Monday through Friday from 8:30am to 8pm, Saturday from 10am to 6pm, and Sunday from noon to 6pm.

Enjoying the Outdoors in Hyde Park

Hyde Park is not only a haven for book lovers and culture aficionados; the community also has open-air attractions. Worthy outdoor environments near Lake Michigan include Lake Shore Drive, where many stately apartment houses follow the contour of the shoreline. A suitable locale for a quiet stroll during the day is Promontory Point, at 55th Street and Lake Michigan, a bulb of land that juts into the lake and offers a good view of Chicago to the north and the seasonally active 57th Street beach to the south.

Farther south, just below the Museum of Science and Industry, is Wooded Island in Jackson Park, the site of the Japanese Pavilion during the Columbian Exposition and today a lovely garden of meandering paths. In the Perennial Garden at 59th Street and Stony Island Avenue in Jackson Park, more than 180 varieties of flowering plants display a palette of colors that changes with the seasons.

Kenwood Historic District

A fun side trip for architecture and history buffs is the Kenwood Historic District, a short walk north of Hyde Park. The area originally developed as a suburb of Chicago, when local captains of industry (including Sears founder Julius Rosenwald) began building lavish mansions in the mid-1850s. The neighborhood's large lots and eclectic mix of architecture (everything from elaborate Italianate to Prairie-style homes) make it unique in Chicago, especially compared to the closely packed buildings in Hyde Park. Although many of the fine homes here became dilapidated after the South Side's "white flight" of the 1950s and '60s, a new generation of black and white middle-class homeowners has lovingly renovated these one-of-a-kind mansions. Today the blocks between 47th and 51st streets (north-south) and Blackstone and Drexel boulevards (east-west) make for a wonderful walking tour, with broad, shady streets full of newly restored buildings.

Best Restaurants in Chicago

Chicago has upped its culinary credentials over the past decade, with high-end spots such as Alinea and The Smyth on the cutting edge of the molecular gastronomy trend (raising the average check price substantially along the way). But the city's thriving deep-dish pizza spots and casual ethnic eateries prove you don't need to be a hard-core foodie to find culinary satisfaction here. Steakhouses continue to be a draw, as they have for decades, and comfort food remains a staple of local restaurant menus.

Price Categories, by Average Entree Price

- ➤ Very Expensive $25-$40
- ➤ Expensive $20-$30
- ➤ Moderate $15-$20
- ➤ Inexpensive $15 or less

The Big Picture

Most restaurants in Chicago are open 7 days a week. A few in the Loop are closed on Sunday evenings, while some others are closed on Mondays (traditionally a slow night). In general, Chicago is not a late-night dining town. Most locals head out to dinner between 6 and 7pm, and the majority of restaurants are closed by 10pm on weeknights and 11pm on weekends. If you plan on heading out for a late dinner, you should definitely check the restaurant's closing time first.

A few restaurants with popular bar areas keep their kitchens open until midnight or later on weekends.

Overall, the restaurant scene in Chicago is casual; the locals go out to enjoy their food, not to score style points or check each other out. Only a handful of restaurants require jackets for men; even ties are optional at all but the most formal places. A business-casual look is appropriate for just about every restaurant in town, and at the moderately priced places, most customers show up in jeans and sneakers. That said, the higher the average entrée price, the more you're expected to make a modest effort: Showing up at Alinea or

Blackbird in scuffed Nikes or shorts won't impress the waitstaff or your fellow diners.

A Spot of Tea

If you're shopping on the Magnificent Mile and feel like having an elegant afternoon tea complete with finger sandwiches, scones, and pastries, head for the stately Palm Courtat The Drake Hotel, 140 E. Walton Place (tel. 312/787-2200); the sophisticated beauty of The Lobby at The Peninsula hotel, 108 E. Superior St. (tel. 312/573-6695); the cozy Seasons Lounge of the Four Seasons Hotel, 120 E. Delaware Place (tel. 312/280-8800); or The Greenhouse in the Ritz-Carlton, 160 E. Pearson St. (tel. 312/266-1000), in the sunny 12th-floor lobby above the Water Tower Place mall. In the Loop, the appropriately named Russian Tea Time, 77 E. Adams St. (tel. 312/360-0000), serves tea from 2:30 to 4:30pm daily.

Dessert Tour

Eli's cheesecake is a Chicago icon the rich, creamy cakes have been served at presidential inaugurations and numerous other high-profile events. For a behind-the-scenes peek at Chicago's most famous dessert, you can take a tour of Eli's Bakery on the northwest side of the city. After watching the cooking and decorating processes, you get to enjoy a full-size slice of your favorite flavor. Tours are given Monday through Friday at 1pm (although reservations aren't necessary, call to make sure the bakery isn't closed for periodic maintenance). The 40-minute tour costs $3 per person; special packages are available for groups. Eli's bakery is at 6701 Forest Preserve Dr., at the corner of Montrose Avenue (tel. 800/ELI-CAKE [354-2253]; www.elischeesecake.com).

Chicago Treats

Deep-dish pizza may be Chicago's culinary claim to fame, but the city has added to the national waistline in other ways. Twinkies and Wonder Bread were invented here, Chicago businessman James L.

Kraft created the first processed cheese, and Oscar Mayer got his start as a butcher in the Old Town neighborhood.

Dining Alfresco in Chicago

Cocooned for 6 months of the year, with furnaces and electric blankets blazing, Chicagoans revel in the warm months of late spring, summer, and early autumn. For locals and visitors alike, dining alfresco is an ideal way to experience the sights, sounds, smells, and social fabric of this multifaceted city.

Loop & Vicinity

Athena This Greektown mainstay offers a stunning three-level outdoor seating area. It's paved with brick and landscaped with 30-foot trees, flower gardens, and even a waterfall. Best of all: An incredible view of the downtown skyline with the Sears Tower right in the middle. It's located at 212 S. Halsted St., between Adams and Jackson streets (tel. 312/655-0000;www.athenarestaurantchicago.com).

Park Grill Millennium Park's restaurant serves upscale versions of American comfort food with panoramic views of Michigan Avenue. In the summer, you can pick up a sandwich and grab a seat on the large patio (converted into an ice-skating rink come winter). It's at 11 N. Michigan Ave., at Madison Street (tel. 312/521-PARK[7275]).

Rhapsody A tranquil oasis amid the Loop high-rises, Rhapsody's outdoor garden is a great spot for a romantic meal downtown. It's located at 65 E. Adams St., at Wabash Avenue (tel. 312/786-9911).

Magnificent Mile & Gold Coast

Charlie's Ale House at Navy Pier One of several outdoor dining options along Navy Pier, this outpost of the Lincoln Park restaurant has lip-smacking pub fare and a great location on the southern promenade overlooking the lakefront and Loop skyline. It's located at 700 E. Grand Ave., near the entrance to the Pier (tel. 312/595-1440).

Le Colonial This lovely French-Vietnamese restaurant, located in a vintage Gold Coast town house and evocative of 1920s Saigon, *does* have a sidewalk cafe, but you'd do better to reserve a table on the tiny second-floor porch, overlooking the street. It's located at 937 N. Rush St., just south of Oak Street (tel. 312/255-0088).

Oak Street Beachstro Suit up and head for this warm-weather-only beachfront cafe literally on the sands of popular Oak Street Beach which serves inventive cafe fare (fresh seafood, sandwiches, and pastas). Beer and wine are available. The address is 1000 N. Lake Shore Dr., at Oak Street Beach (tel. 312/915-4100; www.oakstreetbeachstro.com).

Puck's at the MCA This cafe run by celebrity chef Wolfgang Puck is tucked in the back of the Museum of Contemporary Art, where, from the terrace, you'll get a view of the museum's sculpture garden. (Restaurant-only patrons can bypass museum admission.) The address is 220 E. Chicago Ave., at Fairbanks Court (tel. 312/397-4034; www.mcachicago.org).

River North

SushiSamba Rio For stunning nighttime views of the skyline accompanied by views of some pretty stunning people head to the rooftop deck of this Latin-Asian fusion spot. Canopied banquettes and flickering tea lights create a sultry atmosphere, along with a menu of specialty cocktails. You'll find it at 504 N. Wells St., at Illinois St. (tel. 312/595-2300).

ZED 451 You'll find another great rooftop deck on top of this funky all-you-can-eat spot. Here the wood decor and laid-back vibe let you imagine you're kicking back at a rich friend's penthouse. It's at 739 N. Clark St., 1 block south of Chicago Ave. (tel. 888/493-3451).

Lincoln Park

Charlie's Ale House A true neighborhood hangout, this Lincoln Park pub's wonderful beer garden surrounded by tall, ivy-covered brick walls is spacious and buzzing with activity and good vibes. It's located at 1224 W. Webster Ave., at Magnolia Avenue (tel. 773/871-1440).

North Pond Set on the banks of one of Lincoln Park's beautiful lagoons, the excellent North Pond serves upscale, fresh-as-can-be American cuisine in a romantic and sylvan setting. Also The address is 2610 N. Cannon Dr., halfway between Diversey Parkway and Fullerton Avenue (tel. 773/477-5845).

O'Brien's Restaurant Wells Street in Old Town is lined with several alfresco options, but the best belongs to O'Brien's, the unofficial nucleus of neighborhood life. The outdoor patio has teakwood furniture, a gazebo bar, and a mural of the owners' country club on a brick wall. Order the dressed-up chips, a house specialty. Located at 1528 N. Wells St., 2 blocks south of North Avenue (tel. 312/787-3131;www.obriensrestaurant.com).

Wrigleyville & Vicinity

Tapas Gitana The tapas and sangria at this cozy Wrigleyville restaurant can compete with other, better-known Spanish spots, and the intimate, leafy terrace out back glows with lantern light. Located at 3445 N. Halsted St., at Newport Avenue (tel. 773/296-6046; www.tapasgitana.com).

Moody's For more than 30 years, Moody's has been grilling some of the best burgers in Chicago. It's ideal in winter for its dark, cozy dining room (warmed by a fireplace), but it's better still in summer for its awesome outdoor patio, a real hidden treasure. The address is 5910 N. Broadway Ave., between Rosedale and Thorndale Avenues (tel. 773/275-2696; www.moodyspub.com).

Wicker Park / Bucktown

Northside Café On a sunny summer day, Northside seems like Wicker Park's town square, packed with an eclectic mix of locals catching up and checking out the scene. The entire front of the restaurant opens onto the street, making it relatively easy to get an "outdoor" table.

Located at 1635 N. Damen Ave., just north of North Avenue (tel. 773/384-3555).

Farmers' Markets

If you're lucky enough to be here during good weather, celebrate by enjoying at least one picnic. Peruse the city's farmers' markets and then carry your lunch off to Grant Park or a spot along the lake front.

The city-sponsored farmers' markets operate from late May through October. Two locations in the Loop are easy for visitors to get to: Daley Plaza (at Washington and Dearborn sts.; open on Thurs) and Federal Plaza (at Adams and Dearborn sts.; open on Tues), both open from 7am to 3pm. Both are good places to pick up fresh fruit or bakery treats. For more information, call the Mayor's Office of Special Events at tel. 312/744-3315. At the south end of Lincoln Park (between Clark St. and Stockton Dr.), local chefs and civilian foodies head to the Green City Market (tel. 773/880-1266; greencitymarket.org) for seasonal produce. Pick up some fresh bread, locally produced cheese, and in-season fruit, and enjoy an alfresco meal; Lincoln Park Zoo is just steps away. The market is open Wednesdays and Saturdays from 7am to 1pm, from mid-May through October, and often features cooking demonstrations by chefs from Chicago restaurants.

Ethnic Dining in Chicago

While the term "ethnic restaurant" is often synonymous with casual, low-priced spots, Chicago chefs have taken world cuisine to new, fine-dining heights. At Topolobampo, chef Rick Bayless highlights the flavors of Mexico, including little-known regional specialties, with a focus on fresh, sustainably produced ingredients. Arun's, the namesake restaurant of chef Arun Sampanthavivat, turns Thai dining into a multi-hour, multi-course experience, with a customized menu that varies with the seasons and according to diners' preferences. Ultra-elegant Spiaggia gives Italian cuisine a gourmet upgrade, featuring luxe ingredients such as truffles and caviar.

Ethnic Dining near the Loop

Chinatown Chicago's Chinatown is about 20 blocks south of the Loop. The district is strung along two thoroughfares, Cermak Road and Wentworth Avenue, as far south as 24th Place. Hailing a cab from the Loop is the easiest way to get here, but you can also drive and leave your car in the validated lot near the entrance to Chinatown, or take the Orange Line of the El to the Cermak stop, a well-lit station on the edge of the Chinatown commercial district.

The spacious, fairly elegant Phoenix, 2131 S. Archer Ave. (btw. Wentworth Ave. and Cermak Rd.; tel. 312/328-0848; www.chinatownphoenix.com), has plenty of room for big tables of family or friends to enjoy the Cantonese (and some Szechuan) cuisine. A good sign: The place attracts lots of Chinatown locals. It's especially popular for dim sum brunch, so come early to avoid the wait. Late night, stop by the more casual Saint's Alp Teahouse downstairs (tel. 312/842-1886), an outpost of the Hong Kong chain, which is open until at least midnight daily.

Open since 1927, Won Kow, 2237 S. Wentworth Ave. (btw. 22nd Place and Alexander St.; tel. 312/842-7500), is the oldest continually operating restaurant in Chinatown. You can enjoy dim sum in the mezzanine-level dining room from 9am to 3pm daily. Most of the items cost around $3. Other house specialties include Mongolian chicken and duck with seafood.

Two other great spots for daily dim sum are located in Chinatown Square Mall, an open-air walking pavilion of restaurants, shops, and other businesses along Archer Avenue. Try Shiu Wah, 2162 S. Archer Ave. (tel. 312/225-8811; 8am-3pm), or Happy Chef, 2164 S. Archer Ave. (tel. 312/808-3689; 9am-4pm). They're both great; pick the one with the shortest wait.

Little Italy Convenient to most downtown locations, a few blocks' stretch of Taylor Street is home to a host of time-honored, traditional, hearty Italian restaurants. If you're staying in the Loop (an easy cab ride away), the area makes a good destination for dinner.

Regulars return for the straightforward Italian favorites livened up with some adventurous specials at Francesca's on Taylor, 1400 W. Taylor St. (at Loomis St.; tel. 312/829-2828; www.miafrancesca.com). Standouts include the fresh homemade pastas and the creative fish entrees. This is part of a local chain that includes the popular Mia Francesca, as well as nearby Davanti Enoteca, 1359 W. Taylor St. (tel. 312/226-5550), a cozy, buzzy small-plates spot that's known for its truffle egg toast, bruschetta, and specialty pizzas.

Expect to wait even with a reservation at Rosebud on Taylor, 1500 W. Taylor St. (at Laflin St.; tel. 312/942-1117; www.rosebudrestaurants.com), but fear not your hunger will be satisfied. Rosebud is known for enormous helpings of pasta, most of which lean toward heavy Italian-American favorites: deep-dish lasagna and a fettuccine Alfredo that defines the word *rich.* I highly recommend any of the pastas served with vodka sauce. Another location is near the Mag Mile at 720 N. Rush St. (tel. 312/266-6444).

Family-owned Tuscany, 1014 W. Taylor St. (btw. Morgan and Miller sts.; tel. 312/829-1990; www.tuscanychicago.com), has the comfortable feel of a neighborhood restaurant, unlike the city's more fashionable Italian spots. Specialties include anything cooked on the wood-burning grill and Tuscan sausage dishes. A second location is across from Wrigley Field, at 3700 N. Clark St. (at Waveland Ave.; tel. 773/404-7700).

Greektown A short cab ride across the south branch of the Chicago River will take you to the city's Greektown, a row of moderately priced and inexpensive Greek restaurants clustered on Halsted Street between Van Buren and Washington streets.

To be honest, there's not much here to distinguish one restaurant from the other: They're all standard Greek restaurants with similar looks and similar menus. That said, Greek Islands, 200 S. Halsted St. (at Adams St.; tel. 312/782-9855;www.greekislands.net); Santorini, 800 W. Adams St. (at Halsted St.; tel. 312/829-8820; www.santorinichicago.com); Parthenon, 314 S. Halsted St. (btw.

Jackson and Van Buren sts.; tel. 312/726-2407; www.theparthenon.com); and Costas, 340 S. Halsted St. (btw. Jackson and Van Buren sts.; tel. 312/263-0767; www.costasdining.com), are all good bets for gyros, Greek salads, shish kabobs, and the classic moussaka. On warm summer nights, opt for either Athena, 212 S. Halsted St. (btw. Adams and Jackson sts.; tel. 312/655-0000; www.athenarestaurantchicago.com), which has a huge outdoor seating area, or Pegasus, 130 S. Halsted St. (btw. Monroe and Adams sts.; tel. 312/226-3377; www.pegasuschicago.com), with its rooftop patio serving drinks, appetizers, and desserts. Both have wonderful views of the Loop's skyline. Artopolis, 306 S. Halsted St. (at Jackson St.; tel. 312/559-9000; www.artopolischicago.com), a more recent addition to the neighborhood, is a casual option offering up Greek and Mediterranean specialties, wood-oven pizzas, breads, and French pastries, all of them tasty.

Pilsen Just south of the Loop and convenient to McCormick Place and Chinatown, Pilsen is a colorful blend of Mexican culture, artists, and bohemians, and pricey new residential developments. The area's nascent restaurant scene is showing signs of life, but for now, the local fare is decidedly casual.

Nuevo Leon, 1515 W. 18th St. (at Laflin St.; tel. 312/421-1517;www.nuevoleonrestaurant.com), is a popular Mexican restaurant serving the standard offerings.

On the more bohemian side, linger over a salad, sandwich, cake, or refreshing fruit milkshake *(liquado)* at Café Jumping Bean, 1439 W. 18th St. (at Bishop St.; tel. 312/455-0019; http://cafejumpingbean.org), and admire the artwork from paintings to photographs hanging on the walls.

A Taste of Poland

Chicago has long been a popular destination for Polish immigrants (currently, about one million Chicagoans claim Polish ancestry). It's somewhat mystifying, then, why they haven't made much of an impact on the city's dining scene. There are Polish restaurants here, but they tend to be small, casual, family-run affairs in residential neighborhoods far removed from the usual tourist attractions. If you'd like to try some hearty, stick-to-your-ribs Polish food, the best-known restaurant is Red Apple (Czerwone Jabluszko), 3121 N. Milwaukee Ave. (tel. 773/588-5781; www.redapplebuffet.com). Dining here is strictly buffet, and the lineup includes Polish specialties such as pirogi (meat- or cheese-stuffed dumplings) and blintzes, as well as a huge selection of roast meats, salads, and bread (there's even fruit, should you feel nutrient starved). Best of all is the price: $13 on weekdays and $15 on weekends for all you can eat (lunch prices are $2 less).

A Taste of Thai

Thai restaurants are to Chicago what Chinese restaurants are to many other American cities: ubiquitous, affordable, and perfect for a quick meal that offers a taste of the exotic. If you've never tried Thai, Chicago is a great place to start. Good introductory dishes are pad thai noodles topped with minced peanuts or the coconut-based mild yellow curry.

Arun's is the city's reigning gourmet interpreter of Thai cuisine, but many other low-key places are scattered throughout the residential neighborhoods. Most entrees at these spots don't cost much more $10. A staple of the River North dining scene is the bright and airy Star of Siam, 11 E. Illinois St., at North State Street (tel. 312/670-0100; www.starofsiamchicago.com). On the north end of the Gold Coast where it meets Old Town, Tiparos, 1540 N. Clark St. at North Avenue (tel. 312/712-9900; www.tiparosthai.com), is a very friendly place that features Thai textiles on its brick interior walls and serves delicious specialties such as massaman curry. Thai Classic, 3332 N. Clark St., at Roscoe Street (tel. 773/404-2000; www.thaiclassicrestaurant.com), conveniently located between the busy Belmont/Clark intersection and Wrigley Field, offers an excellent all-you-can-eat buffet on weekends if you want to try a taste of everything. While wandering the Lakeview neighborhood, a good stop for a quick, no-frills meal is the Bamee Noodle Shop, 3120 N. Broadway, at Wellington Street (tel. 773/281-2641; www.bameethai.com), which offers a wide selection of

"Noodles on Plates" and "Noodles in Bowls," as well as a number of soups and fried-rice combinations.

Local Cuisine in Chicago

There is great food to be had in Chicago, but the two dishes that the city truly calls its own are pizza and hot dogs. It may not be haute cuisine, but I promise you've never had anything quite like the city's spin on either of these indulgences.

Pizza

We have three pizza styles in Chicago: Chicago style, also known as deep-dish, which is thick-crusted and often demands a knife and fork; stuffed, which is similar to a pie, with a crust on both top and bottom; and thin crust.

Three of the best places to try the classic Chicago deep-dish are Pizzeria Uno, Pizzeria Due, and Gino's East. In River North, Lou Malnati's Pizzeria, 439 N. Wells St. (at Hubbard St.; tel. 312/828-9800), bakes both deep-dish and thin-crust pizza and even has a low-fat-cheese option. Edwardo's is a local pizza chain that serves all three varieties, but with a wheat crust and all-natural ingredients (spinach pizza is the specialty here); locations are in the Gold Coast at 1212 N. Dearborn St. (at Division St.; tel. 312/337-4490), in the South Loop at 521 S. Dearborn St. (btw. Congress Pkwy. and Harrison St.; tel. 312/939-3366), and in Lincoln Park at 2622 N. Halsted St. (at Wrightwood Ave.; tel. 773/871-3400). Another popular chain known for its stuffed pizza is Giordano's, with downtown locations off the Magnificent Mile at 730 N. Rush St. (at Superior St.; tel. 312/951-0747), and at the Prudential Plaza, 135 E. Lake St. (just east of Michigan Ave.; tel. 312/616-1200).

For a unique twist on the deep-dish phenomenon, head to Chicago Pizza & Oven Grinder, 2121 N. Clark St. (between Webster and Dickens aves.; tel. 773/248-2570), a few blocks from Lincoln Park Zoo. Here the "pizza potpie" is baked in a bowl and then turned over when served.

This neighborhood spot stays popular year after year, so plan on showing up early for dinner to avoid a long wait.

Hot Dogs

The classic Chicago hot dog includes a frankfurter by Vienna Beef (a local food processor and hallowed institution), heaps of chopped onions and green relish, a slather of yellow mustard, pickle spears, fresh tomato wedges, a dash of celery salt, and, for good measure, two or three "sport" peppers, those thumb-shaped holy terrors that turn your mouth into its own bonfire.

Chicago is home to many standout hot-dog spots, but one, Hot Doug's, 3324 N. California Ave. (at Roscoe St.; tel. 773/279-9550), takes encased meats to a new level, featuring several gourmet sausages on a bun every day except Sunday (plan on standing in line no matter which day you show up and it's always worth it). Hot Doug's also serves a great classic Chicago dog just like many other stands in town, including Gold Coast Dogs, 159 N. Wabash Ave. (at Randolph St.; tel. 312/917-1677), in the Loop just a block from Michigan Avenue. Portillo's is another local chain that specializes in hot dogs but also serves tasty pastas and salads. Murphy's Red Hots, 1211 W. Belmont Ave. (at Racine Ave.; tel. 773/935-2882), is a neighborhood spot not too far from Wrigley Field; while The Wieners Circle, in Lincoln Park at 2622 N. Clark St. (btw. Wrightwood Ave. and Drummond Place; tel. 773/477-7444), is a late-night favorite where rude order-takers are part of the shtick.

If you've got a car, head up to Superdawg Drive-In, 6363 N. Milwaukee Ave. (at Devon Ave.; tel. 773/763-0660), on the northwest side of the city (look for the giant hot dogs dressed as Tarzan and Jane on the roof). This classic 1950s-style flashback has been run by the same family for three generations, and, yes, they still have carhops who bring out your order.

Breakfast in Chicago

Near The Loop & Magnificent Mile

You can get a good (and upscale) breakfast at one of the hotels near the Loop or Magnificent Mile. Favorite spots for business travelers looking to impress include The Café, at the Four Seasons Hotel, 120 E. Delaware Place (tel. 312/280-8800); and Drake Bros. Restaurant at The Drake Hotel, 140 E. Walton Place, at Michigan Avenue (tel. 312/787-2200).

A more informal choice in the Loop, overlooking the El tracks, is Heaven on Seven, where the Cajun and Creole specialties supplement an enormous diner-style menu.

For brunch with some soul, head to House of Blues, 329 N. Dearborn St., at Kinzie Street (tel. 312/527-2583), for its popular Sunday gospel brunch. To guarantee seating, it's a good idea to book a spot 2 weeks in advance.

A local breakfast favorite since 1923 is Lou Mitchell's, 565 W. Jackson Blvd. (tel. 312/939-3111; loumitchellsrestaurant.com), across the south branch of the Chicago River from the Loop, a block farther west than Union Station. You'll be greeted at the door with a basket of doughnut holes and Milk Duds so that you can nibble while waiting for a table.

For a Southern-style breakfast of spicy red eggs, cheese grits, or biscuits and gravy, head over to Wishbone, a family-friendly, laid-back spot in a converted warehouse building in the West Loop.

Lincoln Park & The North Side

A perfect breakfast or brunch spot if you're heading up to Wrigleyville for a Cubs game or a walk through Lincoln Park is Ann Sather, famous for its homemade cinnamon rolls.

The Nookies restaurants are Chicago favorites for all the standard morning fare. Locations include 2114 N. Halsted St., in Lincoln Park (tel. 773/327-1400; www.nookiesrestaurants.net); 1748 N. Wells St., in Old Town (tel. 312/337-2454); and 3334 N. Halsted St., in Lakeview (tel. 773/248-9888). Especially in Old Town, be prepared to stand outside on the weekends until a table opens for you. It's quite a scene on the sidewalk, which is packed with baby strollers, dogs on leashes, large groups chatting, and singles reading the newspaper.

Go to Orange, 3231 N. Clark St., at Belmont (tel. 773/549-4400; orangerestaurantchicago.com), for a fun twist on breakfast foods. Try the Green Eggs and Ham eggs scrambled with pesto, tomatoes, mozzarella, and pancetta. There's a kids' menu, too, making this a popular choice for families. But a warning to all those with hungry kids (and parents): Come early or late; the line for a table winds outside during prime weekend brunch hours.

Lincoln Park's Toast, 746 W. Webster St., at Halsted Street (tel. 773/935-5600), is homey yet slightly funky. Pancakes come in all sorts of tempting varieties, from lemon/poppy seed drizzled with honey to the "pancake orgy," a strawberry, mango, and banana-pecan pancake topped with granola, yogurt, and honey. Come early on weekends, though; by 10:30am or so, there's guaranteed to be a lengthy wait.

Wicker Park / Bucktown

The brightly colored and artwork-adorned Earwax Café, 1561 N. Milwaukee Ave., at North and Damen avenues (tel. 773/772-4019; www.earwax-cafe.com), is a Wicker Park institution serving everything from salmon Benedict to vegan options such as the popular tofu scramble. Don't let the unappetizing name, the proliferation of hipsters, or the dearth of meat deter you from this place. The food is delicious, the back patio is delightful, and the tattooed and pierced waitstaff could not be nicer.

Family Friendly Restaurants in Chicago

One of the city's first "theme" restaurants, Ed Debevic's, 640 N. Wells St., at Ontario Street (tel. 312/664-1707), is a temple to America's hometown lunch-counter culture. The burgers-and-milkshakes menu is kid-friendly, but it's the staff shtick that makes this place memorable. The waitresses play the parts of gum-chewing toughies who make wisecracks, toss out good-natured insults, and even sit right down at your table.

If you're in the mood for something a little more funky, Wishbone is a popular option for local families. The food is diverse enough that both adults and kids can find something to their liking (you can mix and match side dishes, a big plus), and there's also a menu geared just toward children. Another all-American choice in the Loop is South Water Kitchen, which offers a kids' menu and coloring books.

A fun breakfast-and-lunch spot in Lincoln Park, Toast, 746 W. Webster St., at Halsted Street (tel. 773/935-5600), serves up all-American favorites (pancakes, eggs, sandwiches) and employs an age-old restaurateur's device for keeping idle hands and minds occupied: Tables at this neighborhood spot are covered with blank canvases of butcher-block paper on which kids of all ages can doodle away with crayons. But be forewarned: This is a very popular spot for weekend brunch.

At Gino's East, the famous Chicago pizzeria, long waits can also be an issue during the prime summer tourist season. But once you get your table, the kids can let loose: Patrons are invited to scrawl all over the graffiti-strewn walls and furniture. For fun and games of the coin-operated and basement rec room variety, seek out Dave & Buster's, 1024 N. Clark St. (tel. 312/943-5151), the Chicago location of the Dallas-based mega entertainment/dining chain.

With heaping plates of pasta served up family style, Maggiano's, 516 N. Clark St. (tel. 312/644-7700), in River North, and Buca di Beppo, 521 N. Rush St., right off Michigan Avenue (tel. 312/396-0001), are good choices for budget-conscious families. These Italian-American restaurants (both parts of national chains) serve up huge portions of pasta and meat to be passed and shared.

Neighborhoods in Chicago

The Loop

In keeping with their proximity to the towers of power, many of the restaurants in the Loop feature expense-account-style prices, but it's still possible to dine here for less than the cost of your hotel room. The South Loop a neighborhood just west of the lake and south of Congress Parkway has seen a mini-boom in restaurants in the past few years, accompanying a rash of condo conversions and new construction in the area. *Note:* Keep in mind that several of the best downtown spots are closed on Sunday.

The West Loop

The stretch of Randolph Street just west of the Chicago River once known as the Market District used to be filled with produce trucks and warehouses that shut down tight after nightfall. In the 1990s, in an echo of New York's Meatpacking District, a few bold restaurant pioneers moved in, bringing their super-hip clientele with them. It wasn't long before industrial buildings began their transformation into condos, and now it seems like there's a construction zone on every corner. Despite the upheaval, the West Loop still feels like a neighborhood in transition. It's home to some of the city's coolest restaurants and clubs, but not much else.

Transportation to the West Loop is easy. You can get there by bus (no. 8 or 9) or El (the Green Line has a stop at Clinton, which is within a few blocks of most restaurants listed), but it takes about 5 minutes and costs less than $10 to take a cab from Michigan Avenue. The walk from the Loop is pleasant and secure in the daytime and early evening, but it's best to catch a cab if you're returning to your hotel late.

The Magnificent Mile & the Gold Coast

Many tourists who visit Chicago never stray far from the Magnificent Mile and the adjoining Gold Coast area. From the array of restaurants, shops, and pretty streets, it's not hard to see why. The Gold Coast is home to some of the city's wealthiest, most tradition-bound families, people who have been frequenting the same restaurants for years. But newer places, such as Table Fifty-Two, have carved out their own culinary niches here as well.

River North

River North, the area north of the Loop and west of Michigan Avenue, is home to the city's most concentrated cluster of art galleries and a something-for-everyone array of restaurants from fast food and themed restaurants to chains and some of our trendiest dining destinations. Whether you seek a quick dog or burger, contemporary American fine dining, or world-class Mexican fare, River North has it all within easy walking distance of many downtown hotels.

Lincoln Park & Old Town

Singles and upwardly mobile young families inhabit Lincoln Park, the neighborhood roughly defined by North Avenue on the south, Diversey Parkway on the north, the park on the east, and Clybourn Avenue on the west. In the southeast corner of this area is Old Town, a neighborhood of historic town houses that stretches out from the intersection of North Avenue and Wells Street. You'll find a few fine-dining spots, but most restaurants here are more casual, with average prices lower than you'll find in River North or along the Magnificent Mile.

Wrigleyville & the North Side

The area surrounding Wrigley Field has a long history as a working-class neighborhood, and although housing prices are now beyond the reach of most blue-collar workers, the neighborhood still attracts hordes of recent college grads who prefer chicken wings to truffles. Overall, restaurants here are more affordable and low-key than downtown, though most aren't worth a special trip if you're staying elsewhere. Throughout the North Side a catch phrase encompassing the neighborhoods north of Lincoln Park you'll find mostly casual, neighborhood restaurants and a good range of ethnic eats.

Wicker Park/Bucktown

The booming Wicker Park/Bucktown area followed closely on the heels of Lincoln Park and Wrigleyville in the race to gentrification. First came the artists and musicians, followed by armies of yuppies and young families all attracted by cheap rents and real estate. The result is a well-established, happening scene, which includes some of the city's hippest restaurants and clubs. Get yourself to the nexus of activity at the intersection of North, Damen, and Milwaukee avenues, and you won't have to walk more than a couple of blocks in any direction to find a hot spot. Cab fares from downtown are reasonable, or you can take the El's Blue Line to Damen.

Vegetarian in Chicago

Yes, Chicago may have a reputation as a carnivore's paradise, but that doesn't mean vegetarians should stuff their bags with dried tofu before coming here. In recent years, more and more local restaurants have made an effort to accommodate non-meat eaters. While you can order a green salad or vegetable pasta almost anywhere, here are some places where veggie offerings are the main event.

At Green Zebra (1460 W. Chicago Ave. [at Greenview St.]; tel. 312/243-7100; www.greenzebrachicago.com), the menu is almost exclusively meat-free, and the creative small-plates menu gives diners a wide range of flavors to sample. Reza's, a sprawling Middle Eastern spot in River North, may specialize in giant mixed-meat kebabs, but their vegetarian plates are generous, flavorful mixes of hummus, tabbouleh, and other traditional dishes, nicely presented in red bento boxes. At the Southern spot Wishbone, in the West Loop, veggie lovers can create their own sampler plates by selecting from a wide range of side dishes.

Going vegetarian also doesn't mean giving up on gourmet dining. Two of the city's best, most creative chefs in town Charlie Trotter at his namesake restaurant and Michael Taus at Zealous offer multicourse vegetarian tasting menus. At Crofton on Wells, in River North, chef Suzy Crofton always includes a few meat-free options on her nightly menu. (She'll customize them for vegans, too.) In Wrigleyville, chef Yoshi Katsumura of Yoshi's Café also offers a regular selection of vegetarian dishes featuring his signature blend of French and Asian flavors.

Vegans may find their options extremely limited on most menus, but local holistic health devotee Karyn Calabrese operates two vegan-friendly restaurants. Karyn's Raw, 1901 N. Halsted St. (tel. 312/255-1590), in Old Town, encompasses both a casual cafe and juice bar and a white-tablecloth restaurant specializing in raw food; Karyn's Cooked, 738 N. Wells St. (tel. 312/587-1050), in River North, offers globally inspired vegan dishes. You can check out both menus at www.karynraw.com. Farther north in Wrigleyville, The Chicago Diner, 3411 N. Halsted St. (tel. 773/935-6696; www.veggiediner.com), might sound like the kind of place you load up on greasy burgers, but it's actually one of the city's best and longest-lasting vegetarian restaurants. (Most dishes are vegan, too.) The wide-ranging menu includes salads, sandwiches (including a "California Reuben" with seitan instead of corned beef), tacos, and pastas; for dessert, try a peanut butter or vanilla chai vegan milkshake.

Best Nightlife in Chicago

Chicago's bustling energy isn't confined to daylight hours. The city offers loads of after-hours entertainment, including Broadway musicals, world-class classical music, and a theater scene that rivals New York's. Late-night hangouts run the gamut from sleek lounges to classic neighborhood taverns and most are refreshingly attitude-free.

The international talent on stage at both the Chicago Symphony Orchestra and the Lyric Opera of Chicago is appealing to culture vultures, while theater buffs can choose between high-profile companies such as Steppenwolf and the scrappy groups that spring up in storefronts around the city. The theater scene here was built by performers who valued gritty realism and a communal work ethic, and that down-to-earth energy is still very much present. Music and nightclub haunts are scattered throughout the city, but Chicago's thriving music scene is concentrated in Lincoln Park, Lakeview, and

Wicker Park, where clubs are devoted to everything from jazz and blues to alternative rock and reggae.

While the city has its share of see-and-be-seen nightspots, Chicagoans in general are not obsessed with getting into the latest hot club; for the most part, chilling out with buddies at a neighborhood bar is the evening activity of choice. To join the locals, you only have to pick a residential area and wander it won't be long before you'll come across a tavern filled with neighborhood regulars and friendly bartenders.

For up-to-date entertainment listings, check the local newspapers and magazines, particularly the Friday editions of the Chicago Tribune and the Chicago Sun-Times; the weekly magazine Time Out Chicago, which has excellent comprehensive listings; and the Chicago Reader or New City, two free weekly tabloids with extensive listings. The Tribune's entertainment-oriented website, www.chicago.metromix.com; the Reader's website, www.chicagoreader.com; and Time Out Chicago's website, www.timeoutchicago.com, are also excellent sources of information, with lots of opinionated reviews.

The Performing Arts in Chicago

Chicago is a regular stop on the big-name entertainment circuit, whether it's musicals such as *Wicked* or pop music acts. High-profile shows that went on to great success in New York, including Monty Python's *Spamalot* and Mel Brooks's stage version of *The Producers,* had their first runs here before moving on to Broadway.

Thanks to extensive renovation of historic theaters, performers have a choice of impressive venues to strut their stuff. The Auditorium Theatre, 50 E. Congress Pkwy., between Michigan and Wabash avenues (tel. 312/922-2110; www.auditoriumtheatre.org), may be the most beautiful theater in Chicago and it's also a certified national landmark. Built in 1889 by Louis Sullivan and Dankmar Adler, this grand hall schedules mostly musicals and dance performances. Even if you don't catch a show here, you can stop by for a tour.

The city's other great historic theaters are concentrated in the North Loop. The Ford Center for the Performing Arts/Oriental Theater, 24 W. Randolph St., and the Cadillac Palace Theater, 151 W. Randolph St., book major touring shows and are well worth a visit for arts buffs. The Oriental's fantastical Asian look includes elaborate carvings almost everywhere you look; dragons, elephants, and griffins peer down at the audience from the gilded ceiling. The Palace features a profusion of Italian marble surfaces and columns, gold-leaf accents a la Versailles, huge decorative mirrors, and crystal chandeliers. (If you'd like to get a look at these historic theaters for a fraction of the standard ticket price, guided tours of both start at 11am Sat and cost $10 per person; meet in the Oriental lobby.) The Bank of America Theatre (formerly the Schubert Theatre), 18 W. Monroe St., was built in 1906 as a home for vaudeville shows; today it books mostly well-known musicals and sometimes comedy performers. For show schedules at all three theaters, call tel. 312/977-1700, or visit www.broadwayinchicago.com.

The Chicago Theatre, 175 N. State St., at Lake Street (tel. 312/443-1130; www.thechicagotheatre.com), is a 1920s music palace reborn as an all-purpose entertainment venue, playing host to pop acts, magicians, stand-up comedians, and more. (Both the Chicago Theatre and the Bank of America Theatre, above, are quite large, so be forewarned that the cheaper seats are in nosebleed territory.) Arie Crown Theater, in the McCormick Place convention center at 23rd Street and Lake Shore Drive (tel. 312/791-6190; www.ariecrown.com), books musicals and pop acts, but compared to the venues listed above, the massive hall feels somewhat impersonal.

Symphony Center, 220 S. Michigan Ave., between Adams Street and Jackson Boulevard (tel. 312/294-3000), is the building that encompasses Orchestra Hall, home of the Chicago Symphony Orchestra (CSO). The building holds a six-story sky-lit arcade, recital spaces, and the fine-dining restaurant Rhapsody. While the CSO is the main attraction, the Symphony Center schedules a series of piano recitals, classical and chamber music concerts, a family matinee series, and the occasional jazz or pop artist.

Chicago has a few other major venues for traveling shows, but they are not as convenient for visitors. The Rosemont Theatre, 5400 River Rd. in Rosemont, near O'Hare Airport (tel. 847/671-5100; www.rosemonttheatre.com), is a top suburban stop for family-friendly musicals and concerts. The North Shore Center for the Performing Arts in Skokie, 9501 Skokie Blvd., in the northern suburb of Skokie (tel. 847/673-6300; www.northshorecenter.org), is home to the well-respected Northlight Theater troupe, the Skokie Valley Symphony Orchestra, and a series of nationally known touring acts, including comics, dance troupes, and children's programs.

Tip: Finding a Better Seat Most of Chicago's grand old theaters have balconies that go way, way up toward the ceiling and if you're stuck in the cheap seats, you'll be straining to see what's happening onstage. While theaters are very strict about checking tickets when you arrive, the ushers relax during intermission, so scope out empty seats during the first act, and then move down to better (and much pricier) spots for the rest of the show.

Classical Music

Not surprisingly, the world-class talent of the Chicago Symphony Orchestra considered one of the best in the country dominates the classical music calendar. However, many orchestra members play in smaller ensembles around town on a semi-regular basis; a few independent musical groups have also built loyal followings with eclectic programming.

To find out what's playing when you're in town, check out the Chicago Classical Music website (www.chicagoclassicalmusic.org), maintained by a consortium of the city's leading music groups.

The Chicago Symphony Orchestra is considered among the best in the world.

The oldest all-volunteer civic chorus in the country, Apollo Chorus of Chicago (tel. 312/427-5620; www.apollochorus.org), was founded in 1872, 1 year after the Great Chicago Fire. Today, it's best known for its annual holiday-season performances of Handel's *Messiah* at Orchestra Hall. The group also presents at least two other concerts during the year at various downtown venues.

The Chicago Chamber Musicians (CCM; tel. 312/819-5800; www.chicagochambermusic.org), a 15-member ensemble drawn from performers from the CSO and Northwestern and DePaul universities, presents chamber music concerts at various locales around the city. The season runs September through May, and you can always find the CCM performing free noontime concerts on the first Monday of the month (except Sept and Mar) on the second floor of the Chicago Cultural Center in the Loop. The Chicago String Quartet is affiliated with the group.

The Chicago Sinfonietta (tel. 312/236-3681; www.chicagosinfonietta.org), with its racially diverse 45-member orchestra and a wide-ranging repertoire, seeks to broaden the audience for classical music. Concerts combine works by masters such as Beethoven and Mendelssohn with music from Latin America, Asia, and others. Playing about 10 times a year at Orchestra Hall and other venues, the group often takes a multimedia approach to its multicultural mission, collaborating with dance troupes, visual artists, museums, rock bands, and gospel choirs.

Music of the Baroque (tel. 312/551-1414; www.baroque.org) is a small orchestra and chorus that pulls members from both the CSO and the Lyric Opera orchestra, and features professional singers from across the country. The ensemble performs the music of the 16th, 17th, and 18th centuries, in appropriately Gothic church settings in various neighborhoods. The group has made several recordings and has introduced lesser-known works by composers such as Mozart and Monteverdi to Chicago audiences.

Dance

Chicago's dance scene is lively, but unfortunately it doesn't attract the same crowds as theater or music performances. Some resident dance troupes have international reputations, but they spend much of their time touring to support themselves. Dance performances in Chicago tend to occur in spurts throughout the year, with visiting companies such as the American Ballet Theatre and the Dance Theater of Harlem stopping in Chicago for limited engagements. Depending on the timing of your visit, you may have a choice of dance performances or there may be none at all.

Dance lovers should schedule their visit for November, when the annual "Dance Chicago" festival (tel. 773/989-0698; www.dancechicago.com) is held at various locations around town. Featuring performances and workshops from the city's best-known dance companies and countless smaller groups, it's a great chance to check out the range of local dance talent. Another phenomenon that has enlivened the local scene is the scintillating Chicago Human Rhythm Project (tel. 773/281-1825; www.chicagotap.com), a non-profit group that brings together tap and percussive dancers from around the world for a series of workshops and performances in the summer and fall.

To find out what's going on at other times of the year, visit the website for the non-profit group See Chicago Dance (www.seechicagodance.com), which gives a comprehensive roundup of local performances. Another good reason to check out the site: You can often find links to discounted tickets.

The major Chicago dance troupes perform at the Harris Theater for Music and Dance, 205 E. Randolph St. (tel. 312/334-7777; www.harristheaterchicago.org), in Millennium Park. The 1,500-seat theater feels fairly stark and impersonal the gray concrete lobby could be mistaken for a parking garage but the sightlines are great, thanks to the stadium-style seating.

Theater

Ever since the Steppenwolf Theatre Company burst onto the national radar in the late '70s and early '80s with in-your-face productions of Sam Shepard's *True West* and Lanford Wilson's *Balm in Gilead,* Chicago has been known as a theater town. As Broadway produced bloated, big-budget musicals with plenty of special effects but little soul, Chicago theater troupes gained respect for their risk-taking and no-holds-barred emotional style. Some of Broadway's most acclaimed dramas in recent years (the Goodman Theatre's revival of *Death of a Salesman* and Steppenwolf's *August: Osage County,* to name a couple) hatched on Chicago stages. With more than 200 theaters, Chicago might have dozens of productions playing on any given weekend and seeing a show here is on my must-do list for all visitors.

The city's theaters have produced a number of legendary comedic actors, including comic-turned-director Mike Nichols *(The Graduate, Postcards from the Edge, Primary Colors),* as well as fine dramatic actors and playwrights. David Mamet, one of America's greatest playwrights and an acclaimed film director and screenwriter, grew up in Chicago's South Shore steel-mill neighborhood and honed his craft with the former St. Nicholas Players, which included actor William H. Macy *(Fargo, Boogie Nights).*

The thespian soil here must be fertile. Tinseltown and TV have lured away such talents as John Malkovich, Joan Allen, Dennis Franz, Gary Sinise, George Wendt, and John Cusack. But even as emerging talents leave for bigger paychecks, a new pool of fresh faces is always waiting to take over. This constant renewal keeps the city's theatrical scene invigorated with new ideas and energy. Many of the smaller theater companies place great emphasis on communal work: Everyone takes part in putting on a production, from writing the script to building the sets. These companies perform in tiny, none-too-impressive venues, but their enthusiasm and commitment are inspiring. Who knows? The group you see performing in some storefront theater today could be the Steppenwolf of tomorrow.

The listings below highlight the troupes that consistently present high-quality work, but they represent only a fraction of Chicago's theater scene. For a complete listing of productions that are playing while you're in town, check the comprehensive listings in the two free weeklies, the *Reader* (which reviews just about every show in town) and *New City;* the weekly *Time Out Chicago* magazine; or the Friday sections of the two daily newspapers. The website of the League of Chicago Theatres(www.chicagoplays.com) also lists all theater productions playing in the area.

Getting Tickets You can buy tickets for most shows directly from each theater's website. Individual box offices also take credit card orders by phone, and many of the smaller theaters will reserve seats for you with a simple request under your name left on the answering machine. For hard-to-get tickets, try Gold Coast Tickets (tel. 800/889-9100; www.goldcoasttickets.com).

Special Value: Half-Price theater Tickets For half-price tickets on the day of the show, drop by one of the Hot Tix ticket centers (tel. 312/977-1755; www.hottix.org), located in the Loop at 72 E. Randolph St. (btw. Wabash and Michigan aves.), and the Water Works Visitor Center, 163 E. Pearson St. The website lists what's on sale for that day beginning at 10am. You can buy tickets to most shows online, but you'll have to pay Ticketmaster's irritating "convenience" charge. Branches are open Tuesday through Saturday 10am to 6pm, Sunday 11am to 4pm; on Friday you can also purchase tickets for weekend performances. Hot Tix also offers advance-purchase tickets at full price.

In addition, a few theaters offer last-minute discounts on leftover seats. Steppenwolf Theatre Company often has $20 tickets available beginning at 11am on the day of a performance; stop by Audience Services at the theater. Also, half-price tickets become available 1 hr. before the show; call or stop by the box office, or visit www.steppenwolf.org. At the Goodman Theatre, if a show doesn't sell out, half-price tickets for that evening's performance are available starting at 10am at the box office; you can also buy them on the theater's website.

Tip: Theater for All Visitors with disabilities will find that some local theaters go the extra mile to make their performances accessible. The Steppenwolf, Goodman, and Lookingglass theaters offer sign-language interpretation for deaf patrons and audio-described performances for visually impaired audiences. Victory Gardens Theater schedules special performances throughout the year customized for audiences with different disabilities. The theater even offers deaf patrons special glasses that project captions of dialogue onto the frame of the glasses.

Comedy & Improv

In the mid-1970s, the nation was introduced to Chicago's brand of comedy through the skit-comedy show *Saturday Night Live.* Back then, John Belushi and Bill Murray were among the latest brood to hatch from the number-one incubator of Chicago-style humor, Second City. Generations of American comics, from Mike Nichols and Robert Klein to Mike Myers and Tina Fey, have honed their skills in Chicago before making it big in film and TV. Chicago continues to nurture young comics, affording them the chance to learn the tricks of improvisational comedy at Second City, the ImprovOlympic, and numerous other comedy and improv outlets.

The Club & Music Scene in Chicago

Jazz
In the first great wave of black migration from the South just after World War I, jazz journeyed from the Storyville section of New Orleans to Chicago. Jelly Roll Morton and Louis Armstrong made Chicago a jazz hot spot in the 1920s, and their music lives on in a whole new generation of talent. Chicago jazz is known for its collaborative spirit and a certain degree of risk-taking which you can experience at a number of lively clubs.

Blues

If there's any music that epitomizes Chicago, it's the blues. As African-Americans migrated northward in the years following World War II, they brought their musical traditions with them, including the mournful, guitar-and-harmonica-based sound known as Delta blues. In Chicago, the addition of electric guitar gave the traditional blues a jolt of new life, and local musicians such as Howlin' Wolf, Muddy Waters, and Willie Dixon influenced generations of rockers that followed. Today, blues clubs remain a staple of the cultural scene, but one that attracts mostly niche audiences. Some spots cater to out-of-towners looking for an "authentic" blues experience, while others keep a relatively low profile, surviving thanks to the loyalty of die-hard blues aficionados.

Rock (Basically)

In the early 1990s, Chicago's burgeoning alternative rock scene produced such national names as the Smashing Pumpkins, Liz Phair, Veruca Salt, Urge Overkill, and Material Issue. Although the city's moment of pop hipness quickly faded (as did most of the aforementioned artists), the live music scene has continued to thrive. Although local groups still occasionally hit it big (Wilco, Fall Out Boy), most Chicago bands concentrate on keeping it real, happy to perform at small local clubs and not obsessing (at least openly) about getting a record contract. The city is also a regular stop for touring bands, from big stadium acts to smaller up-and-coming groups. Scan the *Reader, New City,* or *Time Out Chicago* to see who's playing where.

The biggest rock acts tend to play at the local indoor stadiums: the United Center (tel. 312/455-4500; www.unitedcenter.com), home of the Bulls and Blackhawks, and Allstate Arena (tel. 847/635-6601; www.allstatearena.com), in Rosemont near O'Hare Airport. These venues are about what you expect: The overpriced seats nearest the stage are fine, but you'd better bring binoculars if you're stuck in the more affordable upper decks. During the summer, you'll also find the big names at the outdoor First Midwest Bank Amphitheatre (tel. 708/614-1616; www.livenation.com/venue/getVenue/venueId/785), inconveniently located in the suburb of Tinley Park, about an hour outside the city, and cursed with pretty bad acoustics.

The good news: You can catch midlevel rock acts at local venues with a lot more character. The Riviera Theatre, 4746 N. Racine Ave. (tel. 773/275-6800; www.jamusa.com/Venues/Riviera/Concerts.aspx), is a relic of the Uptown neighborhood's swinging days in the 1920s, '30s, and '40s. A former movie palace, it retains the original ornate ceiling, balcony, and lighting fixtures, but it has definitely gotten grimy with age. (Head upstairs to the balcony seats if you'd rather avoid the crowd that rushes toward the stage during shows.) The Aragon Ballroom, a few blocks away, at 1106 W. Lawrence Ave. (tel. 773/561-9500; www.aragon.com; subway/El: Red Line to Lawrence), was once an elegant big-band dance hall; the worn Moorish-castle decor and twinkling-star ceiling now give the place a seedy charm despite its less-than-ideal acoustics. A former vaudeville house is now the Vic Theatre,3145 N. Sheffield Ave. (tel. 773/472-0366; www.victheatre.com; subway/El: Red or Brown line to Fullerton), a midsize venue that features up-and-coming acts. (Get there early to snag one of the lower balcony rows.)

More sedate audiences love the Park West, 322 W. Armitage Ave. (tel. 773/929-5959; www.jamusa.com/Venues/ParkWest/Concerts.aspx; subway/El: Brown Line to Armitage, or bus no. 22 [Clark St.]), both for its excellent sound system and its cabaret-style seating (no mosh pit here). For tickets to most shows at all these venues, you're stuck going through the service-fee-grabbing Ticketmaster (tel. 312/559-1212).

Chicago Rocks Come summertime, Chicago's indie-music credibility gets a major boost from two high-profile concert festivals. Every August, Lollapalooza (www.lollapalooza.com) takes over a prime section of Grant Park for 3 days of performances by big-name artists and rising stars. The lakefront views are great, but the number of acts and people can get overwhelming and the weather is usually steamy. Hipster music snobs prefer the Pitchfork Music Festival (www.pitchforkmusicfestival.com) in July, which brings edgy young bands to play a series of shows at Union Park in the West Loop. Most are groups that mainstream rock fans haven't heard of, which is just the way hard-core Pitchfork devotees like it.

Country, Folk & Ethnic Music

Known as a musician-friendly town, Chicago attracts artists from a wide range of genres. While the big-name country music stars tend to play at stadium-sized arenas, "alt country" groups are a staple of the local music scene, mixing traditional American tunes with more experimental sounds. One highlight of the city's eclectic offerings is The Old Town School of Folk Music, a flourishing center that regularly hosts well-known singer-songwriters, bluegrass groups, Celtic fiddlers, and other traditional music from around the world.

Cabarets & Piano Bars

Chicago's relatively low-key cabaret scene is concentrated in River North and tends to attract a relaxed but well dressed clientele.

The Club Scene

Chicago is the hallowed ground where house music was hatched in the 1980s, so it's no surprise to find that it's also home to several vast, industrial-style dance clubs with pounding music and an under-30 crowd. Some spots specialize in a single type of music, while others offer an ever-changing mix of rhythms and beats that follow the latest DJ-driven trend. Many clubs attract a different clientele on each day of the week (Sun night, for example, is gay-friendly at many of the clubs), so check the club's website to get an idea of each night's vibe. Given the fickle nature of clubgoers, some places we list might have disappeared by the time you read this, but there is an impressive list of longtime survivors clubs that have lasted more than a decade but continue to draw crowds.

The Bar Scene in Chicago

If you want to soak up the atmosphere of an authentic neighborhood tavern or sports bar, it's best to venture beyond downtown. Lincoln Park, Wrigleyville, and Bucktown/Wicker Park have well-established nightlife zones that abound with bars that range from bright and upscale to borderline-dingy but full of character. You'll also find numerous dives and no-frills "corner taps" in the blue-collar neighborhoods.

As for nightlife downtown, virtually every hotel in Chicago has some kind of bar. Many are little more than undistinguished groupings of tables and chairs in the lobby, but others have become trendy clublike hotspots. If you're looking for an old-school, cocktail-lounge vibe, the piano bar at The Drake Hotel, Coq d'Or, is a standout.

Hotel Hopping Forget the stereotypical bland hotel bar filled with drunken conventioneers. In downtown Chicago, some of the most distinctive watering holes are in hotel lobbies. In the Loop, Encore in the Hotel Allegro, 171 W. Randolph St. (tel. 312/236-0123), is a popular happy hour spot, with a black-and-white color scheme and urban lounge feel. For late-night drinks in a low-lit, intimate space, head to Angels and Kings, the bar in the Hard Rock Hotel, 230 N. Michigan Ave. (tel. 312/345-1000). The look is glam rock, and the music (live acts or a DJ) is always good. If you prefer to stick to tradition, Kitty O'Shea's, 720 S. Michigan Ave. (tel. 312/294-6860), is an authentically appointed Irish pub inside the Hilton Chicago a genuine Irish bartender will even pour your Guinness. Farther north, in the blocks surrounding the Magnificent Mile, you'll find style-conscious spots such as Le Bar, in the Sofitel Chicago Water Tower, 20 E. Chestnut St. (tel. 312/324-4000), a popular after-work hangout with a sophisticated vibe. At Whiskey Sky, on the top floor of the W Chicago-Lakeshore Hotel, 644 N. Lakeshore Dr. (tel. 312/943-9200), there's not much seating and the decor is minimal, but the views of both the surrounding skyline and the gorgeous staff are terrific. Vertigo Sky Lounge, atop the Dana Hotel and Spa, 660 N. State St. (tel. 312/202-6060), is a dark, clublike space with live DJs, but expansive floor-to-ceiling windows make you feel like you're floating amid the high-rises. An added bonus is the outdoor deck, a great spot to take in the views when the weather's nice. But for sheer drama, the current hotel-bar champ is Roof, atop The Wit Hotel, 201 N. State St. (tel. 312/467-0200). The sprawling space includes a Miami Beach-style terrace with fire pits for chilly nights and a large indoor seating area (with cozy fireplaces) so that even winter visitors can enjoy the views. If you dare, you can even book a table with a see-through glass floor that juts out from the roof's edge.

The Great Bar Sting What's now the Brehon Pub was once the site of a notorious Chicago bribery scandal, back in the days when muckraking journalism was still a city specialty. In 1977, the *Chicago Sun-Times* newspaper, in partnership with the Better Government Association, decided to fund an undercover investigation into corruption among city officials who regulated local businesses. They leased the bar and opened it as the appropriately named Mirage, then took notes as a series of city inspectors offered to take bribes to overlook health- and safety-code violations; state liquor inspectors also demanded their cut. A photographer tucked away on a hidden platform overlooking the room caught it all on film. The resulting 5-week newspaper series caused a sensation and eventually led to 34 court convictions. But it also triggered a national controversy over the ethics of undercover journalism. Although the *Sun-Times* was favored to win a Pulitzer Prize for the series, notable Pulitzer board members including legendary *Washington Post* editor Ben Bradlee successfully argued that stories based on deception should not win awards. With that decision, the days of reporters posing as bartenders were doomed and the local papers got a lot less colorful.

Rush & Division Streets

Around Rush Street are what a bygone era called singles bars although the only singles that tend to head here now are suburbanites, out-of-towners, and barely legal partiers. Rush Street's glory days may be long gone, but there are still a few vestiges of the old times on nearby Division Street, which overflows with party-hearty spots that attract a loud, frat-party element. They include Shenanigan's House of Beer, 16 W. Division St. (tel. 312/642-2344); Butch McGuire's, 20 W. Division St. (tel. 312/337-9080); the Lodge, 21 W. Division St. (tel. 312/642-4406); and Mother's, 26 W. Division St. (tel. 312/642-7251). Many of these bars offer discounts for women, as loud pitchmen in front of each establishment will be happy to tell any attractive ladies who pass by.

Old Town

The center of nightlife in Old Town is Wells Street, home to Second City and Zanies Comedy Club, as well as a string of reliable restaurants and bars, many of which have been in business for decades. You're not going to find many trendy spots in Old Town; the nightlife here tends toward neighborhood pubs and casual restaurants, filled mostly with a late-20s and 30-something crowd.

Lincoln Park

Lincoln Park, with its high concentration of apartment-dwelling singles, is one of the busiest nightlife destinations in Chicago. Prime real estate is at a premium in this residential neighborhood, so you won't find many warehouse-size dance clubs here; most of the action is at pubs and bars. Concentrations of in-spots run along Halsted Street and Lincoln Avenue.

Wrigleyville, Lakeview & the North Side

Real estate in Wrigleyville and Lakeview is a tad less expensive than in Lincoln Park, so the nightlife scene here skews a little younger. You'll find a mostly postcollegiate crowd partying on Clark Street across from Wrigley Field (especially after games in the summer). But head away from the ball field, and you'll discover some more exotic choices.

Wicker Park & Bucktown

The closest Chicago has to an alternative scene is Wicker Park and Bucktown, where both slackers and adventurous suburbanites populate bars dotting the streets leading out from the intersection of North, Damen, and Milwaukee avenues. Don't dress up if you want to blend in: A casually bohemian getup and low-key attitude are all you need. While you can reach most of these places relatively easily by public transportation, I recommend taking a cab at night the surrounding neighborhoods are what I'd call "transitional."

Film in Chicago

An Escape from the Multiplex

Chicago has a fine selection of movie theaters, but even the so-called art houses show mostly the same films that you'd be able to catch back home (or eventually on cable). But three local movie houses cater to cinema buffs with original programming. The Gene Siskel Film Center, 164 N. State St. (tel. 312/846-2600; www.siskelfilmcenter.org; subway/El: Red Line to Washington or Brown Line to Randolph), named after the well-known *Chicago Tribune* film critic who died in 1999, is part of the School of the Art Institute of Chicago.

The center schedules a selection of films in two theaters, including lectures and discussions with filmmakers. The Film Center often shows foreign films that are not released commercially in the U.S.

The Music Box Theatre, 3733 N. Southport Ave. (tel. 773/871-6604; www.musicboxtheatre.com; subway/El: Brown Line to Southport), is a movie palace on a human scale. Opened in 1929, it was meant to re-create the feeling of an Italian courtyard; a faux-marble loggia and towers cover the walls and electric "stars" sparkle in the painted sky overhead. The Music Box books a selection of foreign and independent American films everything from Polish filmmaker Krzysztof Kieslowski's epic *Decalogue* to a sing-along version of *The Sound of Music* to the Vincent Price cult classic *House of Wax*. The vintage seats may not be the most comfortable, but the Music Box's funky, shabby feel is part of its charm.

Facets MultiMedia, 1517 W. Fullerton Ave. (tel. 773/281-4114; www.facets.org; subway/El: Red or Brown line to Fullerton), a nonprofit group that screens independent film and video from around the world, is for the die-hard cinematic thrill-seeker. The group mounts an annual Children's Film Festival (Oct-Nov) and the Chicago Latino Film Festival (Apr-May), and rents its impressive collection of classic, hard-to-find films on video and DVD by mail.

Late-Night Bites in Chicago

Chicago's not much of a late-night dining town; most restaurants shut down by 10 or 11pm, leaving night owls with the munchies out of luck. But if you know where to go, you can still get a decent meal past midnight. Here are a few spots that serve real food until real late:

In the Loop, your best and practically only choice is Miller's Pub, 134 S. Wabash Ave. (tel. 312/645-5377), which offers hearty American comfort food until 2am daily. Many late-night visitors to this historic watering hole and restaurant are out-of-towners staying at neighboring hotels.

In the South Loop, food is available until 4am at Bar Louie, 47 W. Polk St. tel. 312/347-0000). The menu is a step above mozzarella sticks and other standard bar food: Focaccia sandwiches, vegetarian wraps, and salads are among the highlights.

After a night out, Wicker Park and Bucktown residents stop by Northside Café, 1635 N. Damen Ave. (tel. 773/384-3555), for sandwiches and salads served until 2am (3am Sat). In nice weather, the front patio is the place to be for prime people-watching.

The bright, welcoming atmosphere at Clarke's Pancake House, 2441 N. Lincoln Ave. (tel. 773/472-3505), is a dose of fresh air after an evening spent in dark Lincoln Park bars. Yes, there are pancakes on the menu, as well as plenty of other creative breakfast choices, including mixed skillets of veggies, meat, and potatoes. If you need to satisfy a *really* late-night craving, Clarke's is open 24 hours.

When the Lincoln Park bars shut down at 2am, the action moves to the Wieners Circle, 2622 N. Clark St. (tel. 773/477-7444). This hot dog stand is strictly no-frills: You shout your order across the drunken crowd, get sassed by the counter staff, then try to snag a spot on one of the picnic tables out front (the only seating provided). Open until 4am during the week and 6am on weekends, the Wieners Circle is the center of predawn life in Lincoln Park and some people swear that the greasy cheese-topped fries are the perfect hangover prevention.

Shopping in Chicago

Forget Rodeo Drive or Fifth Avenue Chicago is the country's original shopping center, the place that helped the United States expand westward by transporting goods to the frontier. Today, the city is the commercial capital of the Midwest, attracting out-of-towners with its mix of designer boutiques, quirky independent clothing shops and cutting-edge home design stores.

The big names in fashion from Prada to Louis Vuitton are all represented here, but you don't have to be a big spender to enjoy a Chicago shopping spree. Indeed, the city's commercial success comes from offering something for everyone. Oak Street is known for its luxury boutiques, while bustling Michigan Avenue has everything from designer labels at Giorgio Armani to low-priced fashion trends at H&M. In the Loop, you can wander the massive Macy's (built in the 19th century as Marshall Field's and a Chicago architectural landmark), or bargain shop at a range of discount department stores. River North is home to a cluster of interior-decor shops, while the fashion-forward can find inspiration at the independent boutiques of Wicker Park.

Shopping Hours As a general rule, store hours are 10am to 6 or 7pm Monday through Saturday, and noon to 6pm Sunday. Stores along Michigan Avenue tend to keep later hours, since they cater to after-work shoppers as well as tourists. Almost all stores have extended hours during the holiday season. Nearly all of the stores in the Loop are open for daytime shopping only, generally from 9 or 10am to no later than 6pm Monday through Saturday. (The few remaining big downtown department stores have some selected evening hours.) Many Loop stores not on State Street are closed Saturday; on Sunday the Loop except for a few restaurants, theaters, and cultural attractions shuts down.

Sales Tax You might do a double-take after checking the total on your purchase: At 9.75%, the local sales tax on nonfood items is one of the steepest in the country.

Shopping A-Z in Chicago

Chicago has shops selling just about anything you could want or need, be it functional or ornamental, whimsical or exotic. Although the following list only scratches the surface, it gives you an idea of the range of merchandise available.

Antiques

If you think half the fun of antiquing is sorting through piles of junk to discover hidden treasures, you'll probably enjoy browsing the series of independently owned antiques stores along Belmont Avenue west of Southport Avenue. (Since it's a haul from the El, I'd recommend shopping here only if you have a car.) Chicago's best-organized and best-stocked antique shops are scattered throughout the city, but if you're willing to venture beyond the usual tourist neighborhoods, you'll be well rewarded.

Art Galleries

Most of the city's major art galleries are concentrated in two neighborhoods. The city's original gallery district is in River North, within easy walking distance of most downtown hotels. More recently, galleries have been opening in the converted loft buildings of the West Loop, which is best reached by taxi.

Artistic Center of The Heartland Chicago may have thrived as a business center and transportation hub, but it's also a gathering spot for artists from throughout the Midwest. In part, that's due to the presence of the School of the Art Institute of Chicago, considered one of the best fine arts colleges in the country. The school produces a steady stream of arts-minded graduates, many of whom stay in town to work at local art galleries or fashion boutiques. Notable Art Institute alumni include painters Georgia O'Keefe and Grant Wood; iconic '70s fashion designer Halston; sculptors Claes Oldenburg, Jeff Koons, and Richard Hunt; alternative cartoonist and illustrator Chris Ware; and humorists Sarah Vowell and David Sedaris. Another downtown academic institution, Columbia College Chicago, also fosters an environment of creativity: The largest private arts and media college in the country, it offers undergraduate and graduate programs in film, arts management, creative writing, journalism, dance, and photography.

Clothing Boutiques

In the not-so-distant past, local fashion addicts had to head for the coasts when they wanted to shop for cutting-edge designer duds. Those days are over. While over-the-top outrageousness doesn't sell here this is still the practical Midwest stylish Chicagoans now turn to local independent boutiques when they want to stay on top of the latest trends without looking like fashion victims.

Shopping With The Pros Want to stay on top of the trends but have limited time to scout out hip boutiques? A guided tour of Chicago's coolest clothing shops is a great way to fit some concentrated shopping into a busy schedule. *An added bonus:* You'll hit the insider places only the locals know about and sometimes get exclusive discounts along the way. Shop Walk Chicago (tel. 773/255-7866;www.chicagoshopwalk.com), run by local image consultant Danielle Lutz, offers a number of different neighborhood tours (let them know the kinds of clothes you like, and they'll suggest where to go); there's also a "Made in Chicago" tour that focuses on local designers. Tours range from $50 to $90 per person for 4 hours of shopping. The company arranges custom tours on request, and for an additional fee, they'll arrange a pick-up from your hotel.

In Search of Specialty Foods

Chicago's got a huge variety of ethnic grocery stores, where you can sample authentic specialties from around the world and stock up on unusual cooking-related gifts. Because most of the shops are in residential neighborhoods far from the usual tourist haunts, the best way to get an overview of them is by taking a culinary tour, led by a guide who knows the cuisine (and, best of all, can organize tastings along the way). Ethnic Grocery Tours (tel. 773/465-8064; www.ethnic-grocery-tours.com), run by Evelyn Thompson, organizes half-day excursions for up to four people that stop at a variety of shops, from Russian to Jamaican, to Middle Eastern. Chef Rebecca Wheeler takes visitors to Southeast Asian and Indian stores and bakeries for her Ethnic Market Tours (tel. 773/368-1336; www.rebeccawheeler.com). She'll even share cooking tips so you can arrive home with a few new recipes to try out.

The Top Shopping Streets & Neighborhoods in Chicago

The nickname "Magnificent Mile" hyperbole to some, an understatement to others refers to the roughly mile-long stretch of North Michigan Avenue between Oak Street and the Chicago River.

In terms of density, the area's first-rate shopping is, quite simply, unmatched. Even jaded shoppers from other worldly capitals are delighted at the ease and convenience of the stores concentrated here. Taking into account that tony Oak Street is just around the corner, the overall area is a little like New York's Fifth Avenue and Beverly Hills's Rodeo Drive rolled into one. Whether your passion is Bulgari jewelry, Prada bags, or Salvatore Ferragamo footwear, you'll find it on this stretch of concrete. And don't think you're seeing everything by walking down the street: Michigan Avenue is home to several indoor, high-rise malls, where plenty more boutiques and restaurants are tucked away. Even if you're not the shop-till-you-drop type, it's worth a stroll because this stretch is, in many ways, the heart of the city, a place that bustles with life year-round (although it's especially crowded around Christmas and during the summer).

For the ultimate Mag Mile shopping adventure, start at one end of North Michigan Avenue and try to work your way to the other. Below I've listed some of the best-known shops on the avenue and nearby side streets.

A North Michigan Avenue Shopper's Stroll

This shopper's stroll begins at Oak Street at the northern end of the avenue and heads south toward the river. It just hits the highlights; you'll find much more to tempt your wallet as you meander from designer landmarks to well-known chain stores. (In general, this is not the place to pick up distinctive, one-of-a-kind items other neighborhoods described cater more to shoppers searching for something unique.)

The parade of designer names begins at the intersection of Michigan Avenue and Oak Street, including a couple housed in The Drake Hotel, such as the legendary Danish silversmith Georg Jensen, 959 N. Michigan Ave. (tel. 312/642-9160; www.georgjensenstore.com), known for outstanding craftsmanship in sterling silver and gold, including earrings, brooches, watches, tie clips, and flatware; and Chanel,935 N. Michigan Ave. (tel. 312/787-5500; www.chanel.com). One block south is another luxury emporium, the spacious Louis Vuitton store at 919 N. Michigan Ave. (tel. 312/944-2010; www.louisvuitton.com), where you'll find trendy handbags and the company's distinctive monogrammed luggage.

On the other side of the street, opposite the dark, soaring Hancock Building, you'll find a quiet oasis that's worth a quick peek. The Fourth Presbyterian Church, 126 E. Chestnut St. (tel. 312/787-4570; www.fourthchurch.org), looks like something out of an English country village, with a Gothic stone exterior and a peaceful, flower-filled courtyard.

One block south, you'll notice a steady stream of mothers and daughters toting distinctive red shopping bags from American Girl Place, on the ground floor of the Water Tower Place mall, 835 N. Michigan Ave. (tel. 877/AG-PLACE [247-5223]; www.americangirl.com/stores). The multistory doll emporium is one of the most-visited attractions in town, thanks to the popularity of the company's historic character dolls. The store's cafe is a nice spot for a special mother-daughter lunch or afternoon tea (but be sure to book ahead during Christmas and summer).

Across the street, overlooking a small park next to the historic Water Tower, is Giorgio Armani's sleek boutique, 800 N. Michigan Ave., in the Park Hyatt Hotel (tel. 312/573-4220; www.armanistores.com). Offering an alternative to high-style minimalism is the Hershey's Chicago candy store, 822 N. Michigan Ave. (tel. 312/337-7711; www.thehersheycompany.com), a multisensory overload of colors and chocolate.

The next block of Michigan Avenue has a New York vibe, thanks to the world's largest Polo Ralph Lauren, 750 N. Michigan Ave. (tel. 312/280-1655; http://stores.ralphlauren.com), a four-floor, wood-paneled mini-mansion, and Tiffany & Co., 730 N. Michigan Ave. (tel. 312/944-7500; www.tiffany.com), with its signature clock, jewels, and tabletop accessories.

A few doors south are high-end department store Neiman Marcus and Niketown, a multilevel complex that helped pioneer the concept of retail as entertainment. Across the street, at the intersection of Michigan Avenue and Erie Street, is the appropriately barrel-shaped Crate & Barrel, 646 N. Michigan Ave. (tel. 312/787-5900). Crate & Barrel was started in Chicago, so this is the company's flagship location. Countless varieties of glassware, dishes, cookware, and kitchen gadgets for everyday use line the shelves. The top two floors are devoted to furniture.

Continuing south, you'll find the iconic British design house Burberry, 633 N. Michigan Ave. (tel. 312/787-2500), where the classic beige plaid shows up on chic purses, shoes, and bathing suits. (If you're looking for luxury souvenirs, check out the collection of baby clothes and dog accessories.) Across Ontario Street, you'll probably see a line of people trailing out from the Garrett Popcorn Shop, 645 N. Michigan Ave. (tel. 312/944-2630), a 50-year-old landmark. Join the locals in line and pick up some caramel corn for a quick sugar rush. Beautifully made (but pricey) Italian lingerie is the draw at La Perla, 535 N. Michigan Ave. (tel. 312/494-0400), a popular stop around Valentine's Day.

The Magnificent Malls Many of the Magnificent Mile's shops are tucked away inside high-rise malls, most of which take up a whole city block.

Chic Shopping on Nearby Oak Street

Oak Street has long been a symbol of designer-label shopping; if a store has an Oak Street address, you can count on it being expensive. The shopping district itself is actually quite limited, taking up only 1 block at the northern tip of the Magnificent Mile (where Michigan Ave. ends and Lake Shore Dr. begins). While big-name designer showcases such as Giorgio Armani and Louis Vuitton pride themselves on having a Michigan Avenue address, Oak Street features smaller, more personal shops (most of them high-priced). Since the stores are tucked into converted town houses, it's also more tranquil than Michigan Avenue. It's well worth a stroll for people-watching: This is Main Street for Chicago socialites. Most of Oak Street is closed on Sunday, except during the holiday season.

Just around the corner from Michigan Avenue, footwear fans can browse Italian shoemaker Tod's, best known for its luxuriously soft (and pricey) driving shoes. Shoes, stationery, and handbags are available at kate spade, 101 E. Oak St. (tel. 312/654-8853), along with the Jack Spade line of men's accessories. The priciest accessories on this very pricey block can likely be found at French luxury house Hermès of Paris,110 E. Oak St. (tel. 312/787-8175). Thread-count fanatics swear by the sheets from Pratesi, 67 E. Oak St. (tel. 312/943-8422), and Frette, 41 E. Oak St. (tel. 312/649-3744), both of which supply linens to top hotels (and where sheet sets cost more than what some people pay in rent).

Anchoring the western end of the block are two haute heavyweights, hip Italian designer Prada, 30 E. Oak St. (tel. 312/951-1113), which offers three floors of sleek, postmodern fashions for men and women and plenty of the designer's signature handbags; and the equally style-conscious department store Barneys New York. When you're ready to take a break, stop for a coffee and treat at Sarah's Pastries & Candies, a cheery cafe where chocolate lovers will find plenty to tempt them.

An Oak Street Bargain Oak Street is not the place to come shopping for bargains, with one exception Bravco, 43 E. Oak St. (tel. 312/943-4305). This crowded, narrow drugstore seems out of place among the luxury boutiques, but it's a popular spot among Chicago hairstylists and makeup artists. You'll find an excellent selection of professional hair and beauty products (including Aveda, Sebastian, and Bumble and bumble) here for much less than they cost at salons. Even if you haven't heard of some of the brands, trust me, if Bravco carries them, they're hot.

State Street & the Loop

Shopping in the Loop is mostly concentrated along State Street, from Randolph Street south to Congress Parkway. State Street was Chicago's first great shopping district by World War I, seven of the largest and most lavish department stores in the world were competing for shoppers' loyalties along this half-mile stretch. The area has long since been eclipsed by Michigan Avenue, but one grand old department store makes it worth a visit: Macy's at State Street (formerly Marshall Field's). A city landmark and one of the largest department stores in the world, it occupies an entire city block and features the largest Tiffany glass mosaic dome in the U.S. If you're in Chicago between Thanksgiving and New Year's, Macy's has maintained a long-time Marshall Field's tradition: lavishly decorated holiday windows and lunch under the Great Tree in the store's restaurant, the Walnut Room.

Aside from Macy's, State Street has become a hot destination for bargain hunters in recent years, thanks to the opening of discount stores such as Loehmann's, 151 N. State St. (tel. 312/705-3810); Nordstrom Rack, 24 N. State St. (tel. 312/377-5500); T.J. Maxx, 11 N. State St. (tel. 312/553-0515); and Filene's Basement, 1 N. State St. (tel. 312/553-1055). If you've got the energy to hunt through racks of not-so-great stuff, you can sometimes find good designer-label deals.

State Street has a no-frills aura compared to Michigan Avenue but it stays busy thanks to the thousands of office workers who stroll around during their lunch hour or after work. On weekends, the street is considerably more subdued.

Point Zero If the quick change from north to south in the Loop confuses you, keep in mind that in Chicago, point zero for the purpose of address numbering is the intersection of State and Madison streets.

Jewelers' Row It's not quite as impressive as the Big Apple's diamond district, but Chicago's own "Jewelers' Row" is certainly worth a detour for rock hunters. Half a dozen high-rises along the Wabash Avenue El tracks in the heart of the Loop service the wholesale trade, but the one at 5 S. Wabash Ave. opens its doors to customers off the street. There's a mall-like retail space on the ground floor crammed with tiny booths manned by smooth-talking reps hawking their wares. It's quite an experience many of the booths are cubbyholes with hunched-over geezers who look as if they've been eyeballing solitaire and marquise cuts since the Roosevelt administration Teddy, that is.

River North

Since the 1960s, when the Chicago Imagists (painters Ed Paschke, Jim Nutt, and Roger Brown among them) attracted international attention with their shows at the Hyde Park Art Center, the city has been a fertile breeding ground for emerging artists and innovative art dealers. Today the primary art gallery district is concentrated in the River North neighborhood the area west of the Magnificent Mile and north of the Chicago River where century-old redbrick warehouses have been converted into lofty exhibition spaces. More recently, a new generation of gallery owners has set up shop in the West Loop neighborhood, where you'll tend to find more cutting-edge work.

The River North gallery season officially gets underway on the first Friday after Labor Day in September. Besides fall, another great time to visit the district is from mid-July through August, when the Chicago Art Dealers Association presents Vision, an annual lineup of programs tailored to the public. The Chicago Reader, a free weekly newspaper available at many stores, taverns, and cafes on the North Side, publishes a very comprehensive listing of current gallery exhibitions, as does the quarterly *Chicago Gallery News* (www.chicagogallerynews.com), which is available free at the city's visitor information centers. Another good resource is the Chicago Art Dealers Association (tel. 312/649-0065; www.chicagoartdealers.org); the group's website has descriptions of all member galleries.

Along with its status as Chicago's primary art gallery district, River North has attracted many interesting home-design shops, with many concentrated on Wells Street from Kinzie Street to Chicago Avenue. The best include Manifesto, 755 N. Wells St., at Chicago Avenue (tel. 312/664-0733; www.manifestofurniture.com), which offers custom-designed furniture, as well as imports from Italy and elsewhere in Europe; edgy Orange Skin, a great place to pick up one-of-a-kind modern decorative accents; and Lightology, 215 W. Chicago Ave., at Wells St. (tel. 312/944-1000;www.lightology.com), a massive lighting store that carries a mind-boggling array of funky lamps, chandeliers, and glowing orbs from more than 400 manufacturers. (Even if you have no intention of flying home with a stack of lamps in your luggage, it's still a fun place for the design-minded to browse.)

Looming above the Chicago River at the southern end of River North is the Merchandise Mart, the world's largest commercial building. The massive complex was built in 1930 by Marshall Field & Company and was bought in 1945 by Joseph P. Kennedy (JFK's dad). The Mart houses mostly interior design showrooms, which are open only to professional designers. Public tours of the whole complex are offered once a week, usually on Fridays ($12 adults; tel. 312/527-7762; www.merchandisemart.com for dates and reservations).

Armitage Avenue

Hovering between the North Side neighborhoods of Old Town and Lincoln Park, Armitage Avenue has emerged as a shopping destination in its own right, thanks to an influx of wealthy young professionals who have settled into historic town homes on the neighboring tree-lined streets. I'd suggest starting at the Armitage El stop on the Brown Line, working your way east to Halsted Street, and then wandering a few blocks north to Webster Street. As you stroll around, you'll get a good sense of the area's strong community spirit, with neighbors greeting each other and catching up on the street corners.

The shops and boutiques here are geared toward sophisticated, well-heeled, predominantly female shoppers (sorry, guys). You'll find trendy clothing boutiques, including that of Chicago-area native Cynthia Rowley, 808 W. Armitage Ave. (tel. 773/528-6160; www.cynthiarowley.com); eclectic home-decor stores; beauty emporiums; and one of my favorite impossible-to-classify gift shops, Art Effect. The upscale pet accessories shop Barker & Meowsky, 1003 W. Armitage Ave. (tel. 773/868-0200; www.barkerandmeowsky.com), has everything you need to spoil furry family members, including catnip cigars, doggy "sushi," and designer-inspired outfits.

Despite the area's upscale feel, you can snag bargains at some top-notch discount and consignment shops, including Lori's Designer Shoes, McShane's Exchange, Fox's, and The Second Child.

Lincoln Park & Lakeview

Radiating from the intersection of Belmont Avenue and Clark Street is a string of shops catering to rebellious kids on tour from their homes in the 'burbs. (The Dunkin' Donuts on the corner is often referred to as "Punkin' Donuts" in their honor.) One constant in the ever-changing youth culture has been the Alley, 3228 N. Clark St., at Belmont Avenue (tel. 773/883-1800; thealley.com), an "alternative shopping complex" selling everything from plaster gargoyles to racks of leather jackets. It has separate shops specializing in condoms, cigars, and bondage wear. Tragically Hip, a storefront women's boutique, 931 W. Belmont Ave. (tel. 773/549-1500), next to the Belmont El train stop, has outlasted many other similar purveyors of cutting-edge women's apparel.

You can get plugged into what the kids are reading at Chicago Comics, 3244 N. Clark St. (tel. 773/528-1983; www.chicagocomics.com), considered one of the best comics shops in the country. Besides the usual superhero titles, you'll find lots of European and Japanese comics, along with underground books and zines.

Southport Avenue

West of Lakeview, a few blocks from Wrigley Field, this commercial strip houses a mix of restaurants, cool (but not *too* cool) clothing boutiques, and cafes appealing to the upscale urban families who live in the surrounding area. It's worth a look if you want to hang out in a neighborhood that's a little more laid-back than the Gold Coast or Wicker Park, and the surrounding tree-lined residential streets are a pleasant place to stroll. Start at the Southport El stop on the Brown Line, and work your way north to Grace Street. (Round-trip, the walk will take you about a half-hour but allow more if you're doing some serious shopping or want to stop for lunch.) Along the way you'll pass the historic Music Box Theatre, at 3733 N. Southport Ave. (tel. 773/871-6604; www.musicboxtheatre.com), north of Addison Street, which shows independent films from around the world. Krista K, 3458 N. Southport Ave. (tel. 773/248-1967; www.kristak.com), caters to hip young women with plenty of disposable income by stocking up-and-coming designers that aren't widely available, while Ceratochampions made-in-Chicago fashion.

Wicker Park/Bucktown

The gentrification of the Wicker Park/Bucktown area was followed by not only a rash of restaurants and bars, but also retailers with an artsy bent that reflect the neighborhood's bohemian spirit. Mixed in with old neighborhood businesses, such as discount furniture stores and religious icon purveyors, is a proliferation of antique furniture shops, edgy clothing boutiques, and eclectic galleries and gift emporiums. Despite the hefty price tags in many of these shops, the neighborhood still feels gritty so come here if you want to feel like you've gotten a real urban fix.

To browse the best of the neighborhood, start at the Damen El stop on the Blue Line, and walk north along Damen Avenue to Armitage Avenue to scope out the trendiest shops. If you've got time, some stores are also scattered along Milwaukee Avenue south of North Avenue.

The friendly modern-day Marco Polos at Pagoda Red, 1714 N. Damen Ave., second floor (tel. 773/235-1188; www.pagodared.com), import beautiful (and expensive) antique furniture and art objects from Asia. Design-conscious shoppers head to Stitchfor one-of-a-kind, stylish gifts the kind of thing you won't find at the mall back home. Damen Avenue is also known for its concentration of independent women's clothing boutiques, which range from body-conscious, urban looks at p45 to flirty dresses and skirts at Tangerine.

Taking a Break in Wicker Park When you're ready to rest your weary self, settle down at a local coffeehouse and soak in Wicker Park's artsy vibe. Earwax Café, 1564 N. Milwaukee Ave. (tel. 773/772-4019), attracts the jaded and pierced set with a no-frills, slightly edgy atmosphere. At Gallery Café, 1760 W. North Ave., 4 blocks east of Milwaukee Ave. (tel. 773/252-8228), the atmosphere isn't quite as memorable, but the laid-back hangout roasts its own coffee and offers a full menu of breakfast and lunch dishes. Both cafes are near the bustling intersection of North, Milwaukee, and Damen avenues the heart of Wicker Park and draw a steady stream of locals. It's here you'll realize that Wicker Park is really just a small town with cooler hair and funkier shoes.

West Division Street

Once home to just a few pioneering restaurants, Division Street is quickly being transformed from a desolate urban landscape to a hot shopping destination. It's a work in progress (you'll still find some boarded-up buildings among the cool boutiques), but for now this is what Wicker Park used to be: a place where rents are still cheap enough for eager young entrepreneurs. Begin your walk at the Division El stop on the Blue Line, and head west along Division Street; most stores are concentrated between Milwaukee Avenue and Damen Avenue (a round-trip walk will take about a half-hour). Along the way, you'll stroll past eclectic clothing and home boutiques, including the hip kids' shop Grow, where eco-conscious urban parents stock up on organic-cotton baby clothes and sustainable-wood furniture.

Chicago Insideout

Chicago has spent the last few years in the national media spotlight, for reasons both inspiring and embarrassing. On the one hand, it's the adopted hometown of President Barack Obama, the place he got his start in politics and where he still maintains his Hyde Park home. His victory rally in downtown's Grant Park signaled Chicago's vitality and influence to the whole world (many of his top presidential advisors were local business and philanthropic leaders before they moved to Washington).

Unfortunately, Chicago must also lay claim to politicians such as former Illinois state governor Rod Blagojevich. "Blago," a product of the city's shady Democratic political machine, stunned even cynical Chicagoans with his blatant moneygrubbing and attempts to sell Obama's former Senate seat to the highest bidder. Obama's talk about a new era of hope in politics turned out to be short-lived, with his ties to Chicago wheeler-dealers a liability. Blagojevich proved that the old ways of doing business aren't so easily erased.

It's easy to be cynical about Chicago politics the miracle is that such cynicism doesn't pervade the way Chicagoans feel about their city. We're proud of our gorgeous skyline and love nothing better than hearing visitors compare our hometown favorably to New York. (You'll make friends for life if you tell us you'd rather live here than the Big Apple.) As the retail, financial, and legal center of the Midwest, Chicago has a thriving, diverse business community and an active arts scene, attracting everyone from thrifty wannabe hipsters to ambitious future CEOs. The one thing they've got in common? A certain humility that comes with living in the Second City. Being down-to-earth is a highly rated local virtue.

In this section, you'll get an overview of the issues facing the city today, as well as a quick primer on Chicago's history. Because architecture plays such an important role in the look of the city and so many influential architects have worked here you'll also find a guide to the major styles of buildings you'll pass by during your visit. But you won't get a full sense of the city's spirit unless you understand the city's role in popular culture, too. Chicago has been home to many great writers and has served as a setting for dozens of films, so we've included a section on recommended books and movies. Check out a few before your trip to put you in a Chicago state of mind.

Sky Train: Chicago's El

Watch any Hollywood film or TV series set in Chicago, and chances are, they'll feature at least one scene set against our screeching elevated train system, more commonly known as the "El" (witness *The Fugitive, ER,* and others). The trains symbolize Chicago's gritty, "city-that-works" attitude, but they actually began as cutting-edge technology.

After the Great Fire of 1871, Chicago made a remarkable recovery; within 20 years, the downtown district was swarming with people, streetcars, and horses (but no stoplights). To help relieve congestion, the city took to the sky, building a system of elevated trains 15 feet above all the madness. The first El trains were steam powered, but by the end of the century, all the lines run by separate companies used electricity. In 1895, the three El companies collaborated to build a set of tracks into and around the central business district that all the lines would then share. By 1897, the "Loop" was up and running.

Chicago's El wasn't the nation's first. That honor belongs to New York City, which started running its elevated trains in 1867, 25 years before Chicago. But the New York El has almost disappeared, moving underground and turning into a subway early last century. With 289 miles of track, Chicago has the biggest El and the second-largest public transportation system in the country.

Architecture in Chicago

Although the Great Chicago Fire leveled almost 3 square miles of the downtown area in 1871, it did clear the stage for Chicago's emergence as a breeding ground for innovative architecture. Some of the field's biggest names Frank Lloyd Wright, Louis Sullivan, and Ludwig van der Rohe made their mark on the city. And today Chicago's skyline is home to iconic buildings, including the John Hancock Center and the (former) Sears Tower.

Early Skyscrapers (1880-1920)
In the late 19th century, important technical innovations including safety elevators, fireproofing, and telecommunications combined with advances in skeletal construction to create a new building type: the skyscraper. These buildings were spacious, cost-effective, efficient, and quick to build in short, the perfect architectural solution for Chicago's growing downtown. Architect Louis Sullivan (1865-1924) was the first to formalize a vision of a tall building based on the parts of a classical column. His theories inspired the Chicago school of architecture, examples of which still fill the city's downtown. Features of Chicago school buildings include a rectangular shape with a flat roof; large windows (made possible by the development of load-bearing interior skeletons); and the use of terra cotta, a light, fireproof material that could be cast in any shape and attached to the exterior, often for decoration.

A good example of the development of the skyscraper is the Monadnock Building, 53 W. Jackson Blvd. (Holabird & Root, 1889-91; Holabird & Roche, 1893). The northern section has 6-foot-thick walls at its base to support the building's 17 stories; the newer, southern half has a steel frame clad in terra cotta (allowing the walls to be much thinner). The Reliance Building, now the Hotel Burnham, 1 W. Washington St. (Burnham & Root and Burnham & Co., 1891-95), was influential for its use of large glass windows and decorative spandrels (the horizontal panel below a window).

Second Renaissance Revival (1890-1920)
The grand buildings of the Second Renaissance Revival, with their textural richness, suited the tastes of the wealthy Gilded Age. Typical

144

features include a cubelike structure with a massive, imposing look; a symmetrical facade, including distinct horizontal divisions; and a different stylistic treatment for each floor, with different column capitals, finishes, and window treatments on each level. A fine example of this style is the Chicago Cultural Center, 78 E. Washington St. (Shepley, Rutan & Coolidge, 1897), originally built as a public library. This tasteful edifice, with its sumptuous decor, was constructed in part to help secure Chicago's reputation as a culture-conscious city.

Beaux Arts (1890-1920)

This style takes its name from the Ecole des Beaux-Arts in Paris, where a number of prominent American architects received their training, beginning around the mid-19th century. In 1893, Chicago played host to the World's Columbian Exposition, attended by 21 million people at a time when Chicago's population was just over 1 million. Overseen by Chicagoan Daniel H. Burnham (1846-1912), the fairgrounds in Hyde Park were laid out in Beaux Arts style, with broad boulevards, fountains, and temporary ornate white buildings, mostly by New York-based architects. (One of the few permanent structures is now the Museum of Science and Industry.)

Grandiose compositions, exuberance of detail, and a variety of stone finishes typify most Beaux Arts structures. Chicago has several Beaux Arts buildings that exhibit the style's main features. The oldest part of the Art Institute of Chicago, Michigan Avenue at Adams Street (Shepley, Rutan & Coolidge, 1893), was built for the World's Columbian Exposition. A later example of yet another skyscraper is the gleaming white Wrigley Building, 400-410 N. Michigan Ave. (Graham, Anderson, Probst & White, 1919-24), which serves as a gateway to North Michigan Avenue.

Art Deco (1925-33)

Art Deco buildings are characterized by a linear, hard edge or angular composition, often with a vertical emphasis and highlighted with stylized decoration. The Chicago Board of Trade, 141 W. Jackson Blvd.

(Holabird & Root, 1930), punctuates LaSalle Street with its dramatic Art Deco facade. High atop the pyramidal roof, an aluminum statue of Ceres, the Roman goddess of agriculture, gazes down over the building. The last major construction project in Chicago before the Great Depression, 135 S. LaSalle St. (originally the Field Building; Graham, Anderson, Probst & White, 1934), has a magnificent Art Deco lobby. A fine example of an Art Deco town house is the Edward P. Russell House, 1444 N. Astor St. (Holabird & Root, 1929), in the city's Gold Coast.

International Style (1932-45)

The International Style was popularized in the United States through the teachings and designs of Ludwig Mies van der Rohe (1886-1969), a German émigré who taught and practiced architecture in Chicago after leaving Germany's influential Bauhaus school of design. In the 1950s, erecting a "Miesian" office building made companies appear progressive. Features of the style include a rectangular shape; the frequent use of glass; an absence of ornamentation; and a clear expression of the building's form and function. (The interior structure of stacked office floors is clearly visible, as are the locations of mechanical systems, such as elevator shafts and air-conditioning units.)

Some famous Mies van der Rohe designs are the Chicago Federal Center, Dearborn Street between Adams Street and Jackson Boulevard (1959-74), and 860-880 N. Lake Shore Dr. (1949-51). Interesting interpretations of the style by Skidmore, Owings & Merrill, a Chicago firm that helped make the International Style a corporate staple, are the Sears Tower (1968-74) and the John Hancock Center (1969) impressive engineering feats that rise 110 and 100 stories, respectively.

Postmodern (1975-90)

As a reaction against the stark International Style, postmodernists began to incorporate classical details and recognizable forms into their designs often applied in outrageous proportions. One example, 190 S.

LaSalle St. (John Burgee Architects with Philip Johnson, 1987), brings the shape of a famous Chicago building back to the skyline. The overall design is that of the 1892 Masonic Temple (now razed), complete with the tripartite divisions of the Chicago school. Another amalgam of historical precedents is the Harold Washington Library Center, 400 S. State St. (Hammond, Beeby & Babka, 1991). An extremely modern interpretation of a three-part skyscraper but you have to look for the divisions to find them is 333 Wacker Dr. (Kohn Pedersen Fox, 1979-83), an elegant green-glass structure that curves along a bend in the Chicago River. Unlike this harmonious juxtaposition, the James R. Thompson Center, 100 W. Randolph St. (Murphy/Jahn, 1979-85), inventively clashes with everything around it.

Only in Chicago: The Master Builders

Visitors from around the world flock to Chicago to see the groundbreaking work of three major architects: Sullivan, Wright, and Mies. They all lived and worked in the Windy City, leaving behind a legacy of innovative structures that still inspire architects today. Here's the rundown on each of them:

Louis Sullivan (1865-1924)

> Quote: "Form ever follows function."

> Iconic Chicago building: Auditorium Building, 430 S. Michigan Ave. (1887-89).

> Innovations: Father of the Chicago school, Sullivan was perhaps at his most original in the creation of his intricate, nature-inspired ornamentation.

Frank Lloyd Wright (1867-1959)

> Quote: "Nature is my manifestation of God."

> Iconic Chicago building: Frederick C. Robie House, 5757 S. Woodlawn Ave., Hyde Park (1909).

> Innovations: While in Chicago, Wright developed the architecture of the Prairie School, a largely residential style combining natural

materials, communication between interior and exterior spaces, and the sweeping horizontals of the Midwestern landscape.

Ludwig Mies van der Rohe (1886-1969)

➢ Quote: "Less is more."

➢ Iconic Chicago building: Chicago Federal Center, Dearborn Street between Adams Street and Jackson Boulevard (1959-74).

➢ Innovations: Mies van der Rohe brought the office tower of steel and glass to the United States. His stark facades don't immediately reveal his careful attention to details and materials.

Food & Drink in Chicago

Joke all you want about bratwurst and deep-dish pizza; Chicago is a genuine culinary hot spot. One of the city's most creative dining spots, Alinea, was even named the top restaurant in the United States by *Gourmet* magazine in 2007 (take that, New York and San Francisco!). What makes eating out in Chicago fun is the variety. We've got it all: stylish see-and-be-seen spots, an amazing array of steakhouses, chef-owned temples to fine dining, and every kind of ethnic cuisine you could possibly crave plus, yes, some not-to-be-missed deep-dish pizza places.

Fueled in part by expense-account-wielding business travelers, high-end dining is a growth industry here. What makes Chicago's top restaurants unique, however, is their inclusive, low-key attitude. This isn't the kind of city where snooty waiters show off their foodie expertise or stare in horror if you have no idea what wine to order. By and large, hospitality is more than just a buzzword here, and as long as you can afford the eye-popping bill, the city's top chefs will welcome you. If you want to splurge on a one-of-a-kind meal the kind you'll be describing to friends weeks later Chicago is the place to do it.

That said, ever-increasing restaurant prices are one of my pet peeves; eating out downtown has become more and more of a luxury. While finding bargains in the Loop or around the Magnificent Mile isn't easy, you can still fill up without going broke by stopping at one of the food courts inside the malls along Michigan Avenue (as many locals on their lunch break do). Ethnic restaurants also tend to be less expensive, whether you're sampling *spanakopita* in Greektown or a noodle dish at a Thai restaurant.

And about that pizza: Yes, Chicagoans hate to be stereotyped as cheese-and-sausage-devouring slobs, but we really do eat deep-dish pizza, which was created in the 1940s at the original Pizzeria Uno restaurant. If you've never had this decadent, cholesterol-raising delicacy, you should definitely try it while you're here (especially on a chilly day it's not as appealing during a summer heat wave)

Recommended Books, Films & Music in Chicago

Books

So many great American writers have come from Chicago, lived here, or set their work in the city that it's impossible to recommend a single book that says all there is to say about the city. But here are a few to get you started.

Upton Sinclair's enormously influential *The Jungle* tells the tale of a young immigrant encountering the brutal, filthy city. James T. Farrell's trilogy *Studs Lonigan,* published in the 1930s, explores the power of ethnic and neighborhood identity in Chicago. Other novels set in Chicago include Saul Bellow's *The Adventures of Augie March* and *Humboldt's Gift,* and Richard Wright's *Native Son. The Time Traveler's Wife,* by local author Audrey Niffenegger, unfolds amid recognizable Chicago backdrops such as the Newberry Library. (The movie version, alas, filmed only a few scenes here.)

For an entertaining overview of the city's history, read *City of the Century,* by Donald Miller (an excellent PBS special based on the book is also available on DVD). Erik Larson's *Devil in the White City,* a history book that reads like a thriller, tells the engrossing story of the 1893 World's Columbian Exposition and the serial killer who preyed on young women who visited from out of town. For another look at the seamy underside of Chicago's history, try *Sin in the Second City,* by Karen Abbott, which focuses on the city's most notorious and expensive brothel.

Two books give a human face to the city's shameful public housing history: Daniel Coyle's *Hardball: A Season in the Projects,* the true story of youngsters on a Little League baseball team; and Alex Kotlowitz's *There Are No Children Here,* a portrait of children growing up in one of the city's most dangerous projects. Kotlowitz also wrote *Never a City So Real: A Walk in Chicago,* which tells the stories of everyday Chicagoans, from a retired steelworker to a public defender, to the owner of a soul-food restaurant.

But no one has given a voice to the people of Chicago like Studs Terkel, whose books *Division Street: America, Working,* and *Chicago* are based on interviews with Chicagoans from every neighborhood and income level; and the late newspaper columnist Mike Royko, author of perhaps the definitive account of Chicago machine politics, *Boss.* His columns have been collected in *One More Time: The Best of Mike Royko* and *For the Love of Mike: More of the Best of Mike Royko.*

Jungle Fever *It's hard to get a man to understand something if his salary depends on him not understanding it.* Upton Sinclair

The most influential work of Chicago-based literature may also be the most disturbing. Upton Sinclair's *The Jungle,* an exposé of the city's meatpacking industry, caused a sensation when it was published in 1906. Although the book is a novel, following the tragic life of a poorly paid Lithuanian immigrant, it was based on Sinclair's firsthand observations at the Union Stockyards; many of its most gruesome scenes, such as when a man falls into a processing tank and is ground up along with the rest of the meat, were based on fact. After *The Jungle* became an international bestseller, U.S. meat exports plummeted and panicked meat-packing companies practically begged for government inspections to prove their products were safe. A Food and Drug Act was passed soon after, which made it a crime to sell food that had been adulterated or produced using "decomposed or putrid" substances; eventually, that led to the founding of the Food and Drug Administration (FDA).

Film

Chicago became a popular setting for feature films in the 1980s and '90s. For a look at Chicago on the silver screen, check out *Ferris Bueller's Day Off* (1985), the ultimate teenage wish-fulfillment fantasy, which includes scenes filmed at Wrigley Field and the city's annual St. Patrick's Day Parade; *The Fugitive* (1993), which used the city's El trains as an effective backdrop; and *My Best Friend's Wedding* (1996). For many Chicagoans, the quintessential hometown movie scene is the finale of *The Blues Brothers* (1979), which features a multicar pileup in the center of downtown Daley Plaza.

Sometimes locally born actors choose to shoot movies in their hometown. A film that fueled a thousand paparazzi photographs was *The Break-Up* (2006), starring local-boy-made-good Vince Vaughn and Jennifer Aniston, and filmed on location throughout the city. Another hometown actor, John Cusack, starred in *High Fidelity* (2000), where hip Wicker Park makes an appropriate backdrop for the tale of a music-obsessed record store owner. Director Michael Mann, a Chicago native, filmed part of the gangster movie *Public Enemies* (2009) in town appropriately enough, since this was the place where bank robber John Dillinger (played by Johnny Depp in the movie) was caught and killed by federal agents.

Though it technically takes place in Gotham City, the setting of the Batman blockbuster *The Dark Knight* is clearly recognizable as Chicago although, rest assured, the real city isn't nearly as dark as the movie version! Swaths of downtown were also overrun by rampaging robots in *Transformers 3* (2011).

Music

If Chicagoans were asked to pick one musical style to represent their city, most of us would start singing the blues. Thanks in part to the presence of the influential Chess Records, Chicago became a hub of blues activity after World War II, with musicians such as Muddy Waters, Howlin' Wolf, and Buddy Guy recording and performing here. (For a glimpse of what the music studio was like in its glory days, rent the 2008 movie *Cadillac Records,* starring Jeffrey Wright as Muddy Waters and Beyoncé Knowles as Etta James.) Buddy Guy is still active on the local scene, making regular appearances at his eponymous downtown blues club, one of the best live music venues in the city.

In the '60s and '70s, Chicago helped usher in the era of "electric blues" low-tech, soulful singing melded with the rock sensibility of electric guitars. Blues-influenced rock musicians, including the Rolling Stones, Led Zeppelin, and Eric Clapton, made Chicago a regular pilgrimage spot.

Today the blues has become yet another tourist attraction, especially for international visitors, but the quality and variety of blues acts is still impressive. Hard-core blues fans shouldn't miss the annual (free) Blues Fest, held along the lakefront in Grant Park in early June.

A Chicago Playlist The classic swingin' anthem of the city is Frank Sinatra's rendition of "Chicago" ("That toddlin' town . . . free and easy town, brassy, breezy town"), overblown versions of which show up regularly at local karaoke bars. Sinatra also sang his praises to the city in "My Kind of Town (Chicago Is)," which mentions the Wrigley Building and the Union Stockyards. But an even better pick for official city theme song is Robert Johnson's "Sweet Home Chicago," with its appropriately bluesy riff ("Come on, baby don't you want to go, to the same old place, Sweet Home Chicago").

The 1970s pop-lite group Chicago didn't sing specifically about the city (probably because they moved to L.A. as soon as they hit it big), but their cheery "Saturday in the Park" captures the spirit of Grant Park and Lincoln Park in the summertime. Fast-forwarding a few decades, the blistering "Cherub Rock" by Smashing Pumpkins is a harsh take on the city's 1990s-era music scene (opening with the line: "Freak out, give in, doesn't matter what you believe in . . ."); more mellow is the elegiac "Via Chicago"by indie darlings Wilco. And no survey of Chicago music would be complete without mentioning the maestros of hip-hop, Common and Kanye West, who name-check their hometown in the songs "Southside" and "Homecoming," respectively.

Today in Chicago

Like other major American cities, Chicago has benefited from a renewed interest in urban living over the past 2 decades, as former suburbanites flock to luxury high-rise condos downtown. Where the Loop used to shut down after dark and on weekends, it's now buzzing all week long, with a busy theater district and lively restaurants. Massive new condo buildings have sprung up along the lakefront south of the Loop, while the West Loop once a no-man's-land of industrial buildings has become another hot residential neighborhood.

In many ways, this building boom has erased the physical legacy of Chicago's past. The stockyards that built the city's fortune have disappeared; the industrial factories that pumped smoke into the sky south of the city now sit vacant. While no one misses the stench of the stockyards or the pollution that came with being an industrial center, the city's character has become muted along the way. Living here no longer requires the toughness that was once a hallmark of the native Chicagoan.

And yet a certain brashness remains. While some people may still have a "Second City" chip on their shoulders, we've gotten more confident about our ability to compete with New York or Los Angeles. We know our museums, restaurants, and entertainment options are as good as any other city's in the country; we just wish everyone else knew it, too.

Relatively affordable compared to New York, Chicago is a popular post-college destination for ambitious young people from throughout the Midwest. The city also draws immigrants from other countries (as it has for more than 100 years). Hispanics (mostly of Mexican origin) now make up about one-third of the city's population. Immigration from Eastern Europe is also common, especially from countries such as

Poland, Russia, and Romania. This constant influx of new blood keeps the city vibrant.

This is not to say the city doesn't have problems. With roughly 2.8 million people total, Chicago has nearly equal numbers of black and white residents a rarity among today's urban areas but the residential districts continue to be some of the most segregated in the country. The South Side is overwhelmingly black; the North Side remains mostly white. As in other major cities, the public school system seems to constantly teeter on the edge of disaster. While fine schools are scattered throughout the city, many families are forced to send their children to substandard local schools with high dropout rates.

However, the waves of gentrification sweeping the city have transformed many neighborhoods for the better. For years, the city's public housing was a particular disgrace, epitomized by decrepit 1960s high-rises that had degenerated into isolated bastions of violence and hopelessness. The largest and worst complexes have been torn down during the last decade, replaced with low-rise, mixed-income housing. Some streets I used to avoid after dark are now lined with brand-new supermarkets, parks, and inevitably a Starbucks or two.

The city's crime problem has been more intractable. Despite a murder rate that's one of the highest in the country, Chicago doesn't strike visitors as a dangerous place, because most of the violence is contained within neighborhoods where gangs congregate and tourists rarely go. But gang-instigated shootings are still shockingly common on the South Side, and children are often innocent victims caught in the crossfire. It's something we've gotten far too blasé about, and it continues to be a blot on Chicago's reputation.

Another continuing embarrassment is our local politics. Time and again, our aldermen and other city officials reward our cynicism with yet another scandal involving insider payoffs and corrupt city contracts. For more than 20 years under Mayor Richard M. Daley (himself the son of another longtime mayor, Richard J. Daley),

Chicagoans accepted a certain level of shady behavior after all, there was no denying that the city blossomed under the Daleys' leadership.

When the younger Daley stepped aside in the spring of 2011, his potential successors were quick to serve up the usual campaign promises about wiping out corruption. Now we're left wondering: Is it possible? Our newest mayor, Rahm Emanuel, is no stranger to political fights: He worked in the Clinton White House, served as a member of the U.S. House of Representatives, and survived 2 years as President Obama's chief of staff. It will be interesting to see how his take-no-prisoners style goes down with the complacent, business-as-usual Chicago City Council. Another test of his leadership will come as he attempts to reform the city's struggling public-school system. Emanuel, a dance- and theater-lover, has also pledged his strong support to the city's sometimes cash-strapped cultural institutions, which is good news for residents and visitors alike. In spite of the local politicians, we Chicagoans passionately defend and boast about our city. Ever since the stockyards were our main source of wealth, we've become masters of overlooking the unsavory. As long as Chicago thrives, we don't seem to really care how it happens.

Well-arranged Tours in Chicago

If you're in town for a limited time, an organized tour may be the best way to get a quick overview of the city's highlights. Some tours such as the boat cruises on Lake Michigan and the Chicago River can give you a whole new perspective on the city's landscape. Many tours go beyond sightseeing to explore important historical and architectural landmarks in depth. These specialized tours can help you appreciate buildings or neighborhoods that you might otherwise have passed by without a second glance.

Insider Tours Free!

Want a personalized view of the city aside from your trusted Frommer's guide? A program called Chicago Greeter matches tourists with local Chicagoans who serve as volunteer guides. Visitors can request a specific neighborhood or theme (everything from Polish heritage sites to Chicago movie locations), and a greeter gives them a free 2- to 4-hour tour. (Greeters won't escort groups of more than six people.) Specific requests should be made at least a week in advance, but "InstaGreeters" are also available on a first-come, first-served basis at the Chicago Cultural Center, 77 E. Randolph St., from Friday through Sunday. For details, call tel. 312/744-8000 or visit www.chicagogreeter.com, where you can browse a list of specific tour topics.

Carriage Rides

Noble Horse (tel. 312/266-7878; www.noblehorsechicago.com/carriages.html) maintains the largest fleet of antique horse carriages in Chicago, stationed around the old Water Tower Square at the northwest corner of Chicago and Michigan avenues. Each of the drivers, outfitted in a black tie and top hat, has his or her own variation on the basic Magnificent Mile itinerary (you can also do tours of the lakefront, river, Lincoln Park, and Buckingham Fountain). The charge is $40 for each half-hour, for up to four people. The coaches run year-round, with convertible coaches in the warm months and enclosed carriages furnished with wool blankets on bone-chilling nights. There are several other carriage operators, all of whom pick up riders in the vicinity.

Neighborhood Tours

It's a bit of a cliché to say that Chicago is a city of neighborhoods, but if you want to see what really makes the place special, that's where you have to go.

Sponsored by the city's Department of Cultural Affairs, Chicago Neighborhood Tours (tel. 312/742-1190; www.chicagoneighborhoodtours.com) are 4- to 5-hour narrated bus excursions to about a dozen diverse communities throughout the city. Departing at 10am from the Chicago Cultural Center, 77 E. Randolph St., every Saturday, the tours visit different neighborhoods, from Chinatown and historic Bronzeville on the South Side to the ethnic enclaves of Devon Avenue and Uptown on the North Side. Neighborhood representatives serve as guides and greeters along the way as tour participants visit area landmarks, murals, museums, and shopping districts. Tickets (including a light snack) are $30 for adults and $25 for seniors, students, and children 8 to 18. Tours do not run on major holidays (call first) or, usually, in January. Regularly available specialty tours include Literary Chicago; the Great Chicago Fire; Roots of Blues, Gospel & Jazz; Irish Chicago; and Magnificent Churches. These tours, which generally run about 4 to 6 hours and include lunch, are more expensive ($50 adults, $45 seniors and children 8-18).

On Saturday mornings in the summer, the Chicago History Museum offers 2-hour walking tours of the neighborhoods surrounding the museum: the Gold Coast, Old Town, and Lincoln Park. Led by museum docents, they average about four per month June through August. Day and evening tours are available, and a few specialty walking tours are usually offered as well. Tours are $15 per person, and registration is recommended but not required. Tours depart from the museum at Clark Street and North Avenue, and light refreshments are served afterward. In the summer and fall, the museum also offers a few half-day trolley tours that cover unique themes or aspects of the metropolitan area's history. Led by historians and scholars, they take place in the city and surrounding areas ($45). Tours depart from the Chicago History Museum at Clark Street and North Avenue. Call tel. 312/642-4600, or visit the museum's website (www.chicagohistory.org) for schedules and to order tickets online.

Groups interested in African-American history should visit Bronzeville (also known as the "Black Metropolis"), the South Side neighborhood where immigrants from the South created a flourishing business-and-artistic community in the 1930s and '40s. Walking and bus tours of the area can be arranged through the Bronzeville Visitor Information Center, 3501 S. Martin Luther King Dr. (tel. 773/373-2842; www.bviconline.info). A locally based company that specializes in black heritage tours, Black CouTours (tel. 773/233-8907; www.blackcoutours.com) offers a "Soul Side of the Windy City" tour, which includes Obama-related sites. Tour Black Chicago (tel. 773/684-9034; www.tourblackchicago.com) sells self-guided tours on CD, which are best if you're visiting with a car.

Cemetery Tours

Don't be scared away by the creepy connotations. Some of Chicago's cemeteries are as pretty as parks, and they offer a variety of intriguing monuments that are a virtual road into the city's history.

One of the best area cemeteries is Graceland, stretching along Clark Street in the Swedish neighborhood of Andersonville, where you can view the tombs and monuments of many Chicago notables. When Graceland was laid out in 1860, public parks were rare. The elaborate burial grounds that were constructed in many large American cities around that time had the dual purpose of relieving the congestion of the municipal cemeteries closer to town and providing pastoral recreational settings for the Sunday outings of the living. Indeed, cemeteries like Graceland were the precursors of such great municipal green spaces as Lincoln Park.

The Chicago Architecture Foundation (tel. 312/922-TOUR [8687]; www.architecture.org) offers walking tours of Graceland on select Sundays during August, September, and October. The tour costs $15 and lasts about 2 hours. Among the points of interest in these 121 beautifully landscaped acres are the Ryerson and Getty tombs, famous architectural monuments designed by Louis Sullivan. Sullivan himself rests here in the company of several of his distinguished colleagues: Daniel Burnham, Ludwig Mies van der Rohe, and Howard Van Doren Shaw. Chicago giants of industry and commerce buried at Graceland include Potter Palmer, Marshall Field, and George Pullman. The Chicago Architecture Foundation offers tours of other cemeteries, including Rosehill Cemetery, suburban Lake Forest Cemetery, and Oak Woods Cemetery, the final resting place for many famous African-American figures, including Jesse Owens, Ida B. Wells, and Mayor Harold Washington.

Planning a Trip in Chicago

As with any trip, a little advance preparation will pay off once you arrive in Chicago. We provide a variety of planning tools, including information on how to get here, local visitor resources, and tips on getting around. As a major American city, Chicago has a variety of public transportation options, from trains and buses to taxis and bike rentals, so finding your way between the sights is relatively easy once you've got your bearings.

Entry Requirements & Customs in Chicago

Passports

Virtually every air traveler entering the U.S. is required to show a passport. All persons, including U.S. citizens, traveling by air between the United States and Canada, Mexico, Central and South America, the Caribbean, and Bermuda are required to present a valid passport. *Note:* U.S. and Canadian citizens entering the U. S. at land and sea ports of entry from within the western hemisphere must now also present a passport or other documents compliant with the Western Hemisphere Travel Initiative (WHTI; visit www.getyouhome.gov for details). Children 15 and under may continue entering with only a U.S. birth certificate, or other proof of U.S. citizenship.

Passport Offices Australia Australian Passport Information Service (tel. 131-232, or visit www.passports.gov.au).

Canada Passport Office, Department of Foreign Affairs and International Trade, Ottawa, ON K1A 0G3 (tel. 800/567-6868; www.ppt.gc.ca).

Ireland Passport Office, Setanta Centre, Molesworth Street, Dublin 2 (tel. 01/671-1633; www.foreignaffairs.gov.ie).

New Zealand Passports Office, Department of Internal Affairs, 47 Boulcott St., Wellington, 6011 (tel. 0800/225-050 in New Zealand or 04/474-8100; www.passports.govt.nz).

United Kingdom Visit your nearest passport office, major post office, or travel agency or contact the Identity and Passport Service (IPS), 89 Eccleston Sq., London, SW1V 1PN (tel. 0300/222-0000; www.ips.gov.uk).

United States To find your regional passport office, check the U.S. State Department website (http://travel.state.gov/passport) or call the National Passport Information Center (tel. 877/487-2778) for automated information.

Medical Requirements

Unless you're arriving from an area known to be suffering from an epidemic (particularly cholera or yellow fever), inoculations or vaccinations are not required for entry into the United States.

Visas

The U.S. State Department has a Visa Waiver Program (VWP) allowing citizens of the following countries to enter the United States without a visa for stays of up to 90 days: Andorra, Australia, Austria, Belgium, Brunei, Czech Republic, Denmark, Estonia, Finland, France, Germany, Greece, Hungary, Iceland, Ireland, Italy, Japan, Latvia, Liechtenstein, Lithuania, Luxembourg, Malta, Monaco, the Netherlands, New Zealand, Norway, Portugal, San Marino, Singapore, Slovakia, Slovenia, South Korea, Spain, Sweden, Switzerland, and the United Kingdom. (*Note:* This list was accurate at press time; for the most up-to-date list of countries in the VWP, consult http://travel.state.gov/visa.)

Even though a visa isn't necessary, in an effort to help U.S. officials check travelers against terror watch lists before they arrive at U.S. borders, visitors from VWP countries must register online through the Electronic System for Travel Authorization (ESTA) before boarding a plane or a boat to the U.S. Travelers must complete an electronic application providing basic personal and travel eligibility information. The Department of Homeland Security recommends filling out the form at least 3 days before traveling. Authorizations will be valid for up to 2 years or until the traveler's passport expires, whichever comes first. Currently, there is a US$14 fee for the online application. Existing ESTA registrations remain valid through their expiration dates. *Note:* Any passport issued on or after October 26, 2006, by a VWP country must be an e-Passport for VWP travelers to be eligible to enter the U.S. without a visa. Citizens of these nations also need to present a round-trip air or cruise ticket upon arrival. E-Passports contain computer chips capable of storing biometric information, such as the required digital photograph of the holder. If your passport doesn't have this feature, you can still travel without a visa if the valid passport was issued before October 26, 2005, and includes a machine-readable zone; or if the valid passport was issued between October 26, 2005, and October 25, 2006, and includes a digital photograph.

Citizens of all other countries must have (1) a valid passport that expires at least 6 months later than the scheduled end of their visit to the U.S.; and (2) a tourist visa.

For information about U.S. visas go to http://travel.state.gov and click on "Visas." Or go to one of the following websites:

Australian citizens can obtain up-to-date visa information from the U.S. Embassy Canberra, Moonah Place, Yarralumla, ACT 2600 (tel. 02/6214-5600) or by checking the U.S. Diplomatic Mission's website at http://canberra.usembassy.gov/visas.html.

British subjects can obtain up-to-date visa information by calling the U.S. Embassy Visa Information Line (tel. 09042-450-100 from within the U.K. at £1.20 per minute; or tel. 866/382-3589 from within the U.S. at a flat rate of $16, payable by credit card only) or by visiting the "Visas to the U.S." section of the American Embassy London's website at http://london.usembassy.gov/visas.html.

Irish citizens can obtain up-to-date visa information through the U.S. Embassy Dublin, 42 Elgin Rd., Ballsbridge, Dublin 4 (tel. 1580-47-VISA [8472] from within the Republic of Ireland at €2.40 per minute; http://dublin.usembassy.gov).

Citizens of New Zealand can obtain up-to-date visa information by contacting the U.S. Embassy New Zealand, 29 Fitzherbert Terrace, Thorndon, Wellington (tel. 644/462-6000; http://newzealand.usembassy.gov).

Getting Around in Chicago

Ticket to Ride Visitors who plan on taking a lot of train or bus trips should consider buying a Visitor Pass, which works like a fare card and allows individual users unlimited rides on the El and CTA buses over a 24-hour period. The cards cost $5.75 and are sold at airports, hotels, museums, transportation hubs, and Chicago Office of Tourism visitor information centers (you can also buy them in advance online at www.transitchicago.com or by calling tel. 888/YOUR-CTA [968-7282]). You can also buy 3- and 7-day passes. While the passes save you the trouble of feeding the fare machines yourself, they're economical only if you plan to make at least three distinct trips at least 2 or more hours apart (remember that you get two additional transfers within 2 hr. for an additional 25¢ on a regular fare).

By Train (the El)

The Chicago Transit Authority, better known as the CTA (tel. 836-7000 or TTY 836-4949 from any area code in the city and suburbs; www.transitchicago.com), operates an extensive system of trains throughout the city of Chicago; both the below-ground subway lines and aboveground elevated trains are know collectively as the El. The system is generally safe and reliable, although I'd avoid long rides through unfamiliar neighborhoods late at night.

Fares are $2.25 per ride, regardless of how far you go. For an additional 25¢, you can transfer to the bus or take a different El ride within 2 hours. Children 6 and under ride free, and those between the ages of 7 and 11 pay $1. Seniors can also receive the reduced fare if they have the appropriate reduced-fare permit (call tel. 312/836-7000 for details on how to obtain one, although this is probably not a realistic option for a short-term visitor).

The CTA uses credit card-size fare cards that automatically deduct the exact fare each time you take a ride. The reusable cards can be purchased with a preset value already stored, or riders can obtain cards at vending machines located at all CTA train stations and charge them with whatever amount they choose (a minimum of $2.25 and up to $100). If within 2 hours of your first ride you transfer to a bus or the El, the turnstiles at the El stations and the fare boxes on buses will automatically deduct from your card just the cost of a transfer (25¢). If you make a second transfer within 2 hours, it's free. The same card can be recharged continuously.

The CTA operates seven major train lines, identified by color: The Red Line, which runs north-south, is most likely the only one you'll need, since it runs parallel to the lakefront and past many tourist attractions. The Green Line runs west-south; the Blue Line runs through Wicker Park/Bucktown west-northwest to O'Hare Airport; the Pink Line branches off from the Blue Line and serves the southwest side of the city; the Brown Line runs in a northern zigzag route; and the Orange Line runs southwest, serving Midway airport. The Purple Line, which runs on the same Loop elevated tracks as the Orange and Green lines, serves north-suburban Evanston and runs only during rush hour.

I highly recommend taking at least one El ride while you're here you'll get a whole different perspective on the city (not to mention fascinating views inside downtown office buildings and North Side homes as you zip past their windows). While the Red Line is the most efficient for traveling between the Magnificent Mile and points south, your only views along this underground stretch will be of dingy stations. For sightseers, I recommend taking the aboveground Brown Line, which runs around the downtown Loop and then north through residential neighborhoods. You can ride all the way to the end of the line at Kimball (about a 45-min. ride from downtown), or hop off at Belmont to wander the Lakeview neighborhood. Avoid this scenic ride during rush hour (before about 9am and 3:30-6:30pm), when your only view will be of tired commuters.

Study your CTA map carefully (there's one printed on the inside back cover of this guide) before boarding any train. Most trains run every 5 to 20 minutes, decreasing in frequency in the off-peak and overnight hours. The Orange Line train does not operate from about 11:30pm to 5am, the Brown Line operates only north of Belmont after about 9:30pm, the Blue Line's Cermak branch doesn't run overnight and on weekends, and the Purple Line operates only during the morning and afternoon rush hours on weekdays. (The Red Line runs 24 hr.)

By Bus

The best way to get around neighborhoods along the lakefront where the trains don't run is by public bus. Look for the blue-and-white signs to locate bus stops,which are spaced about 2 blocks apart. Each bus route is identified by a number and the name of the main street it runs along; the bus that follows Grand Avenue, for example, is the no. 65 Grand.

Buses accept the same fare cards used for the El, but you can't buy a card onboard. That means you have to stop by a train station to buy a card in advance, or pay $2.25 cash when you board. The bus drivers cannot make change, so make sure that you've got the right amount in coins and dollar bills before hopping on.

A few buses that are particularly handy for visitors are the no. 146 Marine/Michigan, an express bus from Belmont Avenue on the North Side that cruises down North Lake Shore Drive (and through Lincoln Park during nonpeak times) to North Michigan Avenue, State Street, and the Grant Park museum campus; the no. 151 Sheridan, which passes through Lincoln Park en route to inner Lake Shore Drive and then travels along Michigan Avenue as far south as Adams Street, where it turns west into the Loop (and stops at Union Station); and the no. 156 LaSalle, which goes through Lincoln Park and then into the Loop's financial district on LaSalle Street.

PACE buses (tel. 836-7000 from any Chicago area code or 847/364-7223; Mon-Fri 8am-5pm; www.pacebus.com) cover the suburban zones that surround Chicago. They run every 20 to 30 minutes during rush hour, operating until midevening Monday through Friday and early evening on weekends. Suburban bus routes are marked with nos. 208 and above, and vehicles may be flagged down at intersections where stops aren't marked.

By Commuter Train

The Metra commuter railroad (tel. 312/322-6777 or TTY 312/322-6774; Mon-Fri 8am-5pm; at other times, call the Transit Information Center at tel. 312/836-7000 or TTY 312/836-4949; www.metrarail.com) serves the six-county suburban area around Chicago with 12 train lines. Several terminals are located downtown, including Union Station at Adams and Canal streets, LaSalle Street Station at LaSalle and Van Buren streets, the Ogilvie Transportation Center at Madison and Canal streets, and Randolph Street Station at Randolph Street and Michigan Avenue.

To view the leafy streets of Chicago's northern suburbs, take the Union Pacific North Line, which departs from the Ogilvie Transportation Center, and get off at one of the following scenic towns: Kenilworth, Winnetka, Glencoe, Highland Park, or Lake Forest.

The Metra Electric (once known as the Illinois Central-Gulf Railroad, or the IC), running close to Lake Michigan on a track that occupies some of the most valuable real estate in Chicago, will take you to Hyde Park. You can catch the Metra Electric in the Loop at the Randolph Street Station and at the Van Buren Street Station at Van Buren Street and Michigan Avenue. (Both of these stations are underground, so they're not immediately obvious to visitors.)

Commuter trains have graduated fare schedules based on the distance you ride. On weekends, on holidays, and during the summer, Metra offers a family discount that allows up to three children 11 and under to ride free when accompanying a paid adult. The commuter railroad also offers a $5 weekend pass for unlimited rides on Saturday and Sunday.

By Taxi

Taxis are a convenient way to get around the Loop and to reach restaurants and theaters beyond downtown, in residential neighborhoods such as Old Town, Lincoln Park, Bucktown, and Wicker Park.

Taxis are easy to hail in the Loop, on the Magnificent Mile and the Gold Coast, in River North, and in Lincoln Park, but if you go far beyond these key areas, you might need to call. Cab companies include Flash Cab (tel. 773/561-4444), Yellow Cab (tel. 312/TAXI-CAB [829-4222]), and Checker Cab (tel. 312/CHECKER [243-2537]).

The meter in Chicago cabs currently starts at $2.25 for the first mile and costs $1.80 for each additional mile, with a $1 surcharge for the first additional rider and 50¢ for each person after that. You will also have to pay an additional $1 fuel surcharge whenever gas prices are above $3 per gallon.

By Car

One of the great things about visiting Chicago is that you don't need to rent a car to get around: Most of the main tourist attractions are within walking distance of downtown hotels or public transportation. If you do drive here, Chicago is laid out so logically that it's relatively easy for visitors to find their way around. Although rush-hour traffic jams are just as frustrating as they are in other large cities, traffic runs fairly smoothly at most times of the day. Chicagoans have learned to be prepared for unexpected delays; it seems that at least one major highway and several downtown streets are under repair throughout the spring and summer months. (Some say we have two seasons: winter and construction.)

Great diagonal corridors such as Lincoln Avenue, Clark Street, and Milwaukee Avenue slice through the grid pattern at key points in the city and shorten many a trip that would otherwise be tedious on the checkerboard surface of the Chicago streets. On scenic Lake Shore Drive (also known as Outer Dr.), you can travel the length of the city (and beyond), never far from the great lake that is Chicago's most awesome natural feature. If you're driving here, make sure you take one spin along what we call LSD; the stretch between the Museum Campus and North Avenue is especially stunning.

Driving Rules Unless otherwise posted, a right turn on red is allowed after stopping and signaling. As in any big city with its share of frustrating rush-hour traffic, be prepared for aggressive drivers and the occasional taxi to cut in front of you or make sudden, unexpected turns without signaling. Chicago drivers almost universally speed up at the sight of a yellow light; you'll most likely hear some honking if you don't make that mad dash before the light turns red.

Gasoline (Petrol) Over the past few years, the price of gas in Chicago has fluctuated between $3 and $4 per gallon. Taxes are already included in the printed price. One U.S. gallon equals 3.8 liters or .85 imperial gallons. In general, you pay more within the Chicago city limits than you will in the suburbs (the city adds an extra tax into the price), so if you're planning a day trip, it pays to fill up once you're out of town.

Parking As in most large cities, parking is at a premium in Chicago, so be prepared to pay up. Throughout downtown, street parking is limited to 2 hours (if you can find a spot); you must purchase a receipt from a designated pay box and display it on your dashboard.

Read signs carefully, because parking regulations are vigorously enforced throughout the city. Many streets around Michigan Avenue forbid parking during rush hour and I know from bitter firsthand experience that your car will be towed immediately. If you're visiting in the winter, make note of curbside warnings regarding snow plowing. Many neighborhoods also have adopted resident-only parking that prohibits others from parking on their streets after 6pm each day (even all day in a few areas, such as Old Town). The neighborhood around Wrigley Field is off-limits during Cubs night games, so look for yellow sidewalk signs alerting drivers about the dozen-and-a-half times the Cubs play under lights. You can park in permit zones if you're visiting a friend who can provide you with a pass to stick on your windshield.

A safe bet is valet parking, which most restaurants provide for $8 to $12. Downtown you might also opt for a public garage, but you'll have to pay premium prices. Several garages connected with malls or other major attractions offer discounted parking with a validated ticket.

If you'll be spending an entire day downtown, the best parking deal in the Loop is the city-run Millennium Park garage (tel. 312/742-7644), which charges $19 for up to 3 hours and $21 for up to 8 hours (enter on Columbus Dr., 1 block east of Michigan Ave., between Monroe and Randolph sts.). A little farther south are two municipal lots underneath Grant Park, with one entrance at Michigan Avenue and Van Buren Street and the other at Michigan Avenue and Madison Street (tel. 312/616-0600). Parking costs $14 for the first hour and $27 for 2 to 8 hours. Other downtown lots (where prices are comparable or even higher) include Midcontinental Plaza Garage, 55 E. Monroe St. (tel. 312/986-6821), and Navy Pier Parking, 600 E. Grand Ave. (tel. 312/595-7437). There's also a large lot next to the McCormick Place Convention Center, 2301 S. Lake Shore Dr. (tel. 312/791-7000).

Car Rental All the major car-rental companies have offices at O'Hare and Midway, as well as locations downtown.

If you're visiting from abroad and plan to rent a car in the United States, keep in mind that foreign driver's licenses are usually recognized in the U.S., but you may want to consider obtaining an international driver's license. International visitors also should note that insurance and taxes are almost never included in quoted rental car rates in the U.S. Be sure to ask your rental agency about additional fees for these. They can add a significant cost to your car rental.

By Bicycle

The city of Chicago has earned kudos for its efforts to improve conditions for bicycling (designated bike lanes have been installed on stretches of Wells St., Roosevelt Rd., Elston Ave., and Halsted St.), but it can still be a tough prospect to compete with cars and their drivers, who aren't always so willing to share the road.

The Active Transportation Alliance (tel. 312/427-3325; www.activetrans.org), a nonprofit advocacy group, has been at the forefront of efforts to make the city more bike-friendly. Their website lists upcoming bike-focused events, including the annual "Bike the Drive," when Lake Shore Drive is closed to cars.

Bike Chicago rents all sorts of bikes, including tandems and four-seater "quadcycles," as well as in-line skates, from three locations: North Avenue Beach, Millennium Park, and Navy Pier (tel. 888/BIKE-WAY [245-3929]; www.bikechicago.com). Bike rentals start at $10 an hour or $30 a day. Helmets, pads, and locks are provided free of charge. The shops are open daily from 9am to 7pm, weather permitting.

Fast Facts in Chicago

Area Codes The 312 area code applies to the central downtown business district and the surrounding neighborhoods, including River North, North Michigan Avenue, and the Gold Coast. The code for the rest of the city is 773. Suburban area codes are 847 (north), 708 (west and southwest), and 630 (far west). You must dial 1 plus the area code for all telephone numbers, even if you are making a call within the same area code.

Business Hours Shops generally keep regular American business hours, 10am to 6pm Monday through Saturday. Many stores in downtown Chicago stay open later at least 1 evening a week. Certain businesses, such as bookstores, are almost always open during the evening hours all week. Most shops are also open on Sundays, usually from 11am to 6pm. Malls are generally open until 7pm and on Sunday as well. Banking hours in Chicago are normally from 9am (8am in some cases) to 5pm Monday through Friday, with select banks remaining open later on specified afternoons and evenings.

Doctors Most hotels in Chicago keep a list of local doctors who are available to tend to guests; in case of health problems, your best bet is to contact your hotel's concierge or manager. Northwestern Memorial Hospital, 251 E. Huron St., a well-regarded downtown hospital, also has a physician referral service (tel. 877/926-4664), if you need to find a specialist.

Drinking Laws The legal age for purchase and consumption of alcoholic beverages is 21; proof of age is required and often requested at bars, nightclubs, and restaurants, so it's always a good idea to bring ID when you go out. Do not carry open containers of alcohol in your car or any public area that isn't zoned for alcohol consumption. The police can fine you on the spot. Don't even think about driving while intoxicated.

In Chicago, beer, wine, and other alcoholic beverages are sold at liquor stores and supermarkets. Bars may sell alcohol until 2am, although some nightclubs have special licenses that allow alcohol sales until 4am.

Electricity Like Canada, the United States uses 110 to 120 volts AC (60 cycles), compared to 220 to 240 volts AC (50 cycles) in most of Europe, Australia, and New Zealand. Downward converters that change 220 to 240 volts to 110 to 120 volts are difficult to find in the United States, so bring one with you.

Embassies & Consulates All embassies are in the nation's capital, Washington, D.C. Some consulates are in major U.S. cities, and most nations have a mission to the United Nations in New York City. If your country isn't listed below, call for directory information in Washington, D.C. (tel. 202/555-1212) or check www.embassy.org/embassies.

The embassy of Australia is at 1601 Massachusetts Ave. NW, Washington, DC 20036 (tel. 202/797-3000; www.usa.embassy.gov.au). Consulates are in New York, Honolulu, Houston, Los Angeles, and San Francisco.

The embassy of Canada is at 501 Pennsylvania Ave. NW, Washington, DC 20001 (tel. 202/682-1740; www.canadainternational.gc.ca/washington). Other Canadian consulates are in Buffalo (New York), Detroit, Los Angeles, New York, and Seattle.

The embassy of Ireland is at 2234 Massachusetts Ave. NW, Washington, DC 20008 (tel. 202/462-3939; www.embassyofireland.org). Irish consulates are in Boston, Chicago, New York, San Francisco, and other cities. See website for complete listing.

The embassy of New Zealand is at 37 Observatory Circle NW, Washington, DC 20008 (tel. 202/328-4800; www.nzembassy.com). New Zealand consulates are in Los Angeles, Salt Lake City, San Francisco, and Seattle.

The embassy of the United Kingdom is at 3100 Massachusetts Ave. NW, Washington, DC 20008 (tel. 202/588-6500; http://ukinusa.fco.gov.uk). Other British consulates are in Atlanta, Boston, Chicago, Cleveland, Houston, Los Angeles, New York, San Francisco, and Seattle.

Emergencies For fire or police emergencies, call tel. 911. This is a free call. If it is a medical emergency, a city ambulance will take the patient to the nearest hospital emergency room. The nonemergency phone number for the Chicago Police Department is tel. 311.

Hospitals The best hospital emergency room in downtown Chicago is at Northwestern Memorial Hospital, 251 E. Huron St. (tel. 312/926-2000; www.nmh.org), a state-of-the-art medical center right off North Michigan Avenue. The emergency department (tel. 312/926-5188 or 312/944-2358 for TDD access) is located at 251 E. Erie St., near Fairbanks Court. For an ambulance, dial tel. 911, which is a free call.

Legal Aid While driving, if you are pulled over for a minor infraction (such as speeding), never attempt to pay the fine directly to a police officer; this could be construed as attempted bribery, a much more serious crime. Pay fines by mail, or directly into the hands of the clerk of the court. If accused of a more serious offense, say and do nothing before consulting a lawyer. In the U.S., the burden is on the state to prove a person's guilt beyond a reasonable doubt, and everyone has the right to remain silent, whether he or she is suspected of a crime or actually arrested. Once arrested, a person can make one telephone call to a party of his or her choice. The international visitor should call his or her embassy or consulate.

Mail At press time, domestic postage rates were 28¢ for a postcard and 44¢ for a letter. For international mail, a first-class letter of up to 1 ounce costs 98¢ (75¢ to Canada and 79¢ to Mexico); a first-class postcard costs the same as a letter. For more information, go to www.usps.com.

If you aren't sure what your address will be in the United States, mail can be sent to you, in your name, c/o General Delivery at the main post office of the city or region where you expect to be. (Call tel. 800/275-8777 for information on the nearest post office.) The addressee must pick up mail in person and must produce proof of identity (driver's license, passport, etc.). Most post offices will hold mail for up to 1 month, and are open Monday to Friday from 8am to 6pm, and Saturday from 9am to 3pm.

Newspapers & Magazines The *Chicago Tribune* (tel. 312/222-3232; www.chicagotribune.com) and the *Chicago Sun-Times* (tel. 312/321-3000; www.suntimes.com) are the city's two major daily newspapers. The *Tribune* focuses on sober, just-the-facts reporting; the *Sun-Times* is a scrappier, attitude-filled tabloid. Both have cultural listings, including movies, theaters, and live music, not to mention reviews of the latest restaurants that have opened since this guidebook went to press. The Friday edition of both papers contains a special pullout section with more detailed, up-to-date information on special events happening over the weekend.

The weekly magazine *Time Out Chicago* (tel. 312/924-9555; www.timeoutchicago.com) lists just about everything going on around town during the week, from art openings to theater performances; if you want to squeeze in as much culture as you can while you're here, I highly recommend picking up a copy. The *Chicago Reader* (tel. 312/828-0350; www.chicagoreader.com) is a free weekly that appears each Thursday, with all the current entertainment and cultural listings.

Chicago magazine (www.chicagomag.com) is a monthly with an especially good restaurant review section.

The *Chicago Defender* (www.chicagodefender.com) covers local and national news of interest to the African-American community. The Spanish-language *La Raza*(www.laraza.com) reports on stories from a Latino point of view. The *Windy City Times*(www.windycitytimes.com) publish both news and feature articles about gay and lesbian issues.

Packing In general, you should be prepared for rapid weather shifts while you're in town, especially in the spring and fall. Unless you'll be here in July or August, bring at least one jacket and warm sweater in case of a sudden cold front. The winds off the lake, in particular, can be frosty well into the spring. Your best bet is to bring a selection of long- and short-sleeved shirts that can be layered to adapt to changing temperatures (it's not unusual to start out the morning shivering only to be sweating by afternoon). If you're brave enough to venture to Chicago in the winter, make room for hats, gloves, scarves, and boots: You'll need them.

Chicago is a casual town, so standard tourist-wear is acceptable at all the city's museums and most of the restaurants and theaters. A few traditional fine-dining restaurants have a jacket requirement for men, but otherwise male travelers probably won't need to pack a suit.

Police For emergencies, call tel. 911. This is a free call (no coins required). For nonemergencies, call tel. 311.

Smoking Smoking is banned in all public buildings in Chicago, including offices, restaurants, and bars. Hotels are still allowed to have smoking rooms available, though, so request one if you plan on lighting up.

Taxes The United States has no value-added tax (VAT) or other indirect tax at the national level. Every state, county, and city may levy its own local tax on all purchases, including hotel and restaurant checks and airline tickets. These taxes will not appear on price tags.

When visiting Chicago, be prepared to pay up: The city's 9.75% sales tax is among the highest in the country, and the hotel room tax is a steep 14.9%.

Time The continental United States is divided into four time zones: Eastern Standard Time (EST), Central Standard Time (CST), Mountain Standard Time (MST), and Pacific Standard Time (PST); Chicago is in the Central time zone. Alaska and Hawaii have their own zones. For example, when it's 9am in Los Angeles (PST), it's 7am in Honolulu (HST),10am in Denver (MST), 11am in Chicago (CST), noon in New York City (EST), 5pm in London (GMT), and 2am the next day in Sydney.

Daylight saving time (summer time) is in effect from 1am on the second Sunday in March to 1am on the first Sunday in November, except in Arizona, Hawaii, the U.S. Virgin Islands, and Puerto Rico. Daylight saving time moves the clock 1 hour ahead of standard time.

Tipping In hotels, tip bellhops at least $1 per bag ($2-$3 if you have a lot of luggage) and tip the chamber staff $1 to $2 per day (more if you've left a big mess for him or her to clean up). Tip the doorman or concierge only if he or she has provided you with some specific service (for example, calling a cab for you or obtaining difficult-to-get theater tickets). Tip the valet-parking attendant $1 every time you get your car.

In restaurants, bars, and nightclubs, tip service staff and bartenders 15% to 20% of the check, tip checkroom attendants $1 per garment, and tip valet-parking attendants $1 per vehicle.

As for other service personnel, tip cab drivers 15% of the fare; tip skycaps at airports at least $1 per bag ($2-$3 if you have a lot of luggage); and tip hairdressers and barbers 15% to 20%.

Toilets You won't find public toilets or "restrooms" on the streets in most U.S. cities but they can be found in hotel lobbies, bars, restaurants, museums, department stores, railway and bus stations, and service stations. Large hotels and fast-food restaurants are often the best bet for clean facilities. Restaurants and bars in resorts or heavily visited areas may reserve their restrooms for patrons.

Visitor Information in Chicago

Before your trip, check in with the Chicago Convention & Tourism Bureau (tel. 877/CHICAGO [244-2246]; www.choosechicago.com) to find out about upcoming events and travel packages. (They'll also mail you a packet of materials, if you want.) Click the "Maps" link on the right side of the home page for links to maps of Chicago neighborhoods. The Illinois Bureau of Tourism (tel. 800/2CONNECT [226-6632], or 800/406-6418 TTY; www.enjoyillinois.com) will also send you information about Chicago and other Illinois destinations.

Once you're here, you may want to stop by one of the city's two official visitors' centers. The Chicago Cultural Center, 77 E. Randolph St. (at Michigan Ave.), once the city's public library, is a beautiful landmark building that's worth a look as you're passing through the Loop. Its visitors' center is open Monday through Friday from 8am to 6pm, Saturday from 9am to 6pm, and Sunday from 10am to 6pm; it's closed on holidays.

The Chicago Water Works Visitor Center is in the old pumping station at Michigan and Chicago avenues in the heart of the city's shopping district. The entrance is on the Pearson Street side of the building, across from the Water Tower Place mall. It's open daily from 7:30am to 7pm. This location has the added draw of housing a location of Hot Tix, which offers both half-price day-of-performance and full-price tickets to many theater productions around the city, as well as a gift shop.

Website Extras Scanning the websites of museums and other attractions before you visit can enhance your trip when you get here. At the Field Museum of Natural History website (www.fieldmuseum.org), you can download an MP3 audio tour of the museum's permanent collection; you can also print out a Family Adventure Tour, which sends kids on a scavenger hunt throughout the museum. The Millennium Park MP3 audio tour (available at www.millenniumpark.org) includes interviews with the artists who created the park's eye-catching artwork. And if you're intimidated by the massive size of the Museum of Science and Industry, check out the website's Personal Planner, which will put together a customized itinerary based your family's interests (www.msichicago.org).

Sustainable Travel & Ecotourism in Chicago

Chicago has become a breeding ground for urban environmental initiatives, starting with the green roof that was installed on the top of City Hall and the appointment of a Chief Environmental Officer on the mayor's staff. Throughout the city, architects and contractors are building according to environmentally responsible principles, and an addition to the already massive McCormick Place Convention Center was the largest new construction building in the country to receive LEED (Leadership in Energy and Environmental Design) certification from the U.S. Green Building Council. An active pro-cycling community has pushed for more bike lanes in the city's streets, and Millennium Park provides secured bike parking and showers for two-wheeled commuters.

A city-wide Green Hotels Initiative has encouraged hotels to become more energy-efficient and change back-room operations to minimize their impact on the environment. The nonprofit organization Green Seal has certified many local hotels for their role in minimizing waste, conserving water, and promoting energy savings; among those getting the highest marks are the Hotel Allegro, Hotel Burnham, Hotel Felix, InterContinental Chicago, Hotel Monaco, and Talbott Hotel.

A focus on locally produced, organic ingredients has become a hallmark of the city's top chefs. Following the lead of well-known chefs such as Charlie Trotter, Bruce Sherman of North Pond, and Paul Kahan of Blackbird, more and more local restaurateurs are highlighting seasonal ingredients on their menus, and the Green City Market has become a popular shopping destination for both culinary professionals and local foodies.

When to Go in Chicago

You'll see Chicago at its best if you visit during the summer or fall. Summer offers a nonstop selection of special events and outdoor activities; the downside is that you'll be dealing with the biggest crowds and periods of hot, muggy weather. Autumn days are generally sunny, and the crowds at major tourist attractions grow thinner you don't have to worry about snow until late November at the earliest. Spring is extremely unpredictable, with dramatic fluctuations of cold and warm weather, and usually fair amounts of rain. If your top priority is indoor cultural sights, winter's not such a bad time to visit: no lines at museums, the cheapest rates at hotels, and the pride that comes with slogging through the slush with the natives.

When planning your trip, book a hotel as early as possible, especially if you're coming during the busy summer tourist season. The more affordable a hotel, the more likely it is to be sold out in June, July, and August, especially on weekends. It's also worth checking if a major convention will be in town during the dates you hope to travel. It's not unusual for every major downtown hotel to be sold out during the Housewares Show in late March or the Restaurant Show in mid-May.

Weather

Chicagoans like to joke that if you don't like the weather, just wait an hour it will change. In spring and autumn, be prepared for a wide range of temperatures; you may be shivering in a coat and gloves in the morning, only to be fine in a T-shirt by mid-afternoon. While Chicago winters get a bad rap, they're no worse than in other northern American cities. January isn't exactly prime tourist season, but the city doesn't shut down; as long as you've got the proper cold-weather gear and sturdy boots, you should be fine. Summers are generally warm and sunny, with temperatures that range from pleasant to steamy.

The closer you are to the lake, the more you'll benefit from the cool breezes that float off the water.

As close to your departure as possible, check the local weather forecast at the websites of the Chicago Tribune newspaper (www.chicagotribune.com) or the Weather Channel (www.weather.com). You'll find packing a lot easier if you know whether to expect snow, rain, or sweltering heat. (That said, bring a range of clothes and an umbrella if you're going to be in town for awhile you should be prepared for anything!)

Holidays

Banks, government offices, post offices, and many stores, restaurants, and museums are closed on the following legal national holidays: January 1 (New Year's Day), the third Monday in January (Martin Luther King, Jr., Day), the third Monday in February (Presidents' Day), the last Monday in May (Memorial Day), July 4 (Independence Day), the first Monday in September (Labor Day), the second Monday in October (Columbus Day), November 11 (Veterans' Day/Armistice Day), the fourth Thursday in November (Thanksgiving Day), and December 25 (Christmas). The Tuesday after the first Monday in November is Election Day, a federal government holiday in presidential-election years (held every 4 years, and next in 2012).

Major Convention Dates

Listed below are Chicago's major (20,000 visitors or more) conventions for 2012, with projected attendance figures. Plan ahead, because hotel rooms and restaurant reservations can be hard to come by when the big shows are in town and even if you snag a room, you'll be paying top price. Contact the Chicago Convention and Tourism Bureau (tel. 877/CHICAGO [244-2246]; www.choosechicago.com) to double-check the latest info before you commit to your travel dates, as convention schedules can change.

Event 2012 Dates Projected Attendance

International Heating and Air Expo Jan 23-25 60,000

Chicago Dental Society Feb 23-25 30,000
America's Beauty Show Mar 3-5 48,000
International Home and Housewares Show Mar 11-13 60,000
Kitchen & Bath Industry Show April 27-29 60,000
National Restaurant Association Show May 19-22 55,000
American Society of Clinical Oncology June 1-5 35,000
Neo-Con: World's Trade Fair June 11-13 40,000
International Manufacturing Tech Show Sept 10-15 80,000
Graph Expo Oct 7-10 30,000
Pack Expo Oct 28-Nov 1 45,000
Process Expo Oct 29-31 90,000
Radiological Society of North America Nov 25-30 55,000

Health & Safety

Although Chicago has one of the highest murder rates in the United States, the vast majority of those crimes are tied to drug dealing or gang activity and take place in areas visitors are unlikely to be walking around. In all my years of living here, I've yet to hear of a violent crime specifically targeted at a tourist.

That said, Chicago has the same problems with theft and muggings as any other major American city, so use your common sense and stay cautious and alert. After dark, stick to well-lit streets along the Magnificent Mile, River North, Gold Coast, and Lincoln Park, which are all high-traffic areas late into the night.

Late at night, avoid wandering dark residential streets on the fringes of Hyde Park and Pilsen, which border areas where gangs are active. You can also ask your hotel concierge or an agent at the tourist visitor center about the safety of a particular area.

The El is generally quite safe, even at night, although some of the downtown stations can feel eerily deserted late in the evening. Buses are a safe option, too, especially nos. 146 and 151, which pick up along North Michigan Avenue and State Street and connect to the North Side via Lincoln Park.

Blue-and-white police cars are a common sight, and officers also patrol by bicycle downtown and along the lakefront and by horseback at special events and parades. There are police stations in busy nightlife areas, such as the 18th District station at Chicago Avenue and LaSalle Street in River North, and the 24th District station (known as Town Hall) at Addison and Halsted streets.

Orientation

Chicago proper has about three million inhabitants living in an area about two-thirds the size of New York City; another five million make the suburbs their home. The Chicago River forms a Y that divides the city into its three geographic zones: North Side, South Side, and West Side. (Lake Michigan is where the East Side would be.) The downtown financial district is called the Loop. The city's key shopping street is North Michigan Avenue, also known as the Magnificent Mile. In addition to department stores and vertical malls, this stretch of property north of the river houses many of the city's most elegant hotels. North and south of this downtown zone, Chicago stretches along 29 miles of Lake Michigan shoreline that is, by and large, free of commercial development, reserved for public use as green space and parkland from one end of town to the other.

Finding an Address

Chicago is laid out in a grid system, with the streets neatly lined up as if on a giant piece of graph paper. Because the city itself isn't rectangular (it's rather elongated), the shape is a bit irregular, but the perpendicular pattern remains. A half-dozen or so major diagonal thoroughfares make moving through the city relatively easy.

Point zero is located at the downtown intersection of State and Madison streets. State Street divides east and west addresses, and Madison Street divides north and south addresses. From here, Chicago's highly predictable addressing system begins. Making use of this grid, it's easy to plot the distance in miles between any two points in the city.

Virtually all of Chicago's principal north-south and east-west arteries are spaced by increments of 400 in the addressing system regardless of the number of smaller streets nestled between them and each addition or subtraction of the number 400 to an address is equivalent to a half-mile. Thus, starting at point zero on Madison Street and traveling north along State Street for 1 mile, you will come to 800 N. State St., which intersects Chicago Avenue. Continue uptown for another half-mile and you arrive at the 1200 block of North State Street at Division Street. And so it goes, right to the city line, with suburban Evanston located at the 7600 block north, 9 1/2 miles from point zero.

The same rule applies when you're traveling south, or east to west. Thus, starting at point zero and heading west from State Street along Madison and Halsted streets, the address of 800 W. Madison St. would be the distance of 1 mile, while Racine Avenue, at the intersection of the 1200 block of West Madison Street, is 1 1/2 miles from point zero. Madison Street then continues westward to Chicago's boundary with the nearby suburb of Oak Park along Austin Avenue, which, at 6000 W. Madison, is approximately 7 1/2 miles from point zero.

Once you've got the grid figured out, you can look at a map and estimate about how long it will take to walk around any given neighborhood. The other convenient aspect of the grid is that every major road uses the same numerical system. In other words, the cross street (Division St.) at 1200 N. Lake Shore Dr. is the same as at 1200 N. Clark St. and 1200 N. LaSalle St.

Calendar of Events in Chicago

The best way to stay on top of the city's current crop of special events is to check in with the Chicago Convention & Tourism Bureau(tel. 877/CHICAGO [244-2246]; www.choosechicago.com). Visit their website to browse the *Chicago Destination Guide,* which surveys special events, including parades, street festivals, concerts, theatrical productions, and museum exhibitions (you can also get a copy mailed to you). The Mayor's Office of Special Events (tel. 312/744-3315) lets you search for upcoming festivals, parades, and concerts on its website, www.explorechicago.org.

January

Chicago Boat, RV & Outdoor Show, McCormick Place, 23rd Street and Lake Shore Drive (tel. 312/946-6200; www.chicagoboatshow.com). All the latest boats and recreational vehicles are on display, plus trout fishing, a climbing wall, boating safety seminars, and big-time entertainment. January 11 to 15, 2012.

Winter Delights. Throughout January and February, the city's Office of Tourism (tel. 877/CHICAGO [244-2246]; www.choosechicago.com) offers special travel deals to lure visitors during tourism's low season. Incentives include bargain-priced hotel packages, affordable prix-fixe dinners at downtown restaurants, and special music and theater performances. Early January through February.

Chinese New Year Parade, Wentworth and Cermak streets (tel. 312/326-5320; www.chicagochinatown.org). Join in as the sacred dragon whirls down the boulevard and restaurateurs pass out small envelopes of money to their regular customers. In 2012, Chinese New Year begins on January 23; call to verify the date of the parade.

February

Chicago Auto Show, McCormick Place, 23rd Street and Lake Shore Drive (tel. 630/495-2282; www.chicagoautoshow.com). More than 1,000 cars and trucks, domestic and foreign, current and futuristic, are on display. The event draws nearly a million visitors, so try to visit on a weekday rather than Saturday or Sunday. Many area hotels offer special packages that include show tickets. February 10 to 19, 2012.

March

St. Patrick's Day Parade. In a city with a strong Irish heritage, this holiday is a big deal. The Chicago River is even dyed green for the occasion. The parade route is along Columbus Drive from Balbo Drive to Monroe Street. A second, more neighborhood-like parade is held on the South Side the day after the Dearborn Street parade, on Western Avenue from 103rd to 115th streets. Visit www.chicagostpatsparade.com for information. The Saturday before March 17.

April

Opening Day. For the Cubs, call tel. 773/404-CUBS [2827] or visit www.cubs.mlb.com; for the White Sox, call tel. 312/674-1000 or go to www.whitesox.mlb.com. Make your plans early to get tickets for this eagerly awaited day. The calendar may say spring, but be warned: Opening Day is usually freezing in Chi-town. (The first Cubs and Sox home games have occasionally been postponed because of snow.) Early April.

Chicago Improv Festival. Chicago's improv comedy scene is known as a training ground for performers who have gone on to shows such as Saturday Night Live or MADtv. Big names and lesser-known (but talented) comedians converge for a celebration of silliness, with large main-stage shows and smaller, more experimental pieces. Most performances are at the Lakeshore Theater on the North Side (3175 N. Broadway; tel. 773/472-3492; www.chicagoimprovfestival.org). Late April.

May

Buckingham Fountain Color Light Show, Congress Parkway and Lake Shore Drive. This massive, landmark fountain in Grant Park operates daily from May 1 to October 1. From sundown to 11pm, a colored light show adds to the drama.

The Ferris Wheel and Carousel begin spinning again at Navy Pier, 600 E. Grand Ave. (tel. 312/595-PIER [7437]; www.navypier.com). The rides operate through October. From Memorial Day through Labor Day, Navy Pier also hosts twice-weekly fireworks shows Wednesday nights at 9:30pm and Saturday nights at 10:15pm.

Art Chicago, the Merchandise Mart, at the intersection of Kinzie and Wells streets (tel. 312/527-3701; www.artchicago.com). The city's biggest contemporary art show brings together collectors, art lovers, and gallery owners from throughout the Midwest. You don't have to be an expert to check out the show: Tours and educational programs are offered to make the work accessible to art novices. The Next show, which runs concurrently, focuses on work by emerging international artists. First week in May.

Celtic Fest Chicago, Pritzker Music Pavilion, Randolph Street and Columbus Drive, in Millennium Park (tel. 312/744-3315; www.explorechicago.org). This festival celebrates the music and dance of global Celtic traditions. But the mood is far from reverential: There's a limerick contest and a "best legs" contest exclusively for men wearing kilts. First weekend in May.

Wright Plus Tour, Frank Lloyd Wright Home and Studio, Oak Park (tel. 708/848-1976; www.wrightplus.org). This annual tour of 10 buildings, including Frank Lloyd Wright's home and studio, the Unity Temple, and several other notable buildings in both Prairie and Victorian styles, is very popular, so plan on buying tickets in advance (they go on sale March 1). Third Saturday in May.

June
Chicago Gospel Festival, Pritzker Music Pavilion, Randolph Street and Columbus Drive, Millennium Park (tel. 312/744-3315;
 www.explorechicago.org). Blues may be the city's most famous musical export, but Chicago is also the birthplace of gospel music: Thomas Dorsey, the "father of gospel," and the greatest gospel singer, Mahalia Jackson, were from the city's South Side. This 3-day festival the largest outdoor, free-admission event of its kind offers music on three stages with more than 40 performances. First weekend in June.

Printers Row Lit Fest, Dearborn Street from Congress Parkway to Polk Street (tel. 312/222-3986; http://printersrowlitfest.org). One of the largest free outdoor book fairs in the country, this weekend event celebrates the written word with everything from readings and signings by big-name authors to panel discussions on penning your first novel. Located within walking distance of the Loop, the fair also features more than 150 booksellers with new, used, and antiquarian books; a poetry tent; and special activities for children. First weekend in June.

Chicago Blues Festival, Petrillo Music Shell, Randolph Street and Columbus Drive, Grant Park (tel. 312/744-3315; www.explorechicago.org). Muddy Waters would scratch his noggin over the sea of suburbanites who flood into Grant Park every summer to quaff Budweisers and accompany local legends Buddy Guy and Lonnie Brooks on air guitar. Truth be told, you can hear the same great jams and wails virtually any night of the week in one of the city's many blues clubs. Still, a thousand-voice chorus of "Sweet Home Chicago" under the stars has a rousing appeal. All concerts at the Blues Fest are free, with dozens of acts performing over 3 days, but get there in the afternoon to get a good spot on the lawn for the evening show. Second weekend in June.

Ravinia Festival, Ravinia Park, Highland Park (tel. 847/266-5100;www.ravinia.com). This suburban location is the open-air summer home of the Chicago Symphony Orchestra and the venue of many first-rate visiting orchestras, chamber ensembles, pop artists, and dance companies. June through September.

Puerto Rican Fest, Humboldt Park, Division Street and Sacramento Boulevard (tel. 773/292-1414; http://prparadechicago.org). One of the city's largest festivals, this celebration includes 5 days of live music, theater, games, food, and beverages. It peaks with a parade that winds its way from Wacker Drive and Dearborn Street to the West Side Puerto Rican enclave of Humboldt Park. Mid-June.

Old Town Art Fair, Lincoln Park West and Wisconsin Street, Old Town (tel. 312/337-1938; www.oldtowntriangle.com). This juried fine arts fair has drawn browsers to this historic neighborhood for more than 50 years with the work of more than 250 painters, sculptors, and jewelry designers from the Midwest and around the country on display. It also features an art auction, garden walk, concessions, and children's art activities. It tends to get crowded, but the overall vibe is low-key festive rather than rowdy. Second weekend in June.

Wells Street Art Festival, Wells Street from North Avenue to Division Street (tel. 312/951-6106; www.oldtownchicago.org). Held on the same weekend as the more prestigious Old Town Art Fair, this event is lots of fun, with 200 arts and crafts vendors, food, music, and carnival rides. Second weekend in June.

Grant Park Music Festival, Pritzker Music Pavilion, Randolph Street and Columbus Drive, in Millennium Park (tel. 312/742-7638; www.grantparkmusicfestival.com). One of the city's greatest bargains, this classical music series presents free concerts in picture-perfect Millennium Park. Many of the musicians are members of the Chicago Symphony Orchestra, and the shows often feature internationally known singers and performers. Bring a picnic and enjoy dinner beforehand with a view of the skyline. Concerts begin the last week in June and continue through August.

Taste of Chicago, Grant Park (tel. 312/744-3315;
 www.explorechicago.org). The city claims that this is the largest free outdoor food fest in the nation. Three and a half million rib and pizza lovers feeding at this colossal alfresco trough say they're right. Over 10 days of feasting in the streets, scores of Chicago restaurants cart their fare to food stands set up throughout the park. To avoid the heaviest crowds, try going on weekdays earlier in the day. Claustrophobes, take note: If you're here the evening of July 3 for the Independence Day fireworks, pick out a vantage point farther north on the lakefront unless dodging sweaty limbs, spilled beer, and the occasional bottle rocket sounds fun. Admission is free; you pay for the sampling. June 27 through July 6, 2012.

Gay and Lesbian Pride Parade, Halsted Street, from Belmont Avenue to Broadway, south to Diversey Parkway, and east to Lincoln Park, where a rally and music festival are held (tel. 773/348-8243; www.chicagopridecalendar.org). This parade is the colorful culmination of a month of activities by Chicago's gay and lesbian communities. Halsted Street is usually mobbed; pick a spot on Broadway for a better view. Last Sunday in June.

July

Independence Day Celebration (tel. 312/744-3315; www.explorechicago.org). Chicago celebrates the holiday on July 3 with a free classical music concert in Grant Park in the evening, followed by fireworks over the lake. Expect huge crowds. July 3.

Old St. Patrick's World's Largest Block Party, 700 W. Adams St., at Des Plaines Avenue (tel. 312/648-1021; www.oldstpats.org). This hugely popular blowout is hosted by the city's oldest church, an Irish Catholic landmark in the West Loop area. It can get pretty crowded, but Old St. Pat's always lands some major acts. Six bands perform over 2 nights on two stages and attract a young, lively crowd. Second weekend in July.

Chicago Yacht Club's Race to Mackinac Island, starting line at the Monroe Street Harbor (tel. 312/861-7777; www.chicagoyachtclub.org). This 3-day competition is the grandest of the inland water races. The public is welcome at a Friday night party. On Saturday, jockey for a good place to watch the boats set sail toward northern Michigan. Mid-July.

Sheffield Garden Walk, starting at Sheffield and Webster avenues (tel. 773/929-9255; www.sheffieldfestivals.org). More than 50 Lincoln Park homeowners open their back yards to visitors at this annual event, giving you a chance to snoop around these normally hidden retreats. The walk isn't just for garden nuts; it has also grown into a lively street festival, with live bands, children's activities, and food and drink tents. It's a popular destination for a wide cross-section of Chicagoans, from singles to young families to retirees. Third weekend in July.

Dearborn Garden Walk & Heritage Festival, North Dearborn and Astor streets (tel. 312/632-1241; www.dearborngardenwalk.com). A more upscale affair than the Sheffield Garden Walk, this event allows regular folks to peer into private gardens on the Gold Coast, one of the most expensive and exclusive neighborhoods in the city. As you'd expect, many yards are the work of the best landscape architects, designers, and art world luminaries that old money can buy. There's also live music, a marketplace, and a few architectural tours. Third Sunday in July.

Chicago SummerDance, east side of South Michigan Avenue between Balbo and Harrison streets (tel. 312/742-4007; www.explorechicago.org). From July through late August, the city's Department of Cultural Affairs transforms a patch of Grant Park into a lighted outdoor dance venue on Thursday, Friday, and Saturday from 6 to 9:30pm, and Sunday from 4 to 7pm. The 4,600-square-foot dance floor provides ample room for throwing down moves while live bands play music from ballroom and klezmer to samba and zydeco. One-hour lessons are offered from 6 to 7pm. Free admission.

Taste of Lincoln Avenue, Lincoln Park, between Fullerton Avenue and Wellington Street (tel. 773/868-3010; www.wrightwoodneighbors.org). This is one of the largest and most popular of Chicago's many neighborhood street fairs; it features 50 bands performing music on five stages. Neighborhood restaurants staff the food stands, and there's also a kids' carnival. Last weekend in July.

Newberry Library Book Fair & Bughouse Square Debates, 69 W. Walton St. and Washington Square Park (tel. 312/255-3501; www.newberry.org). Over 4 days, the esteemed Newberry Library invites the masses to rifle through bins stuffed with tens of thousands of used books, most of which go for a few dollars. Better than the book fair is what happens across the street in Washington Square Park: soapbox orators re-creating the days when left-wing agitators came here to make their case. Late July.

August
Northalsted Market Days, Halsted Street between Belmont Avenue and Addison Street (tel. 773/883-0500; www.northalsted.com). The largest of the city's street festivals, held in the heart of the North Side's gay-friendly neighborhood, Northalsted Market Days offers

music on three stages, lots of food and offbeat merchandise, and some of the best people-watching of the summer. First weekend in August.

Bud Billiken Parade and Picnic, starting at 39th Street and King Drive and ending at 55th Street and Washington Park (tel. 773/536-3710; www.budbillikenparade.com). This annual African-American celebration, which has been held for more than 80 years, is one of the oldest parades of its kind in the nation. It's named for the mythical figure Bud Billiken, reputedly the patron saint of "the little guy," and features the standard floats, bands, marching and military units, drill teams, and glad-handing politicians. Second Saturday in August.

Chicago Air & Water Show, North Avenue Beach (tel. 312/744-3315; www.explorechicago.org). The U.S. Air Force Thunderbirds and Navy Seals usually make an appearance at this hugely popular aquatic and aerial spectacular. (Even if you don't plan to watch it, you can't help but experience it with jets screaming overhead all weekend.) Expect huge crowds, so arrive early if you want a spot along the water, or park yourself on the grass along the east edge of Lincoln Park Zoo, where you'll get good views (and some elbow room). Free admission. Third weekend in August.

September

Chicago Jazz Festival, Petrillo Music Shell, Jackson and Columbus drives, Grant Park (tel. 312/744-3315; www.explorechicago.org). Several national headliners are always on hand at this steamy gathering, which provides a swell end-of-summer bookend opposite to the gospel and blues fests in June. The event is free; come early and stay late. First weekend in September.

The art season, in conjunction with the annual Visions series of art gallery programs for the general public, begins with galleries holding their season openers in the Loop, River North, River West, and Wicker Park/Bucktown gallery districts. Contact the Chicago Art Dealers Association (tel. 312/649-0065; www.chicagoartdealers.org) for details. First Friday after Labor Day.

Boulevard Lakefront Bike Tour (Active Transit Alliance; tel. 312/427-3325; www.activetrans.org). This 35-mile leisurely bicycle excursion is a great way to explore the city, from the neighborhoods to the historic link of parks and boulevards. There's also a 10-mile tour for children and families. The Sunday morning event starts and ends at the University of Chicago in Hyde Park, which plays host to vendors and entertainment at the annual Bike Expo. Mid-September.

Mexican Independence Day Parade, Dearborn Street between Wacker Drive and Van Buren Street (tel. 312/744-3315). This parade is on Saturday; another takes place the next day on 26th Street in the Little Village neighborhood (tel. 773/521-5387). Second Saturday in September.

Viva! Chicago Latin Music Festival, Pritzker Music Pavilion, Randolph Street and Columbus Drive, in Millennium Park (tel. 312/744-3315; www.explorechicago.org). This free musical celebration features salsa, mambo, and performances by the hottest Latin rock acts. Free admission. Third weekend in September.

October
Chicago International Film Festival (tel. 312/683-0121; www.chicagofilmfestival.org). The oldest U.S. festival of its kind screens films from around the world, as well as a few high-profile American independent films. It's a great way to catch foreign movies that may never be released in the U.S. Screenings take place over 2 weeks, with most held at downtown movie theaters that are easily accessible to visitors. First 2 weeks of October.

Chicago Country Music Festival, Pritzker Music Pavilion, Randolph Street and Columbus Drive, in Millennium Park (tel. 312/744-3315; www.explorechicago.org). Chicago may be a long way from Dixie, but country music still has a loyal Midwest fan base. This popular event features free concerts from big-name entertainers. First weekend in October.

Chicago Marathon (tel. 312/904-9800; www.chicagomarathon.com). Sponsored by Bank of America, Chicago's marathon is a major event on the international long-distance running circuit. It begins and ends in Grant Park but can be viewed from any number of vantage points along the route. Second Sunday in October.

November

The Chicago Humanities Festival takes over locations throughout downtown, from libraries to concert halls (tel. 312/661-1028; www.chfestival.org). Over a 2-week period, the festival presents cultural performances, readings, and symposiums tied to an annual theme (recent themes included "Brains & Beauty" and "Crime & Punishment"). Expect appearances by major authors, scholars, and policymakers, all at a very reasonable cost (usually $5-$10 per event). Early November.

Dance Chicago (tel. 773/989-0698; www.dancechicago.com). All of the city's best-known dance troupes (including Hubbard Street and Joffrey Ballet) and many smaller companies participate in this month-long celebration of dance, with performances and workshops at the Athenaeum Theatre, 2936 N. Southport Ave., on the city's North Side. It's a great chance to check out the range of local dance talent.

Magnificent Mile Lights Festival (tel. 312/642-3570; www.magnificentmilelightsfestival.com). Beginning at dusk, a colorful parade of Disney characters makes its way south along Michigan Avenue, from Oak Street to the Chicago River. Thousands of lights are entwined around trees, and street lights switch on as the procession passes. Carolers, elves, and minstrels appear with Santa along the avenue throughout the day and into the evening, and many retailers offer hot chocolate and other treats. It's a great, family-friendly event, but get to the parade route early if you want your little ones to see the procession. Saturday before Thanksgiving.

Christmas Tree Lighting, Daley Plaza, in the Loop (tel. 312/744-3315). The arrival of the city's official tree signals the beginning of the Christmas season. The mayor flips the switch the day after Thanksgiving, around dusk.

December

Christkindlmarket, Daley Plaza, in the Loop (tel. 312/644-2662; www.christkindlmarket.com). This annual holiday event is inspired by traditional German Christmas festivals. A mini-European village springs up in downtown's Daley Plaza, where German-speaking vendors showcase handcrafted ornaments and other seasonal decorations. Of course, it wouldn't be a German celebration without beer, sausages, and hot spiced wine, too. The fair is open from Thanksgiving Day until Christmas Eve but is usually packed Thanksgiving weekend; visit on a December weekday for a more enjoyable visit.

A Christmas Carol, Goodman Theatre, 170 N. Dearborn St. (tel. 312/443-3800; www.goodman-theatre.org). This seasonal favorite, performed for more than 2 decades, runs from Thanksgiving to the end of December.

The Nutcracker ballet, Joffrey Ballet of Chicago, Auditorium Theatre, 50 E. Congress Pkwy. For tickets, call tel. 312/559-1212 (Ticketmaster) or contact the Joffrey office (tel. 312/739-0120; www.joffrey.com). The esteemed company performs its Victorian-American twist on the holiday classic. Late November to mid-December.

Getting There in Chicago

By Plane

Chicago's O'Hare International Airport (tel. 773/686-2200; www.flychicago.com; online airport code ORD) has long battled Atlanta's Hartsfield-Jackson Airport for the title of the world's busiest airport. O'Hare is about 15 miles northwest of downtown Chicago. Depending on traffic, the drive to or from the city center can take anywhere from 30 minutes to more than an hour during the busy morning and afternoon rush hours.

O'Hare has information booths in all five terminals; most are on the baggage level. The multilingual employees, who wear red jackets, can assist travelers with everything from arranging ground transportation to getting information about local hotels. The booths, labeled "Airport Information," are open daily from 9am to 8pm.

Every major U.S. airline and most large international airlines fly in to O'Hare. You'll find the widest range of choices on United Airlines (which is headquartered in Chicago) and American Airlines (which has a hub at O'Hare).

At the opposite end of the city, on the southwest side, is Chicago's other major airport, Midway International Airport (tel. 773/838-0600; www.flychicago.com; online airport code MDW). Although it's smaller than O'Hare and handles fewer airlines, Midway is closer to the Loop and attracts more discount airlines, so you may be able to get a cheaper fare flying into here. (Always check fares to both airports if you want to find the best deal.) A cab ride from Midway to the Loop usually takes between 20 and 30 minutes. You can find the latest information on both airports at the city's Department of Aviation website: www.flychicago.com.

Getting into Town from O'Hare & Midway Taxis are plentiful at both O'Hare and Midway, but you can get downtown relatively easily by public transportation as well. A cab ride into the city will cost about $35 from O'Hare and $25 from Midway. One warning: Rush-hour traffic can be horrendous, especially around O'Hare, and the longer you sit in the traffic, the higher the fare will be.

If you're not carting a lot of luggage and want to save money, I highly recommend taking public transportation, which is convenient from both airports. For $2.25, you can take the El (elevated train) straight into downtown.

O'Hare is on the Blue Line; a trip to downtown takes about 40 minutes. (If you're staying on or near Michigan Ave., you'll want to switch to the Red Line, which will add another 10 or 15 min. to your trip.) Trains leave every 6 to 10 minutes during the day and early evening, and every half-hour at night.

Getting downtown from Midway is much faster; the ride on the Orange Line takes 20 to 30 minutes. (The Orange Line stops operating each night at about 11:30pm and resumes service by 5am.) Trains leave the station every 6 to 15 minutes. The train station is a fair walk from the terminal without the benefit of O'Hare's moving sidewalks so be prepared if you have heavy bags.

Though you can see all the major sights in the city without a car, both airports have outposts for every major car-rental company.

GO Airport Express (tel. 888/2-THEVAN [284-3826]; www.airportexpress.com) serves most first-class hotels in Chicago with its green-and-white vans; ticket counters are at both airports near baggage claim (outside Customs at the international terminal at O'Hare). For transportation to the airport, reserve a spot through one of the hotels (check with the bell captain). The cost is $28 one-way ($50 round-trip) to or from O'Hare, and $22 one-way ($37 round-trip) to or from Midway. Group rates for two or more people traveling together are less expensive than sharing a cab, and children ages 6 to 12 ride for $15 each. The shuttles operate from 4am to 11:30pm.

For limo service from O'Hare or Midway, call Carey Limousine of Chicago (tel. 773/763-0009; www.carey.com) or Chicago Limousine Services (tel. 312/726-1035). Depending on the number of passengers and whether you opt for a sedan or a stretch limo, the service will cost about $100 to $150 from Midway and $150 to $200 from O'Hare, excluding gratuity and tax.

By Car

Interstate highways from all major points on the compass serve Chicago. I-80 and I-90 approach from the east, crossing the northern sector of Illinois, with I-90 splitting off and emptying into Chicago on the Skyway and the Dan Ryan Expressway. From here, I-90 runs through Wisconsin, following a northern route to Seattle. I-55 snakes up the Mississippi Valley from the vicinity of New Orleans and enters Chicago from the west along the Stevenson Expressway; in the opposite direction, it provides an outlet to the Southwest. I-57 originates in southern Illinois and forms part of the interstate linkage to Florida and the South, connecting within Chicago on the west leg of the Dan Ryan. I-94 links Detroit with Chicago, arriving on the Calumet

Expressway and leaving the city on the Kennedy Expressway en route to the Northwest.

Here are approximate driving distances in miles to Chicago: From Milwaukee, 92; from St. Louis, 297; from Detroit, 286; from Denver, 1,011; from Atlanta, 716; from Washington, D.C., 715; from New York City, 821; and from Los Angeles, 2,034.

By Train

Chicago's central train station is Union Station, 210 S. Canal St., between Adams and Jackson streets (tel. 312/655-2385). A hub for both national train routes operated by Amtrak and local commuter lines that run to the Chicago suburbs, it's located just across the river from the Loop. Although Union Station is relatively convenient to downtown, you'll most likely want to take a taxi or bus to your hotel if you have luggage. Bus nos. 1, 60, 125, 151, and 156 all stop at the station on their routes through downtown. The nearest El stop is at Adams and Wells streets (Brown Line), a 4-block walk.

For train tickets to Chicago from other cities in the U.S., consult your travel agent or call Amtrak (tel. 800/USA-RAIL [872-7245] in the U.S. or Canada; tel. 001/215-856-7953 outside the U.S.; www.amtrak.com). Ask the reservations agent to send you Amtrak's travel planner, with useful information on train accommodations and package tours.

International visitors can buy a USA Rail Pass, good for 15, 30, or 45 days of unlimited travel. The pass is available online or through many overseas travel agents. See Amtrak's website for the cost of travel within the western, eastern, or northwestern United States. Reservations are generally required and should be made as early as possible. Regional rail passes are also available.

By Bus

Bus travel is often the most economical form of public transit for short hops between U.S. cities. Greyhound (tel. 800/231-2222; www.greyhound.com) is the sole nationwide bus line. International visitors can obtain information about the Greyhound North American

Discovery Pass from foreign travel agents or through www.discoverypass.com. The ticket allows for unlimited travel and stopovers in the U.S. and Canada. Chicago's Greyhound station is at 630 W. Harrison St. (tel. 312/408-5821), just southwest of downtown.

If you're planning on traveling elsewhere in the Midwest, Megabus (tel. 877/GO2-MEGA [462-6342]; www.megabus.com) offers low-cost trips to cities such as Milwaukee, Minneapolis, and St. Louis. The well-kept double-decker buses which come equipped with free Wi-Fi are a popular option for students. Buses leave from the city's main train station, Union Station.

Neighborhoods in Brief in Chicago

Downtown

The Loop The Loop refers literally to a core of high-rises surrounded by a rectangular "loop" of elevated train tracks. But when Chicagoans use the term, they're referring to the city's downtown, bounded by the Chicago River to the north and west, by Michigan Avenue to the east, and by Roosevelt Avenue to the south. For the most part, the Loop is strictly business, filled with office buildings rather than residential developments. For a suggested walking tour of the Loop,

The North Side

Magnificent Mile North Michigan Avenue from the bridge spanning the Chicago River to its northern tip at Oak Street is known as the Magnificent Mile (or, simply, "Michigan Avenue," although the street itself stretches much farther). Many of the city's best hotels and most concentrated shopping can be found here. The area stretching east of Michigan Avenue to the lake is sometimes referred to as "Streeterville" the legacy of George Wellington "Cap" Streeter. Streeter was an eccentric, bankrupt showman who lived in Chicago in the mid-1880s. Looking for a new way to make money, Streeter bought a steamship with a plan to become a gun runner in Honduras. The steamship ran aground during a test cruise in Lake Michigan, and Streeter left the ship where it was, staking out 200 acres of self-created landfill. He then declared himself "governor" of the "District of Lake Michigan." True story.

River North Just to the west of the Mag Mile is an old warehouse district called River North. These formerly industrial buildings have been transformed into one of the city's most vital commercial districts, with many of the city's hottest restaurants and nightspots; you'll also find the city's highest concentration of art galleries here. Large-scale residential loft developments have sprouted on its western and southwestern fringes.

The Gold Coast Some of Chicago's most desirable real estate and historic architecture is found along Lake Shore Drive, between Oak Street and North Avenue and along the adjacent side streets. Despite trendy pockets of real estate that have popped up elsewhere, the moneyed class still prefers to live by the lake. On the neighborhood's southwestern edge, around Division and Rush streets, a string of raucous bars and late-night eateries contrasts sharply with the rest of the area's sedate mood. For a suggested walking tour of the neighborhood,

Old Town West of LaSalle Street, principally on North Wells Street between Division Street and North Avenue, is the residential district of Old Town, which boasts some of the city's best-preserved historic homes (a few even survived the Great Chicago Fire of 1871). This area was a hippie haven in the 1960s and '70s; now the neighborhood is one of the most expensive residential areas in the city. Old Town's biggest claim to fame, the legendary Second City comedy club, has served up the lighter side of life to Chicagoans for more than 30 years.

Lincoln Park Chicago's most popular residential neighborhood for young singles and urban-minded families is Lincoln Park. Stretching from North Avenue to Diversey Parkway, it's bordered on the east by the huge park of the same name, which is home to one of the nation's oldest zoos (established in 1868). The trapezoid formed by Clark Street, Armitage Avenue, Halsted Street, and Diversey Parkway also contains many of Chicago's liveliest bars, restaurants, retail stores, music clubs, and off-Loop theaters including the nationally acclaimed Steppenwolf Theatre Company.

Lakeview & Wrigleyville Midway up the city's North Side is a one-time blue-collar, now mainstream middle-class quarter called Lakeview. It has become the neighborhood of choice for many gays and lesbians, recent college graduates, and residents priced out of Lincoln Park. The main thoroughfare is Belmont Avenue, between Broadway and Sheffield Avenue. Wrigleyville is the name given to the neighborhood in the vicinity of Wrigley Field home of the Chicago Cubs at Sheffield Avenue and Addison Street. Not surprisingly, the ball field is surrounded by sports bars and memorabilia shops.

Uptown & Andersonville Uptown, which runs along the lakefront as far north as Foster Avenue, has traditionally attracted waves of immigrants. While crime was a major problem for decades, the area has stabilized, with formerly decrepit buildings being converted into you guessed it condominiums. Vietnamese and Chinese immigrants have transformed Argyle Street between Broadway and Sheridan Road into a teeming market for fresh meat, fish, and all kinds of exotic vegetables. Slightly to the north and west is the old Scandinavian neighborhood of Andersonville, whose main drag is Clark Street, between Foster and Bryn Mawr avenues. The area has an eclectic mix of Middle Eastern restaurants, a distinct cluster of women-owned businesses, and a burgeoning colony of gays and lesbians.

Lincoln Square West of Andersonville and slightly to the south, where Lincoln, Western, and Lawrence avenues intersect, is Lincoln Square, a neighborhood that still retains traces of Chicago's once-vast German-American community. The surrounding leafy residential streets have attracted many families, who flock to the Old Town School of Folk Music's theater and education center, a beautiful restoration of a former library building.

Rogers Park Rogers Park, which begins at Devon Avenue, is located on the northern fringes of the city bordering suburban Evanston. Its western half has been a Jewish neighborhood for decades. The eastern half, dominated by Loyola University's lakefront campus, has become the most cosmopolitan enclave in the entire city: African Americans, Asians, East Indians, and Russian Jews live side by side with the ethnically mixed student population drawn to the Catholic university. The western stretch of Devon Avenue is a Midwestern slice of Calcutta, colonized by Indians who've transformed the street into a veritable restaurant row serving tandoori chicken and curry-flavored dishes.

The West Side

West Loop Also known as the Near West Side, the neighborhood just across the Chicago River from the Loop is the city's newest gentrification target, as old warehouses and once-vacant lots have been transformed into trendy condos and stylish restaurants. Chicago's old Greektown, still the Greek culinary center of the city, runs along Halsted Street between Adams and Monroe streets. Much of the old Italian neighborhood in this vicinity was the victim of urban renewal, but remnants still survive on Taylor Street. The same is true for a few old delis and shops on Maxwell Street, dating from the turn of the 20th century when a large Jewish community lived in the area.

Bucktown/Wicker Park Centered near the intersection of North, Damen, and Milwaukee avenues, this resurgent area has hosted waves of German-, Polish-, and, most recently, Spanish-speaking immigrants (not to mention writer Nelson Algren). In recent years, it has morphed into a bastion of hot new restaurants, alternative culture, and loft-dwelling yuppies, although the neighborhood still feels somewhat gritty. The terms Bucktown and Wicker Park are often used interchangeably, but Bucktown is technically the neighborhood north of North Avenue, while Wicker Park is to the south. For a walking tour of the area,

The South Side

South Loop The generically rechristened South Loop area was Chicago's original "Gold Coast" in the late 19th century, with Prairie Avenue (now a historic district) as its most exclusive address. But in the wake of the 1893 World's Columbian Exposition in Hyde Park, and continuing through the Prohibition era of the 1920s, the area was infamous for its Levee vice district, home to gambling and prostitution, some of the most corrupt politicians in Chicago history, and Al Capone's headquarters at the old Lexington Hotel. However, in recent years, its prospects have turned around. The South Loop stretching from Harrison Street's historic Printers Row south to Cermak Road (where Chinatown begins), and from Lake Shore Drive west to the south branch of the Chicago River is now one of the fastest-growing residential neighborhoods in the city.

Pilsen Originally home to the nation's largest settlement of Bohemian-Americans, Pilsen (named for a city in what's now the Czech Republic) was for decades the principal entry point in Chicago for immigrants of every ethnic background. Centered at Halsted and 18th streets just southwest of the Loop, Pilsen now contains one of the largest Mexican-American communities in the U.S. This vibrant and colorful neighborhood, which was happily invaded by the outdoor mural movement launched years earlier in Mexico, boasts a profusion of authentic taquerías and bakeries. The artistic spirit that permeates the community isn't confined to Latin American art. In recent years, artists of every stripe, drawn partly by the availability of loft space in Pilsen, have nurtured a small but thriving artists' colony here.

Hyde Park Hyde Park is like an independent village within the confines of Chicago, right off Lake Michigan and roughly a 30-minute train ride from the Loop. Fifty-seventh Street is the main drag, and the University of Chicago with all its attendant shops and restaurants is the neighborhood's principal tenant. The most successful racially integrated community in the city, Hyde Park is an oasis of furious intellectual activity and liberalism that, ironically, is hemmed in on all sides by neighborhoods suffering some of the highest crime rates in Chicago. Its main attraction is the world-famous Museum of Science and Industry.

Money in Chicago

Frommer's lists exact prices in the local currency. However, rates fluctuate, so before departing consult a currency exchange website such as www.oanda.com/currency/converter to check up-to-the-minute rates.

While not as expensive as New York or London, Chicago's hotel and restaurant prices are near the high end compared to other American cities. It's hard to find a hotel room for less than $200 a night in the summer (prime tourist season), and entrees at the city's best restaurants can set you back around $30.

Credit cards are accepted just about everywhere, aside from a few hole-in-the-wall restaurants. You should have no trouble using traveler's checks at most hotels and downtown restaurants (places that are used to accommodating international visitors), but they may not be accepted at smaller businesses in the city's residential neighborhoods.

ATMs are easy to find throughout the city, especially downtown and near tourist attractions. (Most Chicagoans refer to them as "cash stations".) Most ATMs belong to one of two networks: Cirrus (tel. 800/424-7787; www.mastercard.com) or PLUS(tel. 800/843-7587; www.visa.com). Go to your bank card's website to find convenient ATM locations before you leave, and be sure you know your daily withdrawal limit before you depart.

Beware of hidden credit-card fees while traveling. Check with your credit or debit card issuer to see what fees, if any, will be charged for overseas transactions. Recent reform legislation in the U.S., for example, has curbed some exploitative lending practices. But many banks have responded by increasing fees in other areas, including fees for customers who use credit and debit cards while out of the country even if those charges were made in U.S. dollars. Fees can amount to 3% or more of the purchase price. Check with your bank before departing to avoid any surprise charges on your statement.

What Things Cost in Chicago US$

- Taxi from O'Hare Airport to downtown 35.00

- Taxi from Midway Airport to downtown 25.00

- Double room, expensive 300.00-500.00

- Double room, moderate 200.00-250.00

- Double room, inexpensive 100.00-150.00

- Three-course dinner for one (without wine), moderate 30.00-50.00

- Bottle of beer 3.00-8.00

- Cup of coffee 1.50-3.00

- 1 gallon/1 liter of gasoline 3.50

- Admission to most museums 10.00-20.00

o

Tips for Travelers with Disabilities in Chicago

Almost all public establishments in Chicago, including restaurants, hotels, and museums, provide accessible entrances and other facilities for those with disabilities. All city buses are equipped to accommodate wheelchairs, but not all El stations are accessible (some can be reached only via stairs). Contact the Chicago Transit Authority (CTA) at tel. 312/836-7000 for a list of accessible stations. For more information on facilities for people with disabilities, contact the Mayor's Office for People with Disabilities,121 N. LaSalle St., Room 1104, Chicago, IL 60602 (tel. 312/744-7050 for voice, or 312/744-4964 for TTY; www.cityofchicago.org/disabilities). The office is staffed from 8:30am to 4:30pm Monday through Friday.

Horizons for the Blind, 2 N. Williams St., Crystal Lake, IL 60014 (tel. 815/444-8800), is a social service agency that provides information about local hotels equipped with Braille signage and cultural attractions that offer Braille signage and special tours. The Illinois

Relay Center enables hearing- and speech-impaired TTY callers to call individuals or businesses without TTYs 24 hours a day. Calls are confidential and billed at regular phone rates. Call TTY at tel. 800/526-0844 or voice 800/526-0857. The city of Chicago operates a 24-hour information service for hearing-impaired callers with TTY equipment; call tel. 312/744-8599.

Walking Tours in Chicago

According to novelist Nelson Algren, "Chicago is an October kind of city even in spring." Actually, October happens to be a great month to wander around town: The weather is cool but not freezing, most of the tourist hordes have moved on, and the crisp air is invigorating. But you can meander through Chicago in any season. With the right coat, scarf, and mittens, you can even brave the streets in January or February then brag about it to friends back home. The following tours give a taste of Chicago's diversity, from the bustling downtown business center to a couple of distinctive residential neighborhoods.

Walking Tour 1 in Chicago

Walking Tour 1: The Loop
Start: The Sears Tower.
Finish: Harold Washington Library Center.
Time: 1 1/2 hours.
Best Time: Daytime, particularly weekdays when downtown businesses are open.
Worst Time: Late evening, after shops and offices have closed.

Walk through the Loop's densely packed canyon of buildings, and you'll feel the buzzing pulse of downtown. While you'll pass plenty of modern high-rises, you'll also get a minilesson in architectural history as you survey the progression of the city's skyscrapers.

Start the tour at:

1. The Sears Tower

Okay, so this 110-story megatower is no longer the world's tallest building. It's not even the Sears Tower anymore, since the naming rights were bought by the London-based insurance broker Willis Group in early 2009. But "Willis Tower" (gulp) is still referred to as the Sears Tower by defiant Chicagoans and remains a bold symbol of the city. If it's a clear day (and you've got the time), take a trip up to the Skydeck before heading off on your tour: To the east you'll look out over the lake, to the northwest you can watch planes take off from O'Hare Airport, and to the north you'll be able to see all the way to Wisconsin.

Walk north along Wacker Drive until you arrive at:

2. 333 W. Wacker Dr.

Proof that Chicago inspires architectural creativity, this 1983 office building was designed to fit a rather awkward triangular plot (previously thought suitable only for a parking lot). But architectural firm Kohn Pedersen Fox came up with a brilliant solution, designing a curved facade that echoes the bend of the Chicago River. Walk out to the Franklin Street Bridge to get the full effect of the building's mirrored surface, which reflects the surrounding cityscape in ever-changing shades of blue, green, and gray.

Across the river you'll see:

3. The Merchandise Mart

Touted as the world's largest commercial building, the Mart is a Chicago landmark as much for its place in the history of American merchandising as for its hulking institutional look. Completed in 1931, it's occupied mostly by furniture and interior-design businesses. Perched on top of the pillars that run the length of the building are oversized busts of American retail icons, including Julius Rosenwalk (Sears), Frank W. Woolworth, and Aaron Montgomery Ward.

Walk 2 blocks east along Wacker Drive. At LaSalle Street, turn right and continue 2 blocks to Randolph Street. Turn left (east), go half a block, and you'll be standing in front of:

4. The James R. Thompson Center

This postmodern cascade of glass and steel is depending on your point of view the pinnacle or the low point of architect Helmut Jahn's career. Home to offices of the Illinois state bureaucracy, it was designed to promote the idea of open government: The transparent glass walls inside allow citizens to see their tax dollars at work. Step into the atrium to check out the beehivelike atmosphere; you can even ride a glass elevator up to the 17th floor if you're not afraid of heights.

Cross Randolph Street and head south along Clark Street. On the left you'll come to an open space known as:

5. Daley Plaza

Shadowed by the looming tower of the Richard J. Daley Center a blocky dark monolith of government offices this square was named for the legendary mayor and longtime czar of Cook County politics. While you're here, go ahead and do what tourists do: Take a picture in front of the Picasso sculpture.

Walk back up to Randolph Street and head east. At the corner of Randolph and State sts., you'll see two local landmarks: the marquee of the Chicago Theatre to your north and the block-long Macy's (previously Marshall Field's) to the south. Continue south along State Street until you reach:

6. The Reliance Building

Now known as the Burnham Hotel, this building may not look impressive, but it's famous in the world of architecture. Completed in 1895, it had a remarkably lighter look than its bulky predecessors, thanks to steel framing that allowed for the extensive use of glass on the facade. It also marked the first use of the "Chicago window": a large central pane of glass flanked by two smaller, double-hung windows used for ventilation. To get a glimpse of what it looked like when it was an office building, take one of the hotel elevators up to one of the guest room floors, which still have the original tile flooring and glass-windowed office doors.

Continue south along State Street until you reach Adams Street. Ready to pause for a bite or a drink? Then turn right (west), go half a block, and stop at:

7. Take a Break

In a world of chain coffee shops and fast-food joints, the **Berghoff,** 17 W. Adams St. (tel. **312/427-3170**), feels like a flashback to Old Chicago. The bar of this 100-year-old restaurant serves several different house brews on tap, along with sandwiches and appetizers. (For a nonalcoholic treat, try the homemade root beer.) If it's lunchtime, grab a table in the main dining room; although the menu has been modified for modern, lighter tastes, the Wiener schnitzel and spaetzle are house classics.

Go 2 blocks west along Adams Street until you reach LaSalle Street. Turn left (south) and you'll be at:

8. The Rookery

Built between 1885 and 1888, the Rookery represents a dramatic transition in Chicago architecture. (It's also one of the only surviving buildings designed by noted architect Daniel Burnham, along with the Reliance Building, above.) The name refers to the previous building that sat on this site, Chicago's original City Hall, which was a favorite spot for nesting birds; today it's an office building. The imposing Romanesque exterior has thick masonry walls, but the inside is surprisingly open and airy, thanks to an innovative use of iron framing. The building is essentially a square built around an open interior court that rises the full height of the building's 11 stories. Walk upstairs and follow the staircase to get a glimpse of the Rookery's interior courtyard and the sublime stairway spiraling upward.

Continue south along LaSalle Street. At Jackson Boulevard, the street appears to dead-end at the:

9. Chicago Board of Trade

The city's temple to high finance, this building houses the city's commodities exchange, an echo of the days when corn and wheat from the prairie passed through Chicago on its way east. Opened in 1930, the setbacks on the upper stories are typical of the Art Deco styling of the era, as are the geometric decorative elements over the entrance. Along the building's rear (southern) wall, a 24-story postmodern addition by Helmut Jahn repeats the original's pyramid-shaped roof, maintaining the symmetry between old and new. When it was built, the 45-story Board of Trade was considered so tall that the aluminum sculpture of Ceres, the Roman goddess of architecture who adorns the building's peak, was left faceless, because the builders figured no one in neighboring buildings would ever be high enough to see it.

Head 2 blocks east along Jackson Boulevard to the southwest corner of Dearborn Street and Jackson Boulevard. At 53 W. Jackson Blvd. is the:

10. Monadnock Building

This mass of stonework forms two office buildings that occupy an entire narrow block all the way to Van Buren Street. Only 2 years separate the construction of these architectural twins, but they are light-years apart in design and engineering. (You'll need to step across Dearborn Street to fully appreciate the differences.)

Monadnock I, on the northern end, was built by the architectural firm of Burnham and Root between 1889 and 1891. To support a building of this size at the time, the masonry walls had to be built 6 to 8 feet thick (note the deeply recessed windows at street level). Monadnock II, on the southern wing, was built by Holabird & Roche in 1893. Here steel framing was used, allowing the lower walls to be significantly narrower. The second building may have been an engineering marvel at the time, but the original Monadnock has a certain gravitas that the later addition lacks.

Walk south along Dearborn Street until you reach Congress Parkway. At 431 S. Dearborn St. you'll find the:

11. Manhattan Building

Constructed in 1891 by William Le Baron Jenny, this broad structure was viewed as an architectural wonder by many who visited Chicago during the Columbian Exposition 2 years later. To some, the eclectic use of materials and varied design of the facade give the Manhattan Building an appearance of complete chaos; others see a dynamic rhythm in the architect's choices. Today this former office building has been converted into condos.

From the corner of Dearborn and Van Buren streets, look a few blocks west along Van Buren until you spot a triangular tower, carved with slivers of window. That building is the Metropolitan Correctional Center, a 27-story jail for defendants preparing for trial in federal court downtown. The building's three-sided design derives from an attempt by the U.S. Bureau of Prisons to reform prison conditions: Cells were built along the edges surrounding a central lounge area. But it's still not a great place to hang out: To foil jailbreaks, the windows are only 5 inches wide (and have bars, to boot); although there's a recreation yard on the roof, it's enclosed on the sides and topped with wire mesh.

Walk 2 blocks east along Congress Parkway until you reach State Street. Turn left (north) to reach the entrance of the:

12. Harold Washington Library Center

This block-long behemoth, named for the city's first African-American mayor, is the world's largest municipal library. Designed by a firm led by Thomas Beeby, then dean of Yale University's School of Architecture, and completed in 1991, it self-consciously echoes the city's original grand buildings, such as the Auditorium Theater a few blocks east. Many Chicagoans think the place looks more like a fortress than a welcoming library but judge for yourself. The Winter

Garden on the ninth floor a lovely retreat drenched with natural light is a good place to relax at the end of your walking tour.

Walking Tour 2 in Chicago

Walking Tour 2: The Gold Coast
Start: Oak Street Beach.
Finish: Bellevue Place and Michigan Avenue.
Time: 1 hour, more if you stop to eat along the way.

Best Time: Weekends are ideal for this walk at any time of the year. On weekdays, wait until after the morning rush before setting out.
Worst Time: After dusk, when it's too dark to appreciate the buildings' decorative elements.

The Gold Coast, as its name implies, is Chicago's ritziest neighborhood, site of its most expensive and exclusive houses. Its reputation dates back to 1882, when Potter Palmer, one of the city's richest businessmen, built a lakeshore castle here, in what was then a relative wilderness north of the city. The mere presence of the Palmers served as an instant magnet, drawing other social climbers in their wake (and Palmer, who owned vast parcels of northside land, saw his holdings shoot up in value). This itinerary begins with a walk overlooking Lake Michigan before heading down charming tree-lined residential streets.

Begin the tour at:

1. Oak Street Beach

This confluence of city and lakeshore epitomizes what Chicagoans love about the city: Facing downtown, you've got the ultimate urban vista; stare at the shoreline, and the seemingly endless expanse of water makes you feel like you've escaped the city completely. You can stroll along the sand or keep to the concrete path (but beware of speeding bikes and rollerbladers). As you head north, look across Lake Shore Drive to see a few remaining historic mansions scattered among the more modern high-rises.

The first mansion you'll pass, just north of Scott Street, is:

2. The Carl C. Heissen House

Both the Heissen House (1250 N. Lake Shore Dr.), built in 1890, and its neighbor, the Starring House (1254 N. Lake Shore Dr.), built in 1889, show the popularity of the sturdy Romanesque style among wealthy Chicagoans.

A second cluster of former private mansions, all vaguely neoclassical in outline, faces Lake Michigan north of Burton Place. The first of these is:

3. 1516 N. Lake Shore Dr.

This building is home to the International College of Surgeons; its neighbor at 1524 N. Lake Shore Dr. is a museum belonging to the same institution. The International Museum of Surgical Science houses a fascinating collection of exhibits and artifacts that portray the evolution of medical surgery, but it's worth visiting for its elegant interior as well, designed by Chicago architect Howard Van Doren Shaw in 1917 as a private mansion (highlights include a massive stone staircase and the second-floor library, with fine wood paneling). A third structure, 1530 N. Lake Shore Dr., is today the Polish Consulate.

Follow the lakefront path to the Chess Pavilion on your left, and continue past the patch of green where the jetty leads out to a harbor light and into the parking lot. Straight ahead is:

4. North Avenue Beach

One of the city's prime summer spots, North Avenue Beach swarms with beach volleyball players and sun worshippers from June through August. But I think it's just as worth a visit maybe more so in spring and fall, when you can take in the view without the crowds. Check out the retro-style beach house, which was designed to look like an old ocean liner.

Double back and cross Lake Shore Drive by way of the North Avenue underpass, directly west of the Chess Pavilion. From the cul-de-sac here, continue west on North Avenue 2 blocks to North State Parkway.

The imposing residence on your left, surrounded by spacious grounds, is the:

5. Residence of the Roman Catholic Archbishop of Chicago

Catholicism has strong roots in Chicago, thanks to generations of German, Irish, and Polish immigrants who brought their faith along with them; the city's current archbishop, Francis Cardinal George, is a well-known local figure who receives regular press coverage. This Queen Anne-style mansion was built in 1885 for the first archbishop of Chicago, Patrick Feehan; it sits on the site of what used to be a cemetery that stretched between present-day North Avenue and Schiller Street. Of the 19 chimneys that march across the roofline, only 3 are still in use.

Across the street on the opposite corner of North Avenue is:

6. 1550 N. State Pkwy.

Each apartment in this 1912 vintage luxury high-rise, known as the Benjamin Marshall Building, originally occupied a single floor and contained 15 rooms spread over 9,000 square feet. The architects were Marshall & Fox, highly regarded in their day as builders of fine hotels. There was once a garden entryway at the ground-floor level. Among the noteworthy architectural features adorning the exterior of this Beaux Arts classic are the many small balconies and the bowed windows at the corners of the building.

Continue west for 1 block on North Avenue and turn left, following Dearborn Street to Burton Place and the:

7. Bullock Folsom House

As its mansard roof reveals, this 1877 landmark, at 1454 N. Dearborn St., on the southwest corner, takes its inspiration from the French Second Empire. (That roof, incidentally, is shingled in slate, not asphalt.) Neighboring houses at nos. 1450 and 1434 have some of the same French-influenced ornamentation and styling. Across Burton Place just to the north, at 1500 N. Dearborn St., is another example of a rival architectural fashion of the day, the Richardsonian or Romanesque Revival.

Return to the east along Burton, but before crossing North State Parkway, stop at:

8. 4 W. Burton Place

Built as a private residence in 1902 by Richard E. Schmidt for a family named Madlener, this striking building today houses the Graham Foundation for Advanced Studies in the Fine Arts. There is something very modern about its appearance: The structure's clean lines and the ornamentation around the entrance were inspired by the work of architects Louis Sullivan and Frank Lloyd Wright. The Society of Architectural Historians offers tours of the home on Saturdays, along with the Charnley-Persky house.

Continue 1 block farther east to Astor Street. On the northwest corner, at 1500 N. Astor St., is the former:

9. Cyrus McCormick Mansion

New York architect Stanford White designed this building, which was constructed for the Patterson family in 1893. Cyrus McCormick, Jr., bought it in 1914, and David Adler's north addition doubled the size of the building in 1927. The senior McCormick made his fortune by inventing the mechanical reaper, which made it possible to farm vast tracts of wheat on the prairie without depending on seasonal labor at harvest time. Cyrus Sr.'s heirs shared in the wealth, and eventually so many members of the family owned homes near Rush and Erie streets, just south of the Gold Coast, that the neighborhood was known as "McCormicksville."

Like the Fifth Avenue mansions White and his contemporaries built in New York, the McCormick palazzo is an essay in neoclassical detailing. Square and grand, like a temple of antiquity, the construction combines Roman bricks of burnt yellow with touches of terra-cotta trim. The building now is divided into condominiums.

Head north briefly on Astor Street to check out a home with a connection to presidential history:

10. 1525 N. Astor St.

This attractive town house was once the residence of Robert Todd Lincoln, the only surviving child of Abraham and Mary Todd Lincoln. The younger Lincoln started a private law practice after the Civil War. He remained in Chicago for much of his life, leaving twice during the 1880s and 1890s to serve under presidents James Garfield and Chester Arthur as Secretary of War, and later under Benjamin Harrison as ambassador to Britain. On the death of George Pullman, one of his major corporate clients, Lincoln became president of the Pullman Palace Car Company in 1897.

Reversing direction, walk south along Astor Street. Notice the houses at:

11. 1451 & 1449 N. Astor St.

The former, occupying the corner lot, is the work of Howard Van Doren Shaw, built in 1910 according to the so-called "Jacobethan" fashion; a combination of Jacobean and Elizabethan, it revives certain 16th- and 17th-century English architectural features, including narrow, elongated windows, split-level roofs, and multiple chimney stacks. The house at no. 1449 was built around the turn of the century, but the architect of this glorious chateau remains a mystery. Guarding the home's entrance is a somewhat intimidating stone porch, seemingly out of scale. Among the home's other unique characteristics are the big front bay and frieze below the cornice, a scroll decorated with a pattern of shells.

Another neighboring home of interest across the street is:

12. 1444 N. Astor St.

While most of the homes in this area were built in the late 1800s and early decades of the 1900s and most took their cues from architectural fashions from centuries before this house was on the cutting edge of style when it was built in 1929. An Art Deco masterpiece, it was designed by Holabird & Roche, the same firm that designed Soldier Field football stadium a few years earlier.

Next, walk to 1412 N. Astor St., site of the:

13. Thomas W. Hinde House

This 1892 home, designed by Douglas S. Pentecost, is an homage to the Flemish architecture of the late Middle Ages. The facade has been altered, but some of the original stone ornamentation remains, as do such dominant features as the multipaned diamond-shaped windows.

On the same side of the street, at 1406 N. Astor St., is the:

14. Joseph T. Ryerson House

David Adler designed this 1922 landmark home in the manner of a Parisian hotel. Adler himself supervised the 1931 addition of the top floor and the mansard roof. Woven into the wrought-iron grillwork above the entrance are the initials of the original owners.

Walk to 1365 N. Astor St. to see the landmark:

15. Charnley-Persky House

Shortly before he left the firm of Adler & Sullivan, a then-obscure draftsman, Frank Lloyd Wright, played a major role in designing this 1892 home. The house's streamlined structure gives it a far more contemporary look than its neighbors, making the case that there is something timeless in Wright's ideas. The building appropriately enough is now the headquarters of the Society of Architectural Historians, which gives tours of the house on Wednesday and more extensive tours including the surrounding area on Saturday. (Visit www.sah.org or call tel. 312/915-0105 for details.)

Walk back to Schiller Street. Cross the street and turn left on North State Parkway, continuing south until the middle of the block to 1340 N. State Pkwy., the original:

16. Playboy Mansion

Little did the original owner of this building, an upright Calvinist named George S. Isham, know how his house would be transformed a mere half-century after it was built in 1899. Playboy founder Hugh Hefner lived here from 1959 to 1974, romping with his Bunnies and celebrities in the indoor pool and lounging in silk pajamas while perusing page layouts in his bedroom. Today that hedonistic past has been erased, and the building has been converted into high-priced condos.

Continue south on State Parkway, then swing east on Goethe Street, back to Astor Street. On opposite corners diagonally across Goethe Street are apartment towers that represent the trend toward high-rise living that began in the 1930s:

17. 1301 & 1260 N. Astor St.

Constructed by architect Philip B. Maher in 1932 and 1931, respectively, these apartment buildings are classics of the sleek modernism that characterized American commercial architecture after World War I. Contrast their timeless style with the 1960s apartment tower at 1300 N. Astor St., by architect Bertrand Goldberg; avant-garde at the time, it has not aged as well.

If you're ready for a snack, turn back north to Goethe Street and head west 2 blocks to Dearborn Street. Turn left (south) and go halfway down the block until you reach:

18. Take a Break

The welcoming Third Coast coffeehouse, 1260 N. Dearborn St. (tel. 312/649-0730), is more laid-back than the elegant neighborhood surrounding it. Tucked below street level, it has a shabby-cozy vibe and makes a good stop for midmorning coffee or lunch (there's a full menu of sandwiches and salads).

Head south on Dearborn Street to Division Street. Walk 1 block east to State Street, then turn right (south), staying on the east side of the street where State and Rush streets merge, and proceed 2 blocks south to:

19. East Cedar Street

This long block between Rush Street and Lake Shore Drive deserves a look because much of its turn-of-the century scale has been so well preserved, in particular the two clusters of "cottages," nos. 42 to 48 (built in 1896 by businessman Potter Palmer) and 50 to 54 (built in 1892).

Return to Rush Street, walk to the next block south, and turn left on Bellevue Place. At 120 E. Bellevue Place stands the:

20. Bryan Lathrop House

New York architect Charles F. McKim, partner of Stanford White, built this mansion for a local real estate agent and civic leader while staying in Chicago as a lead designer of the World's Columbian Exposition. It helped introduce the Georgian fashion in architecture that replaced the Romanesque Revival throughout the Gold Coast

Walking Tour 3 in Chicago

Walking Tour 3: Wicker Park
Start and Finish: The Damen El stop (Blue Line).
Time: 1 hour, not including shopping or eating stops.
Best Time: Any time during the day.
Worst Time: After dark, when you'll have trouble seeing homes' decorative details.

Wicker Park, along with adjacent Bucktown, is mostly known today as a place to shop at edgy clothing boutiques or try out the latest hip restaurant. This tour takes you along the residential side streets that many tourists overlook but that testify to the rich history of this neighborhood. Middle-class artisans, mostly Germans and Scandinavians, began settling here around 1870. In the following decades, wealthy families whose foreign roots made them unwelcome along the Gold Coast built luxurious homes here as well. In the 20th century, the neighborhood's respectability gradually declined, and many of the grandest homes were converted into rooming houses. It was not until the 1980s that the distinctive homes here began to be rediscovered and renovated, just as the gritty main streets of Milwaukee and Damen avenues began sprouting new shops and cafes.

Walk south along Damen Avenue to:

1. Wicker Park

Two brothers who were beginning to develop their extensive real estate holdings in the area donated this land to the city in 1870, hoping the green space would make the surrounding area more attractive to prospective builders. Unfortunately, little remains of the 19th-century landscaping, which once included a pond spanned by a rustic bridge.

Cross the park to the corner of Damen Avenue and Schiller Street. Follow Schiller east, along the park, stopping first at:

2. 1959-1961 W. Schiller St.

Built in 1886 for a ship's captain and a medical doctor, this double home reflects the fashionable Second Empire style. The building became a rooming house in the 1920s but has been restored to its original style. Note the lively Victorian colors of the cornices, tower, and trim. Other distinctive features are the large mansard roof and the decorative saw-toothed pattern in the brickwork.

Next move to:

3. 1941 W. Schiller St.

Built for clothing manufacturer Harris Cohn in 1888, this home is also known as the Wicker Park Castle. Essentially Queen Anne in design, its limestone facade made it pricier and more luxurious than its neighbors. Granite columns were polished to look like marble, and a turret rests on a shell-shaped base.

At the end of the block, turn right on Evergreen Avenue until you come to:

4. 1958 W. Evergreen Ave.

Novelist Nelson Algren lived in a third-floor apartment here from 1959 to 1975. After he was caught stealing a typewriter in 1933, Algren (1909-81) spent 3 months in jail. This experience, which brought him in contact with criminals, outsiders, drug addicts, and prostitutes, was a strong influence on his work. Algren is best remembered for his two dark novels of the urban semiunderworld, *A Walk on the Wild Side* and *The Man with the Golden Arm* (which was set near here, around Division St. and Milwaukee Ave.), and for his tough but lyrical prose poem *Chicago: City on the Make.*

Continue to Damen Avenue, then turn right (north) back to Schiller Street. Take Schiller west 1 block to Hoyne Avenue, then turn right (north), where you'll see:

5. 1407 N. Hoyne Ave.
Built by German wine and beer merchant John H. Rapp in 1880, this was the largest single-family estate in Wicker Park at the time. The original coach house, behind the mansion, is now a separate residence. This was not a happy home. Mrs. Rapp went insane, a son was convicted of embezzlement, and Rapp was murdered by his female bookkeeper. The home itself is of Second Empire style, with a large, curved mansard roof. The original wrought-iron fence defines the boundaries of the original grounds.

Heading north, you'll pass other late 19th-century mansions and, at 1426 N. Hoyne Ave., an example of a worker's cottage, a reminder that in these immigrant neighborhoods, artisans and their patrons often lived side by side. On the next corner, at Hoyne Avenue and Le Moyne Street, is the:

6. Wicker Park Lutheran Church
The city's oldest Lutheran church, it was modeled from plans of Holy Trinity Church in Caen, France, dating from the 12th century. The stone for this Romanesque structure was recycled from a demolished brothel. When one of the scandalized parishioners protested, the pastor remarked that the building material "has served the devil long enough; now let it serve the Lord."

Walk on to:

7. 1558 N. Hoyne St.

The building permit for this Queen Anne-style home was issued in 1877, making it one of the oldest homes in the area. It was built for C. Hermann Plautz, founder of the Chicago Drug and Chemical Company. Ever conscious of the Great Chicago Fire, the builders created all the decorative trim on both towers, the cornices, and the conservatory of the south side from ornamental pressed metal. The seemingly misplaced cannon in the front yard is a relic of the years (1927-72) when the building housed the local American Legion.

Return to Pierce Avenue and walk west to:

8. 2137 W. Pierce Ave.

This well-preserved gem is one of the highlights of historic Wicker Park. Built for the German businessman Hermann Weinhardt in 1888, it's a fanciful combination of elements that defies categorization. Notable details include the elaborate carved-wood balcony and the unusual juxtaposition of green stone and redbrick limestone around the large front window. The large lot used to be flooded in the winter for ice-skating.

Across the street is another notable home:

9. 2138 W. Pierce Ave.

The original owner of this home, Hans D. Runge, was treasurer of a wood milling company, so it's no surprise that elaborate wood carvings characterize the home inside and out; among the unique designs are the Masonic symbols flanking the pair of dragon heads under the rounded arch. A well-heeled local banker and politician, John F. Smulski, acquired the house in 1902, about the time many Poles were moving into the neighborhood. Smulski committed suicide here after the stock market crash in 1929, and the house served for a time as the Polish consulate.

Continue west until you reach Leavitt Street. Turn right (north) and walk 3 blocks until you reach:

10. Caton Street

Many of the houses on this street were built in the early 1890s by the same architectural firm, each with its own style, including German Burgher (no. 2156) and Renaissance (no. 2152). The Classical Revival home at 2147 W. Caton St. was built by the owner of a metal company, hence the extensive metal ornamentation on the exterior. (If you peek at the porch, you'll see it has a tin ceiling.)

Retrace your steps along Caton Street and Leavitt Street to North Avenue, and turn left (east). As you pass Hoyne Street, take a quick look at 1617-1619 N. Hoyne Ave.; the building used to house the neighborhood livery stables, where local families kept their horses and carriages. (It's now condos.) The final stop on the tour is at 2039 W. North Ave., an address that used to house the:

11. Luxor Baths

These public baths were built in the 1920s and were reportedly once a hangout for local politicians and wheeler-dealers. Today the building has been transformed into what else? condos. Still, it's a fitting end to the tour, a reminder of the days when this was a neighborhood of European immigrants trading news from home in the Luxor Baths steam room.

Head east to the three-way intersection of Milwaukee, Damen, and North avenues. From here, you can hop on the Blue Line El train, or walk a block and a half north on Damen toward a favorite local hangout:

12. Take a Break

Long-time residents gripe about the encroaching suburbanization of Wicker Park, where sterile bank branches have replaced funky-divey coffee shops and million-dollar houses no longer raise eyebrows. Still, many independently owned businesses remain, among them Caffe de Luca, 1721 N. Damen Ave. (tel. 773/342-6000), an Italian-inspired hangout where you can grab a coffee and pastry in the morning, a salad or panini at lunchtime, or a midafternoon dessert pick-me-up. Best of all, it's a place the locals come, where you can check out a cross-section of Wicker Park residents, from grungy wannabe artists to hip moms.

Active Pursuits in Chicago

Perhaps because winters can be brutal, Chicagoans take their summers seriously. In the warmer months, with the wide blue lake and the ample green parks, it's easy to think that the city is one big grown-up playground. Whether you prefer your activity in the water or on dry ground, you'll probably find it here. For information, contact the city's park district (tel. 312/742-PLAY[7529]; www.chicagoparkdistrict.com); for questions about the 29 miles of beaches and parks along Lake Michigan, call the park district's lakefront region office at tel. 312/747-2474.

Beaches

Public beaches line Lake Michigan all the way up north into the suburbs and Wisconsin, and southeast through Indiana and into Michigan. The best known is Oak Street Beach. Its location, at the northern tip of the Magnificent Mile, creates some interesting sights as sun worshippers sporting swimsuits and carting coolers make their way down Michigan Avenue. The most popular is massive North Avenue Beach, about 6 blocks farther north, where Lincoln Park singles come to play, check each other out, and fly by on bikes and in-line skates. Rows of beach volleyball courts stretch out beside a vintage steamship-shaped beach house; there's also a Venice Beach-style outdoor gym; Hollywood-Ardmore Beach (officially Kathy Osterman Beach), at the northern end of Lake Shore Drive, is a lovely crescent that's less congested and has steadily become more popular with gays who've moved up the lakefront from the Belmont Rocks, a longtime hangout.

For more seclusion, try Ohio Street Beach, an intimate sliver of sand in tiny Olive Park, just north of Navy Pier, which, incredibly enough, remains largely ignored despite its central location. If you have a car, head up to Montrose Beach, a beautiful unsung treasure about midway between North Avenue Beach and Hollywood-Ardmore Beach (with plenty of free parking). It has an expanse of beach mostly uninterrupted by piers or jetties, and a huge adjacent park with soccer fields, one big hill that's great for kite flying, and even a small bait shop where anglers can go before heading to a nearby long pier designated for fishing.

If you've brought the pooch along, you might want to take him for a dip at the doggie beach south of Addison Street, at about Hawthorne and Lake Shore Drive (although this minute spot aggravates some dog owners because it's in a harbor where the water is somewhat fouled by gas and oil from nearby boats). A tip: Try the south end of North Avenue Beach in early morning, before it opens to the public for the day. (Also consider that, in the off season, all beaches are fair game for dogs. The police won't hassle you, I promise.)

Beaches officially open with a full retinue of lifeguards on duty around June 20, though swimmers can wade into the chilly water from Memorial Day to Labor Day. Only the bravest souls venture into the water before July, when the temperature creeps up enough to make swimming an attractive proposition. Please take note that the entire lakefront is not beach, and don't go do anything stupid such as dive off the rocks.

Biking

Biking is a great way to see the city, particularly along the lakefront bike path that extends for more than 18 miles. The stretch between Navy Pier and North Avenue Beach gets extremely crowded in the summer (you're jostling for space with in-line skaters, joggers, and dawdling pedestrians). If you're looking to pick up some speed, I recommend biking south (once you're past the Museum Campus, the trail is relatively wide open, and you can zip all the way to Hyde Park). If you want a more leisurely tour with people-watching potential, head north (through the crowds). After you pass Belmont Harbor, the traffic lets up a bit. Ride all the way to Hollywood Beach (where the lakefront trail ends) for a good but not exhausting workout.

To rent bikes, try Bike and Roll Chicago (www.bikechicago.com), which has locations at Navy Pier (tel. 312/595-9600), North Avenue Beach (tel. 773/327-2706), and Millennium Park (tel. 888/BIKE-WAY [245-3929]). Open from 8am to 8pm May through October (weather permitting), Bike Chicago stocks mountain and touring bikes, kids' bikes, strollers, and most fun of all quadcycles, which are four-wheel contraptions equipped with a steering wheel and canopy that can accommodate four or five people. Rates for bikes start at $10 an hour, $30 a day, with helmets, pads, and locks included. If you'd like to cycle your way past some Chicago landmarks, guided tours are also available.

Both the park district (tel. 312/742-PLAY [7529]) and the Active Transportation Alliance (tel. 312/427-3325; www.activetrans.org) offer free maps that detail popular biking routes. The latter, which is the preeminent organization for cyclists in Chicago, sells a much larger, more extensive map ($10) that shows routes within a seven-county area. The federation sponsors a number of bike rides throughout the year, including the highly enjoyable Boulevard Lakefront Tour, held in September, which follows the historic circle of boulevards that had their genesis in the Chicago Plan of 1909. It starts in Hyde Park at the University of Chicago campus.

A word of caution: Never head anywhere on the city's streets without first strapping on a helmet. Designated bike lanes have been added to many main thoroughfares, but most cabbies and drivers tend to ignore them. Bike with extreme caution on city streets (you can get a ticket for biking on the sidewalk), and stick to the lakefront path if you're not an expert rider. Locking your bike anywhere you go is a no-brainer.

Golfing

For a major metropolis, Chicago has an impressive number of golf options within the city limits (not to mention many plush and pricey suburban courses). The closest you'll get to golfing downtown is the Green at Grant Park (tel. 312/987-1818; www.thegreenonline.com), an 18-hole putting course on Monroe Street between Columbus Avenue and Lake Shore Drive, just east of Millennium Park. It's not exactly tournament-level play, but it's more challenging than miniature golf and the setting can't be beat. The course is open daily from May through October from 10am to 10pm, and putters and golf balls are provided. Rates are $12 per round for adults, $6 for children 12 and under.

To warm up your swing, head to the Diversey Driving Range, 141 W. Diversey Pkwy. (tel. 312/742-7929), in Lincoln Park just north of Diversey Harbor. This two-level range attracts all levels from show-off heavy hitters to beginners and is very popular on weekends with young singles who live in the surrounding apartment buildings. The price is right ($14 for a bucket of 100 balls), and the setting is pretty much perfect.

The Chicago Park District runs six golf courses in the city. One of the most popular is the 9-hole Sydney Marovitz Course, 3600 N. Lake Shore Dr. (at Waveland Ave.), which many Chicagoans simply call Waveland. Thanks to its picturesque lakefront location, it's always full on weekends, so make a reservation well in advance (and don't expect a quick game this is where beginners come to practice). Another good bet and usually less crowded is the 18-hole course in Jackson Park on the South Side (63rd St. and Stoney Island Ave.). These city-run courses are open from mid-April through November; for information on greens fees, location, and hours, call the Chicago Park District golf office (tel. 312/245-0909; www.cpdgolf.com).

For information about suburban golf courses, visit the website of the Chicago District Golf Association (www.cdga.org).

Ice Skating

The city's premier skating destination is the McCormick-Tribune Ice Rink at Millennium Park, 55 N. Michigan Ave. (tel. 312/742-5222). The location is pretty much perfect: You're skating in the shadows of grand skyscrapers and within view of the lake. The rink is open daily from 10am to 10pm November through March. Admission is free, and skate rentals are $10.

The park district runs dozens of other skating surfaces throughout the city, along the lakefront and in neighborhood parks. Call tel. 312/742-PLAY [7529] for locations. There's also a relatively small rink at Navy Pier, 600 E. Grand Ave. (tel. 312/595-PIER [7437]).

In-Line Skating

The wheeled ones have been battling bikers over control of Chicago's lakefront paths since the early 1990s. If you want to join in the competition, Londo Mondo, 1100 N. Dearborn St. (tel. 312/751-2794; www.londomondo.com), on the Gold Coast, rents blades for $7 an hour or $20 a day. The best route to skate is the lakefront trail that leads from Lincoln Park down to Oak Street Beach. Beware, though, that those same miles of trail are claimed by avid cyclists, and collisions between distracted 'bladers and bikers have been known to happen. On busy summer days, approach Chicago lakefront traffic as carefully as you would a major expressway.

Sailing

It seems a shame just to sit on the beach and watch all those beautiful sailboats gliding across the lake, so go on, get out there. Chicago Sailing, in Belmont Harbor (tel. 773/871-SAIL [7245]; www.chicagosailing.com), rents J-22 and J-30 boats from 9am to sunset, weather permitting, May through October. A J-22, which holds four or five adults, rents for $55 to $75 an hour; a J-30, which accommodates up to 10 people, costs $95 to $110 per hour. If you want to take the boat out without a skipper, you need to demonstrate your skills first (for an additional $15 fee). If you'd rather sit back and relax, you can charter a boat. Reservations are recommended.

Swimming

The Chicago Park District maintains about 30 indoor pools for lap swimming and general splashing around, but none is particularly convenient to downtown. The lakefront is open for swimming until 9:30pm Memorial Day to Labor Day in areas watched over by lifeguards (no swimming off the rocks, please). *But be forewarned:*The water is usually freezing. If you're willing to take a dip anyway, a good place for lake swimming is the water along the wall beginning at Ohio Street Beach, slightly northwest of Navy Pier. The Chicago Triathlon Club marks a course here each summer with a buoy at both the quarter- and half-mile distances. This popular swimming route follows the shoreline in a straight line. The water is fairly shallow. For more information, call the park district's beach and pool office (tel. 312/742-PLAY [7529]).

Spectator Sports in Chicago

Baseball

Until 2016, the Chicago Cubs hadn't made a World Series appearance since 1945 and hadn't been world champs since 1908. That finally changed when the lovable losers finally won the World Series against the Cleveland Indians. But win or lose, historic Wrigley Field is always worth a visit, with its ivy-covered outfield walls, its hand-operated scoreboard, its view of the shimmering lake from the upper deck, and its "W" or "L" flag announcing the outcome of the game to the unfortunates who couldn't attend. After all the strikes, temper tantrums, and other nonsense, Wrigley has managed to hold onto something like purity. Yes, Wrigley eventually installed lights (it was the last major-league park to do so), but by agreement with the residential neighborhood, the Cubs still play most games in the daylight, as they should. Because Wrigley is small, just about every seat is decent.

No matter how the Cubs are doing, tickets ($15-$90) go fast; most weekend and night games sell out by Memorial Day. Your best bet is to hit a weekday game, or try your luck buying a ticket on game day outside the park, when you'll often find some season ticket holders looking to unload a few seats.

Wrigley's easy to reach by El; take the Red Line to the Addison stop, and you're there. Or take the no. 22 bus, which runs up Clark Street. To buy tickets in person, stop by the ticket windows at Wrigley Field Monday through Friday from 9am to 6pm, Saturday from 9am to 4pm, and on game days. Call tel. 800/THE-CUBS [843-2827] for tickets through Tickets.com (tel. 866/652-2827 outside Illinois); you can also order online through the team website.

Despite their stunning World Series win in 2005, the Chicago White Sox still struggle to attract the same kind of loyalty (despite the fact that they regularly win more games than the Cubs). Longtime fans rue the day owner Jerry Reinsdorf replaced admittedly dilapidated Comiskey Park with a concrete behemoth that lacks the yesteryear charm of its predecessor. That said, the current stadium, U.S. Cellular Field, 333 W. 35th St. (tel. 312/674-1000; www.whitesox.mlb.com), in the South Side neighborhood of Bridgeport, has spectacular sightlines from every seat (if you avoid the vertigo-inducing upper deck), and the park has every conceivable amenity, including above-average food concessions, shops, and plentiful restrooms. The White Sox's endearing quality is the blue-collar aura with which so many Cubs-loathing Southsiders identify. Games rarely sell out an effect, presumably, of Reinsdorf's sterile stadium and the blighted neighborhood that surrounds it. All of this makes it a bargain for bona fide baseball fans. Tickets cost $20 to $68 and are half-price on Monday.

To get Sox tickets, call Ticketmaster (tel. 866/SOX-GAME [769-4263]), or visit the ticket office, open Monday through Friday from 10am to 6pm, Saturday and Sunday from 10am to 4pm, with extended hours on game days. To get to the ballpark by El, take the Red Line to Sox/35th Street.

Field of Dreams Built in 1914, Wrigley Field is the second-oldest major-league ballpark, after Boston's Fenway Park, and remains one of the only surviving old-time baseball stadiums in the country (no luxury boxes here!). Known as the "friendly confines," Wrigley Field was the site of Babe Ruth's "called shot," when Ruth allegedly pointed to a bleacher location in the 1932 World Series and then hit a home run to that exact spot. For an intimate look at the historic ballpark, take one of the behind-the-scenes tours offered almost daily throughout the summer; stops include the visitors' and home team locker rooms, press box, security headquarters, and, yes, a walk around the field itself (be sure to check out the original scoreboard, built in 1937). Some dates do sell out, so buy tickets ($25) in advance online, if possible. Keep in mind that if you take a tour on a game day, some areas (such as the locker rooms) will be off-limits. Call tel. 773/404-CUBS [2827], or stop by the box office at 1060 W. Addison St.; you can also buy tickets online through the Cubs website (www.mlb.com/chc/ballpark/wrigley_field_tours.jsp).

Basketball

When it comes to basketball, Chicagoans still live in the past, associating the Chicago Bulls (tel. 312/455-4000; www.nba.com/bulls) with the glory days of Michael Jordan and the never-ending championships of the 1990s. The fact that Jordan chose to remain in town after his playing days were over a decision almost unheard of in professional sports has only burnished his image here, and locals are still wowed by occasional Jordan sightings. The downside is that he's a constant reminder of our ever-more-distant winning past.

Although the current players don't inspire the same city-wide fervor, the Bulls have rebounded somewhat from the dismal seasons following Jordan's departure and even made some respectable showings in post-season play. The Bulls don't consistently sell out, which means you might be able to catch a game at the cavernous United Center,1901 W. Madison St. (tel. 312/455-4500; www.unitedcenter.com). Yes, the space is massive and impersonal, but the pre-game buildup, with flashing lights and thumping music, is undeniably dramatic. Most tickets run $20 to $100 through Ticketmaster(tel. 312/559-1212), although be aware that the cheap seats are practically in the rafters. If money is no object, you can usually score good seats through local ticket brokers without much advance notice.

Football

The Chicago Bears play at Soldier Field, Lake Shore Drive and 16th Street (tel. 847/295-6600; www.chicagobears.com), site of a controversial renovation that added what looks like a giant space ship on top of the original stadium's elegant colonnade. Architecturally, it's a disaster, but from a comfort perspective, the place is much improved although that doesn't impress longtime fans who prided themselves on surviving blistering-cold game days and horrifying bathrooms. The Bears themselves have been inspiring high hopes most recently, winning a trip to the Super Bowl in 2007. But even during losing seasons, tickets are hard to come by. (Most are snapped up by season ticket holders long before the season starts.) If you plan ahead, individual tickets run $45 to $300; expensive seats are usually available through ticket brokers or online sites.

The Northwestern Wildcats play Big Ten college ball at Ryan Field, 1501 Central St., in nearby Evanston (tel. 847/491-CATS [2287]). Unfortunately, Northwestern grads are not particularly loyal to their long-suffering team. In fact, fans of the visiting team often outnumber NU supporters in the stands.

Hockey

The Chicago Blackhawks have devoted, impassioned fans who work themselves into a frenzy with the first note of "The Star-Spangled Banner," but for years, they had to put up with mediocre play and less-than-stellar management. Over the past few seasons, though, the team that once boasted legends such as Bobby Hull and Tony Esposito has made a comeback, winning the Stanley Cup in 2010. Going to a Hawks games has once again become a rousing and sometimes rowdy experience. The Blackhawks play at the United Center, 1901 W. Madison St. (tel. 312/455-7000; www.chicagoblackhawks.com). Tickets cost $15 to $100.

For a more affordable and family-friendly outing, catch the semipro Chicago Wolvesat Allstate Arena, 6920 N. Mannheim Rd., Rosemont (tel. 847/724-GOAL [4625]; www.chicagowolves.com). The team has been consistently excellent over the past few years, and the games are geared toward all ages, with fireworks beforehand and plenty of on- and off-ice entertainment (tickets $13-$30).

Horse Racing

Thoroughbreds race at Arlington International Racecourse, 2200 W. Euclid Ave., Arlington Heights (tel. 847/385-7500; www.arlingtonpark.com), in the northwest suburbs. Live local bands and DJs add to the party atmosphere on Fridays and Saturdays from Memorial Day weekend until Labor Day, starting at 2:30pm. For more details, The Chicago area's other major racetrack, Hawthorne Race Course, 3501 S. Laramie Ave., Stickney (tel. 708/780-3700; www.sportsmanspark.com), is located in the southwest suburbs, about a half-hour drive from downtown.

Soccer

Chicago's Major League Soccer team, the Chicago Fire, plays at its own 20,000-seat stadium in suburban Bridgeview (about 12 miles southwest of downtown). The season runs from late May through October (tel. 888/MLS-FIRE [657-3473]; www.chicago-fire.com). Games have a family feel, with plenty of activities for kids and affordable ticket prices ($15-$60).

The End

Lightning Source UK Ltd.
Milton Keynes UK
UKHW022313131120
373344UK00010B/560